Psychoanalytic Case Studies from an Interpersonal-Relational Perspective

Psychoanalytic Case Studies from an Interpersonal-Relational Perspective contains reports of long-term treatments, including many dialogues and dreams, with commentaries following each one. Drawing upon theories that have been developed since Freud, the analysts focus on problems in living as opposed to diagnoses and repressed sexual and aggressive urges. They also express their own feelings toward patients and even their own dreams.

The cases themselves include sexual abuse, a man whose father killed his mother, a change in sexual orientation, as well as those of depression, physical problems, and difficulties relating interpersonally, such as fear of rejection and rejecting help. Actual dialogues of sessions are featured, so that readers can see what takes place in psychoanalysis. The analysts here draw upon the theories of Sullivan, Fromm, Horney, and Fromm-Reichmann, Kohut, Winnicott, and more recently Levenson, Mitchell, Bromberg, Donnell Stern, and Aron, to name a few.

Most contemporary case reports come from short-term therapies and many rely on techniques of changing conscious cognitions and encouraging new behaviors. The treatments in this book, while often including such interventions, explore more in-depth processes that may be unconscious and related to transferential expectations from previous relationships, encouraging new experiences and not simply explanations.

Psychoanalytic Case Studies from an Interpersonal-Relational Perspective will be of great interest to interpersonal and relational psychoanalysts and psychoanalytic psychotherapists in clinical practice.

Rebecca Coleman Curtis, PhD, Professor of Psychology at Adelphi University and Faculty, William Alanson White Institute, is author of *Desire, Self, Mind and the Psychotherapies: Unifying Psychological Science and Psychoanalysis*, editor of *Self-Defeating Behaviors and the Relational Self*, and co-editor of books on change, death, loneliness, taboos, identity, and failure resilience.

Psychoanalytic Case Studies from an Interpersonal-Relational Perspective

Edited by
Rebecca Coleman Curtis

Routledge
Taylor & Francis Group
LONDON AND NEW YORK

First published 2018
by Routledge
2 Park Square, Milton Park, Abingdon, Oxon OX14 4RN

and by Routledge
711 Third Avenue, New York, NY 10017

Routledge is an imprint of the Taylor & Francis Group, an informa business

British Library Cataloguing in Publication Data
A catalogue record for this book is available from the British Library

Library of Congress Cataloging in Publication Data
Names: Curtis, Rebecca C., editor.
Title: Psychoanalytic case studies from an interpersonal-relational perspective / edited by Rebecca Coleman Curtis.
Description: Abingdon, Oxon ; New York, NY : Routledge, 2018. | Includes bibliographical references and index.
Identifiers: LCCN 2017035356 (print) | LCCN 2017044346 (ebook) | ISBN 9780203709832 (Master) | ISBN 9781351356701 (Web PDF) | ISBN 9781351356695 (ePub) | ISBN 9781351356688 (Mobipocket/ Kindle) | ISBN 9781138560758 (hardback : alk. paper) | ISBN 9781138560765 (pbk. : alk. paper)
Subjects: LCSH: Psychoanalysis–Case studies. | Psychotherapy– Case studies.
Classification: LCC RC509.8 (ebook) | LCC RC509.8 .P764 2018 (print) | DDC 616.89/17–dc23
LC record available at https://lccn.loc.gov/2017035356

ISBN: 978-1-138-56075-8 (hbk)
ISBN: 978-1-138-56076-5 (pbk)
ISBN: 978-0-203-70983-2 (ebk)

Typeset in Times New Roman
by Wearset Ltd, Boldon, Tyne and Wear

Contents

Contributors

Robert U. Akeret received his doctorate in counseling psychology from Teachers College, Columbia University and his certificate in psychoanalysis from the William Alanson White Institute, where he trained with Rollo May and Erich Fromm. He is the author of five previous books: *Not by Words Alone*, *Photoanalysis*, *Family Tales Family Wisdom*, *Tales from a Traveling Couch*, and *Photolanguage.* Dr. Akeret worked in the counseling services at Columbia University and the City College of New York, and is a past President of the Association of Psychoanalytic Psychologists.

David Braucher, LCSW, PhD, is a graduate of The William Alanson White Institute. He is on the Editorial Board of the journal, *Contemporary Psychoanalysis*, and is Associate Editor of the blog, Contemporary Psychoanalysis in Action. He has lectured at the New York University School of Social Work and has written on relationships and identity. He is in private practice in The West Village/Chelsea in Manhattan.

Cory K. Chen, PhD, completed his doctoral training in clinical psychology at the University of North Carolina – Chapel Hill and his psychoanalytic training at the William Alanson White Institute. He is currently Director of the Psychotherapy Research and Development Program at the VA New York Harbor Healthcare System – Manhattan and an Assistant Clinical Professor in the Department of Psychiatry at New York University.

Olga Cheselka, PhD, is a Training and Supervising Analyst at the William Alanson White Institute, and faculty member of the Postdoctoral Externship Program. She has written and lectured about issues concerning the development of the self in relationship to others, including topics relating to the anxiety of creativity, interpersonal power, and intimacy. She is in private practice in Manhattan and Mamaroneck, New York, seeing adults, adolescents, and couples. She has published in *Contemporary Psychoanalysis*, *Hungers and Compulsions*, and *Essential Psychotherapies.*

Rebecca Coleman Curtis, PhD, Editor, is Professor of Psychology at Adelphi University in Garden City, New York, and faculty at the William Alanson

White Institute in New York City. She is the author of *Desire, Self, the Mind, and the Psychotherapies: Unifying Psychological Science and Psychoanalysis.* She is Editor of *Self-defeating Behaviors, The Relational Self,* and *How People Change*, and co-editor of *Taboo or Not Taboo, On Loneliness and Longing, Understanding and Coping with Failure, Deaths and Endings*, and *Psychoanalytic Perspectives on Identity and Difference*. Editor of the section on relational psychoanalysis for the *Edinburgh Encyclopedia of Psychoanalysis*, she has also published articles in the *Journal of Personality and Social Psychology*, *Contemporary Psychoanalysis*, and *Psychoanalytic Psychology*. She has presented papers in Europe, Israel, China, Japan, Viet Nam, Australia, New Zealand, Chile, Argentina, Uruguay, India, South Africa, Malta, Mexico, and the USA.

Eric J. Dammann graduated from Bucknell University, and his PhD in clinical psychology was from Michigan State University. He completed psychoanalytic training at the William Alanson White Institute, where he is currently Co-director of their Artists Program. An Associate Editor of *Contemporary Psychoanalysis* and the *Journal of Financial Therapy*, he is a clinical supervisor at Columbia and the W. A. White Institute. His publications appear in *Fortune*, *Clinical Psychology Review*, *Sex Roles*, and the *Journal of Health and Social Policy*.

Alyson Feit, PhD, consults and writes in the fields of creative and artistic expression, interpersonal relationships, romance, and sexuality. She teaches at the St. Louis Psychoanalytic Institute and at the Chinese American Psychoanalytic Alliance. An Associate Editor of the journal *Contemporary Psychoanalysis*, she is a member of the Artist Group and the Sexual Abuse Service at the William Alanson White Institute in New York.

Daniel Gensler, PhD, is Director of Training of the Child Adolescent Psychotherapy Training Program at the William Alanson White Institute as well as training and supervising analyst at White. He has published many articles in the *Journal of Infant, Child, and Adolescent Psychotherapy* and *Contemporary Psychoanalysis*, as well as chapters in many edited books.

Evelyn Berger Hartman, PhD, is Faculty, Training and Supervising Analyst at the William Alanson White Institute, Manhattan Institute and the Institute for Contemporary Psychotherapy. She is on the Editorial Board of *Contemporary Psychoanalysis* and has contributed to *Loneliness and Longing*, *Contemporary Psychoanalysis*, and *Contemporary Psychoanalysis and the Legacy of the Third Reich: History, Memory and Tradition.* Writing and teaching on the subjects of the intergenerational trauma of the Holocaust, dreams, psychodynamics of love, and Freud, she is in private practice in Manhattan and Riverdale.

Elizabeth Hegeman, PhD, is a Professor at John Jay College of Criminal Justice, City University of New York, a Training and Supervising Analyst at

William Alanson White Institute, on the Editorial Board of *Contemporary Psychoanalysis*, and faculty at New York University's Postdoctoral Institute of Psychoanalysis. Together with Michael Stocker, Dr. Hegeman has written *Valuing Emotions* (Cambridge University Press), and has published in *Contemporary Psychoanalysis* and *Psychoanalytic Dialogues.*

Orsoly Hunyady, PhD, is a graduate of the William Alanson White Institute. She serves as an Associate Editor for the journal *Contemporary Psychoanalysis*, and teaches and supervises in affiliation with the Derner Institute at Adelphi University. She has published papers on infidelity and jealousy, as well as on psychoanalytic topics with an emphasis on social-societal processes. Her private practice is in Midtown Manhattan.

Jenny Kahn Kaufmann is Faculty, Training, and Supervising Analyst at the William Alanson White Institute, Associate Editor for the journal *Contemporary Psychoanalysis*, and Adjunct Professor at Mt. Sinai Beth Israel Medical Center and the National Institute for the Psychotherapies. Her many publications about working with patients who have experienced trauma appear in *Contemporary Psychoanalysis*, *Psychoanalysis and Psychotherapy*, as well as edited volumes.

Peter Kaufmann, PhD, is a clinical psychologist/psychoanalyst and is Faculty and Supervisor at the Institute for the Psychoanalytic Study of Subjectivity and the National Institute for the Psychotherapies. He is currently Co-director of the IPSS program. Teaching such courses as "Kohut and his Critics," he has a particular interest in comparative psychoanalysis and in efforts to integrate the clinical approaches. He has also published several papers, including "The Guilt of Tragic Man," "Working with Men Who Please Too Much," and "On Transforming the Reparative Quest" which reflect his additional interest in the topics of mourning and pathological accommodation.

Susan Kolod, PhD, is a supervising and training analyst, Faculty, and Co-editor of the blog Contemporary Psychoanalysis in Action at the William Alanson White Institute. She is Chair of the Committee on Public Information of the American Psychoanalytic Association. Dr. Kolod has written numerous chapters and articles about the impact of hormones upon the psyche. She has contributed chapters in two new books: *Identity and Difference: Psychoanalytic Perspectives on Navigating the Divide* and *Unknowable, Unspeakable and Unsprung: Navigating the Thrill and Danger of Living amidst Truth, Fantasy and Privacy.*

Sigalit Levy, PhD, is a clinical psychologist and psychoanalyst. Dr. Levy is Faculty and Supervisor at the William Alanson White Institute and Fordham University. She is an Associate Editor for the journal *Contemporary Psychoanalysis*. Dr. Levy is in private practice in midtown New York City.

Suzanne Little, PhD, is Faculty, Fellow, and Supervising Analyst, William Alanson White Institute, past President of the White Psychoanalytic Society, and a member of the Editorial Board of the journal *Contemporary Psychoanalysis*. Dr. Little is Assistant Professor of Psychiatry at the Icahn School of Medicine at Mount Sinai and has a private practice in New York's West Village.

Heather MacIntosh holds a PhD in Clinical Psychology and is a post-academic candidate in psychoanalysis at the Institute for the Advancement of Self Psychology in Toronto, Ontario, Canada. She is currently Assistant Professor in the MScA in Couple and Family Therapy in the School of Social Work at McGill University, Montreal, Quebec, Canada. In addition to her academic work, Dr. MacIntosh maintains a private practice focusing on the treatment of individuals, couples, and families dealing with the after-effects of trauma from a psychoanalytic perspective.

Ira Moses, PhD, is Training, Supervising Analyst, and Faculty at the William Alanson White Institute in New York City. He has published papers in *Contemporary Psychoanalysis*, the *International Forum of Psychoanalysis*, *Psychotherapy*, the *Handbook of Interpersonal Psychoanalysis*, and the *Edinburgh International Encyclopedia of Psychoanalysis.*

John O'Leary, PhD, is Faculty and Supervisor at the William Alanson White Institute. He is also on PT staff at Columbia Presbyterian. With a full-time private practice in Manhattan, he has published articles in *Contemporary Psychoanalysis*, *Psychoanalytic Psychology*, and many chapters in edited books.

Helen Quinones, PhD, is a licensed psychologist and psychoanalyst, private practice in New York City, Psychotherapy Supervisor at the William Alanson White Institute and Teachers College, Columbia University, and Faculty at William Alanson White Institute Child/Adolescent Psychotherapy Program. She has published in the *International Federation of Psychoanalytic Societies*, *Espacio Psicoanalitico*, and presented at the annual meetings of American Orthopsychiatry and the International Psychoanalytic Association.

Nicholas Samstag, PhD, is a Training, Supervising Analyst, and member of the Faculty at the William Alanson White Institute. He has published in *Contemporary Psychoanalysis* and *Psychotherapy: Theory, Research and Training.* He maintains a private practice in Manhattan.

Carol Valentin, PhD, is a clinical psychologist in private practice with children and adults. With a doctorate from the City University of New York, she is also a graduate of the William Alanson White Institute. Dr. Valentin has been Clinical Director of the Sheltering Arms Therapeutic Nursery in New York since 1985 where she is responsible for training psychologists and clinical social workers to apply psychoanalytic thinking to their work with traumatized children and their families. She is currently a co-founder and facilitator of The Race and Psychoanalysis Study Group at The William Alanson White Institute.

Robert Watson, PhD, is a Supervising Psychoanalyst at the William Alanson White Institute; a Staff Psychologist, Department of Psychiatry, Columbia University; Faculty Member of the Institute of Contemporary Psychology; and in private practice. He has published a variety of articles on dreams, paranoia, group process, and borderline personality disorder.

Brent Willock, PhD, is President of the Toronto Institute for Contemporary Psychoanalysis, Board Member of the Canadian Institute for Child and Adolescent Psychoanalytic Psychotherapy, and is on the Faculty of the Institute of the Advancement of Self Psychology. Author of *Comparative-integrative Psychoanalysis: A Relational Perspective for the Second Century*, he is editor of numerous volumes with Rebecca Curtis.

Introduction

Rebecca Coleman Curtis

"The patient needs an experience, not an explanation." This remark, usually attributed to Frieda Fromm-Reichmann (May, 1958, p. 81), is often quoted by interpersonal psychoanalysts. Harry Stack Sullivan, Clara Thompson, Erich Fromm, Frieda Fromm-Reichmann, and Karen Horney all broke away from the dominant Freudian thinking of their time and came to be known as the Interpersonal or Cultural School of psychoanalysis. In more recent years, Stephen Mitchell, Jay Greenberg, Philip Bromberg, Jody Davies, Lewis Aron, Donnell Stern, and many others have continued this break with Freudian analysis in what has come to be known as relational psychoanalysis. In these overlapping traditions, the relationship with the analyst and other people is considered foremost, not only the sexual and aggressive drives of the patient. The intrapsychic is considered along with the interpersonal. Drawing from the influence of Sandor Ferenczi, these analysts have questioned the idea that the analyst should be a blank screen who encourages idealization and transferential distortions. They also see the patient's problems as stemming from problems in living and dehumanizing conditions, not only as repressed sexual urges. The self is not conceived of as a "true" and "false" self, but as a system with multiple self-with-other states. Inquiry is used so that the analyses will not be as prolonged as those involving only the patient's free associations and the analyst's interpretations of them. The goal is to increase "a patient's skill in living" (Sullivan, 1953, p. 175). "Change in experience of self in relation to others – and in analytic treatment, in relation to the analyst – is the goal of Interpersonal psychoanalysis" (Mann, 1995, p. 558). There is no blueprint for this work. Kavanaugh states that there is a "willingness to be drawn in the patient's relational field and to *be with him* rather than *know about him* as in orthodox analysis" (1995, p. 573). The problems seem more complicated than those of simple symptom reduction.

Interpersonal/relational psychoanalysts often look at the anxiety level of the patient. If it is too low, and the patient is speaking of inconsequential material, the analyst may intervene to raise the anxiety by being inquiring or being confrontational. If the anxiety is too high, the analyst may engage in actions to move to a safer space. The analyst is on the lookout for topics and feelings that are avoided. There is also attention to shifts in self-states and experiences that do not seem to be connected to other experiences – those that are dissociated in a broad sense of the word. The task of the analyst is then to bring these experiences into awareness simultaneously so that the conflict is apparent. The analyst is dedicated to listening to the patient's experience, not to imposing a theory on those experiences. Dreams are considered to be a way to understand what is not fully conscious – both dreams of the patient and of the analyst. For a complete description of interpersonal psychoanalysis, see the *Handbook of Interpersonal Psychoanalysis* (Lionells et al., 1995). A chapter on relational psychoanalysis by Curtis (2014) is available in *Essential Psychotherapies* edited by Messer and Gurman.

Although it is possible to find case studies from an interpersonal or relational perspective in *Contemporary Psychoanalysis* or *Psychoanalytic Dialogues*, or perhaps in *In Session*, it is usually not possible to tell from the title that a case lies therein. The current cases and commentaries are all written by analysts with an interpersonal/relational perspective. There is little mention of Freud. The analysts, instead, draw heavily upon the work of Levenson, Bromberg, Donnell Stern, and other interpersonal and relational theorists. Freudians may think that the cases are not psychoanalytic, as they are not primarily focused on the Oedipus complex. But the cases do focus on unconscious processes and transference. A number of the cases were written by candidates prior to graduation; others by more experienced analysts. The reader will see that diagnoses are usually not given. Instead, the analysts see the patients as unique people with problems. The cases were not selected because they were "successes" or made some theoretical point. The cases are basically those for whom we could obtain permission to publish – not a simple task. Permission was given in all cases – the identifying information is disguised, and in one case a combination of patients is presented. The patients by and large are in a pre-contemplation or contemplation stage of change. In most cases depression was the presenting problem, but was complicated by other factors. Trauma is another frequent occurrence, with anxiety about the future and anger being other reasons for seeking analysis.

In the first case, Robert Akeret states that the role of empathy is more important than knowledge of theory and technique. His depressed, handsome young patient tells him he cannot date because he has psoriasis. Dr. Akeret engages in the unconventional intervention of telling him to take off his clothes – but not his underwear. Dr. Akeret tells him that any woman would be lucky to sleep with him. The young man's family has been destroyed by the suicide of his older brother, and Dr. Akeret asks to meet with them as well. Although the psoriasis breaks out again, eventually, with his at-times unconventional interventions, the young man becomes more optimistic and enters graduate school. Years later they meet up and the psoriasis has almost totally cleared up and the patient has a wonderful lover.

In the next case, reported by Nicholas Samstag, a young man does not seem to relate personally to people. He has never experienced good relations and uses quotations from literature and TV to express his thoughts and feelings. He turns other people off. During his analysis he begins to have more sexual encounters with men and realizes he prefers them over those with women. He begins to speak more using his own voice. He finally develops a full relationship with a man, not simply a sexual hook-up.

In his comments on the case, Dr. Watson charts the progress in interpersonal relatedness with Dr. Samstag, noting also that the payment of the fees by the father might be discussed more, and wondering if the patient's lack of professional success could have been dealt with if the analysis had continued longer. He sees the use of dreams as very important to the success of the treatment.

Dr. Quinones describes the case of a man whose father beat his mother to death. Although he said he had been in post-traumatic stress therapy and did not wish to talk about the murder, he eventually began to speak about Jeffrey Dahmer, quoted brutal songs, and reported a dream in which he drugged and raped a woman (another therapist), continuing after she was dead. Dr. Quinones felt victimized and said he would have to find another therapist if he continued to talk in this way, as she was not able to listen to it. Nevertheless, they did continue. She reported that her visual images helped more in the treatment than her thoughts.

In her commentary, Dr. Little notes how the two initially feigned being present and later on the role of the analyst being quiet and facilitating a sense of communion. She sees the analysis in terms of Ghent's (1990) differentiation between masochistic submission and surrender – an acceptance of uncertainty, openness, and acts of shared spontaneity.

Dr. O'Leary notes Dr. Quinones' emphasis on "state-sharing" – experiencing a similar, frequently overwhelming emotion that the patient has reported feeling. He sees the patient as being severely depressed and questions the analyst's insistence that he is identified with his aggressor father, given how badly he feels about himself already. He does believe, however, that her intervention – "I will follow you past the grave to make sure you feel the guilt of killing off those who care about you" – when the patient was suicidal, was helpful. He also explicates his different understanding of the term "enactment."

In her report of the case of "Michael," Olga Cheselka helps a young man with his depression and his career, noting that she seems to be in a role similar to that of his father, acting to make this young man "great." He develops a sense of self that is different from his sense of self as someone "doomed," due to the substance abuse, crime, and suicide in the history of his family. She provides some of the nurturing that Michael's parents did not provide and attributes the success of the treatment to their relationship, to the deconstruction of Michael's presenting sense of self, and to recognizing the enactment that is going on in their relationship.

Dr. Gensler notes that Dr. Cheselka helped her patient move from the alternation between being "great" and being "doomed" to alternating between feelings of being the more powerful one and the less powerful one. He comments that she lets her annoyance be known when Michael avoids self-states of passivity and anger, as well as his conflict between dependence and independence. Observing this successful treatment, he wonders, nevertheless, about some of Michael's "ambivalence" toward women.

Heather MacIntosh also sees enactment and dissociation as central to the case of "William." She sees her own traumatic past as contributing to the way in which both she and her patient moved into dissociation. The patient had been sexually assaulted by his father, and his mother apparently went into hospital periodically for ECT treatments of her depression. He had a history of alcoholism and, using the name "Geoffrey," of trysts with men in the park from which he would sometimes run off, becoming the aggressor in the relationship. The analyst would enter into feelings of "lurking darkness, creepiness, and swirling unspoken traumas." Eventually, when William switched topics, she was able to get William to return to the difficult issues and feelings he was avoiding. Gradually he made a few friends, had more control over his addictive urges, and gained more responsibility at work.

Dr. Kolod believes there must have been something more to William's creepiness than his dissociation. Usually people who dissociate are not seen as creepy. Perhaps it was the sociopathic tendencies he had revealed in his guise as Geoffrey in the park. He stated that he was evil. Dr. Kolod wanted to know a lot more about William, but he had said at the outset that he could afford only 18 months of therapy, so more was not known.

Alyson Feit's patient "Peter" arrived in analysis stating that he felt repellent, reminiscent of the analyst of Kafka's Gregor Artsa. His emotionally absent mother told him he was strange and peculiar. He was sexually molested by his father and coerced into sex by his sister. He developed a maternal view of the analyst and, with her help, moved forward in his work, maintained a relationship with another man, and asked her to tell him to engage in creative work, which he began and in which he was successful. She first helped him link up his fragmented experiences so that he formed a more coherent sense of self. He gradually became more playful and consolidated his many different identities.

Hegeman comments that it is hard to understand the degree of change in Peter in so short a time. Although Feit attributes it largely to his incredible intelligence, Hegeman wonders if there were some relationship or hobbies along the way that were helpful. She believes it was fortunate that Feit recognized that the patient needed parenting as well as analysis. She sees the mirror as a reflection to be feared and shattered. In his art, Peter plays with the pieces of the broken mirror. This may represent a sort of putting himself together again.

Sigalit Levy presents a case of a gay man who entered treatment owing to increasing anxiety and depression. Underlying these symptoms was a dissociated rage. The analysis revealed that instead of putting his thoughts and feelings into words, he used his senses to express himself. Over time he became better at using words to communicate his feelings.

Dr. Moses comments on the case differentiating interpersonal from relational psychoanalysis. Whereas Dr. Levy offered many interpretations to her patient, he suggests the use of inquiry as the interpersonal technique. Dr. Moses sees inquiry as the way to help the patient give form to unformulated experiences, whereas interpretations can place the analyst's understanding onto the patient.

The fear of death permeates the work of Orsoli Hunyady in two cases. In the first case, Hunyady dreams that her patient "Sally" tries to choke her. With the second patient, "Mr. Z," Hunyady dreams that she gets closer to his face under a hood and finds that it is the face of death. In real life Mr. Z was rapidly deteriorating with an as yet undiagnosed illness. With Sally, Hunyady engaged in a power struggle. The patient was always angry. Sally had difficulties in all relationships and was seen as strong, feisty, combative, and demanding but competent by men. Over time, Sally became less combative and feisty, let her vulnerable side show, developed a relationship with a man, and was going to move out of her hated New York City. Mr. Z progressed to seeming better able to make decisions for himself and, although reluctant to sell his house below what he thought was the value, planned to do so and move to sunny California where his son was living. For him, this meant losing all of his possessions.

Cory Chen uses the analogy of swimming in the sea with the patient or standing on the shore watching the patient. He suggests that Orsoli swims in the same water as the patient. Her dreams reflect her involvement with her patients. She had to face her own feelings of loss and facing death, which was terrifying. Chen notes that in the treatments, swimming with the patients meant relaxing and allowing the process to unfold.

The case of a depressed woman who had two not good-enough mothers was described by Carol Valentin. Dr. Valentin moved from empathy to challenging the patient's defenses which kept her feeling like a victim by externalizing responsibility. Eventually, as the patient gave up on life after five attempts at in-vitro fertilization, Dr. Valentin let her know that she loved her. This made a large difference in the patient's outlook on life.

In the case of a young woman seen by Jenny Kaufmann, Jenny is initially empathic. When Jenny does not tell her the secrets of "getting a man," however, the patient becomes angry but more independent. As her responsibilities at work increase, she cannot get to therapy appointments at times of emergencies and has to be late at other times. This conflict is eventually settled without the acrimony that occurred when her mother caught her leaving on a secret date. "Marie-Helene" learned that others can respond differently from her mother.

Peter Kaufmann applies a self-psychological approach to understanding the case. He sees the patient as in a "reparative quest" to undo traumas from the past and to make up for missing meaningful experiences. He sees Jenny as making up for a developmental deficit. Jenny realizes that Marie-Helene's mother wanted her to be "just like me" (her mother), with her mother being annihilating and not wanting Marie-Helene to be independent. He sees Jenny as noting when the idealization has gone too far and it is time for the patient to develop her own separate identity.

Dr. Hartman describes the analysis of a man who had not received the help and affection he needed from his parents. Not surprisingly, he would not accept what he needed from his analyst, either. He was very self-critical and believed others were criticizing him as well. Over time, he was able to feel his vulnerabilities and become more human. He heard his analyst when she praised him.

Dr. Willock comments that the patient's mother vacillated between being an exciting and rejecting presence, leaving the patient wary of her empathic attunement. He also sees the father, and perhaps the mother, as parents who appear to need the father to maintain superiority over the son in a traditional Oedipal struggle that did not allow mutuality, but instead fostered alienation.

Throughout these cases and comments, one sees the importance of experiencing, enactments, dissociation, challenging, and the analyst's feelings and fantasies. There is also considerable mention of fragmentation and the development of a cohesive sense of self. Most of the analysts work in the tradition referred to previously, namely that "the patient needs a new experience, not an explanation." There is no simple diagnosis and treatment plan. There is actually little mention of the Oedipus complex or repression, yet transference and unconscious processes play a central role. The analysts encourage the patients to discover more about their experiences.

References

Curtis, R. C. (2014). Relational psychoanalytic psychotherapy. In S. B. Messer & A. Gurman (Eds.), *Essential Psychotherapies* (pp. 72–105). New York: Guilford Press.

Ghent, E. (1990). Masochism, submission, surrender – Masochism as a perversion of surrender. *Contemporary Psychoanalysis*, *26*, 108–136.

Kavanaugh, G. (1995). The nature of therapeutic action. In M. Lionels, J. Fiscalini, C. H. Mann, & D. B. Stern (Eds.), *Handbook of Interpersonal Psychoanalysis* (pp. 569–602). Hillsdale, NJ: Analytic Press.

Lionells, M., Stern, D. B., Mann, C., & Fiscalini, J. (Eds.) (1995). *Handbook of Interpersonal Psychoanalysis*. Hillsdale, NJ: Analytic Press.

Mann, C. (1995). The goals of interpersonal psychoanalysis. In M. Lionells, J. Fiscalini, C. Mann, & D. Stern (Eds.), *Handbook of Interpersonal Psychoanalysis* (pp. 555–568). Hillsdale, NJ: Analytic Press.

May, R. (1958). Contributions of existential psychotherapy. In R. May, E. Angel, & H. Ellenberger (Eds.), *Existence* (pp. 37–91). New York: Basic Books.

Sullivan, H. S. (1953). *The Interpersonal Theory of Psychiatry*. New York: Norton.

Chapter 1

Mark the leper

Robert U. Akeret

As Krishnamurti (1998) stated, when you are listening to someone completely, you are listening to the feeling of what is being said, not just the words. For a therapist, the ability to empathize with another human being is infinitely more valuable than all the psychoanalytic training in the world.

There, I said it! And I absolutely stand by it.

I have known therapists with years of intense training at highly respected institutions – brilliant scholars, fully versed in the most accepted psychological theories and therapeutic techniques – who nonetheless lacked the capacity for simple human empathy. The result is far too often a complete inability to foster meaningful, positive change in the lives of patients.

I have also known talented therapists with a natural inclination toward empathy who do all they can to suppress those feelings during sessions. They do this, against their own instincts, in the mistaken belief (reinforced by their supervisors) that any empathic response on their part will create obstacles to effective therapy.

The reasoning put forward in support of this attitude is that if one becomes too close to a patient personally it will block transference. The patient who sees you as a "friend" will never be able to express his or her true emotions to you – or so it is claimed.

I believe just the opposite: that a well-developed capacity for empathy is one of a therapist's most valuable tools, and is absolutely necessary to forging the kind of bond required for truly effective work. During my more than 40 years of practicing therapy I have seen colleagues with less than stellar training who nonetheless manage to effect wonderful, life-affirming transformations in their patients – due almost entirely to their innate talent for human empathy.

I also see the power of empathy every day as I walk through Riverside Park and observe the mothers and nannies who congregate there with their charges. I notice that there is almost always one woman who shines as the magnetic center of the group. She is the one to whom all the rest flock for understanding and guidance. *This woman exudes empathy!* I think, as I sit and listen to the conversations taking place only a few feet away from me:

> If I were in charge of selecting candidates for a top psychoanalytic institute, I would choose this intuitive and empathic woman over any of the supposedly brilliant psychology students who excel at "left brain" anatomizations of the human psyche, yet too often shut out their own "right brain" intuitions as untrustworthy.

For me, that choice would be a "no brainer," but for many therapists (and for almost all of the people who train them today) the idea of trusting one's empathetic intuition is unacceptable. They believe empathy is too imprecise to be meaningful. It cannot be measured by tests or quantified into discrete units, so they relegate it to the pseudo-scientific waste dump they reserve for numerologists, invisible energy practitioners, and religious healers.

Empathy as an effective tool for healing has little appeal to the scientific or medical mind. It is in the arts that empathy is respected and cultivated – particularly among writers and actors. These artists must learn to see and feel the world intuitively from inside someone else's skin in order to do their jobs properly. But while most people are willing to grant the vital importance of empathy to artists, they stop short of recognizing how essential a highly developed capacity for empathy is to be a truly successful therapist.

I believe an individual's basic talent for empathic response, much like a talent for music or mathematics, is a gift. Some are blessed with a great deal of it; others not so much. But just as a talent for music or mathematics can be nurtured and developed, so too can one's talent for empathy – even if there is very little there to begin with. It starts with learning how to become aware of one's empathetic powers, faint as they may be, and allowing them to grow. That isn't easy for some people.

The two most critical elements to developing robust empathetic powers are, first, an appetite (or at the very least, a willingness) for taking risks; and second, having the patience and faith necessary to gradually begin believing in and trusting one's own empathic instincts. At its most extreme, empathy can mean entering into what the German philosopher Edmund Husserl (1970, p. 108) called a person's *Lebenswelt* (lived world) experiencing viscerally the way in which that person parcels out and evaluates the contents of his or her world.

Probably the greatest risk a therapist takes when it comes to this level of empathy is that of temporarily abandoning his or her own personality in order to "become" this other person, if only for a few moments. It can feel like jumping out of an airplane without a parachute. But taking personal risks in the pursuit of helping our patients is what we do.

Ultimately, I see empathy as a supreme act of love. It is precisely this willingness to "become" another person that conveys – more forcefully than words ever could – a loving belief in the patient's potential to overcome the issues that are preventing them from leading a rich, full life.

Like love, empathy can be daunting and tricky; inevitably, empathetic "misreadings" will occur along the way. But even misreadings can turn out to be valuable in the end.

This is what happened in the following case, which I call "Mark the Leper." With this patient, the empathic experience that I thought would help me relate to him most deeply turned out to be only skin deep literally. I had to delve much more deeply into my own most painful fears and regrets to understand fully what "the Leper" was really going through – to truly empathize with him.

I could tell immediately that Mark, my new potential patient, was going to be more difficult than most. He was perched on the edge of a chair in my waiting room when I first saw him, his back to my office door: a clear sign that he didn't want to be here.

"Hello. I'm Dr. Akeret," I said by way of my usual greeting. "Come on into my office and we'll get started."

Even from behind him I could see weariness and despair in his body as he forced himself to stand. When he turned around, I was surprised to see that he was unusually handsome – he could have easily been the young leading actor in a romantic film.

But his face, as handsome as it was, displayed nothing: no life energy, no appetite for experience – no interest in anything at all.

"I'm not even sure I should be here, Doctor Akeret," he said, tonelessly. "My brother had two years of therapy and then killed himself."

I knew all about this from Mark's aunt, a former patient. She also warned me to expect difficulties with Mark, as well as serious opposition to any kind of psychoanalytic therapy from his parents.

"Do you think that if we decide to work together you might commit suicide?" I asked. "Are you considering suicide, Mark?"

"Nah," he said, as if he were so dispirited he didn't even have the energy to kill himself.

"That's my mother's fear, really. She's a total pessimist."

"Well, I'm just the opposite, Mark. I'm a total optimist. Makes life much more interesting, wouldn't you say?"

He shrugged. We were still standing in the waiting room. He'd made no move to come into the office, and I was determined he should initiate that move. "How about your Dad?" I asked. "What does he think about therapy?"

"He says there is absolutely no scientific proof therapy works. And there really isn't, is there?"

He gave me a smug, self-satisfied look, as if he'd gotten me.

"Absolutely none," I said cheerfully. "No scientific proof whatsoever. But I'll tell you this, based on more than 40 years of working with patients: when it works it *really* works!"

"And when it doesn't work?" he asked, "What then?"

"I can't promise it will work with you," I told him honestly. "But I will promise you this: that if we do decide to work together, it will be an experience you'll never forget."

"If you say so," he muttered.

"I do. And I promise something else. There will be change. Positive? Negative? I don't know. But you won't be the same, stuck in this same rut you are now when we're through."

"How do you know I won't be the same?" "Because I won't let that happen," I said.

I saw the first glint of life in his eyes since he'd stood up. I could tell he liked what I had said. What I couldn't tell yet was how it was going to go. Usually I can see in the first few minutes whether a new patient and I will be able to forge a working relationship, but in this case I was stumped. It could go either way.

We were still standing in the waiting room. He wasn't about to make a move.

"We could keep standing out here or we can go into my office and sit down," I said finally.

Another thing 40 years of therapy had taught me: sometimes you have to be flexible to move forward.

"Tell me about any previous therapists you have worked with," I said after we were settled inside.

"I've seen a few therapists, but I could always tell pretty much what they were going to say next. So I gave up on them. You guys are so predictable."

I took that as a direct challenge. I hesitated briefly, deciding whether I should do something unpredictable – then decided that would be the most predictable thing of all to do.

"So, what changed your mind and brought you here?" I asked. "The hell I have to go through every morning," he replied.

"And what hell would that be?"

"I tried to masturbate this morning, as I do most mornings, but it's just too painful. I have psoriasis all over my body, even my penis. You can't possibly imagine what it's like to live with all those sores and pus."

"Maybe I can; I have a pretty good imagination."

"Then imagine this, Dr. Akeret: being a young guy like me, with normal urges, and realizing you'll never ever have sex with a woman or have children."

"You sound as if you don't believe your psoriasis will ever get better."

"Why should it? It hasn't really changed since the first outbreak five years ago, just two weeks after Luke jumped out of a hotel window."

"So why did you decide to give yourself psoriasis right after your brother committed suicide?" I asked.

He was instantly outraged.

"What an incredibly stupid thing to say!" he exploded. "'Give' myself psoriasis? That's just crazy. Why would I do that?"

"I don't know. That's why I'm asking you."

He looked at me, breathing heavily. I could tell he was on the verge of walking out.

"I guess you didn't see that one coming, did you?" I added, finally meeting the challenge he had thrown down at me earlier. "Maybe not all therapists are as predictable as you think."

He almost smiled.

"No. I didn't," he said, then added, "My aunt said you were very unconventional, Dr. Akeret – but maybe you're just cruel."

"I think I'm just honest," I pressed. "Why psoriasis?"

"I don't know. But I think you have an idea," he said. "Why don't you just tell me? That's what you're paid for, isn't it?"

"I think that maybe you wanted to join your brother in a kind of living death, but without actually committing suicide. No sex. No mate. No children. No life in your life."

He was quiet, thinking. I reconsidered my approach.

"Mark, listen to me carefully," I said. "Listen and take your time in answering: *What kind of a therapist do you want me to be?*"

"I don't have to think about it, Akeret. I want a drill sergeant in my life. That's what I need. Someone who'll be tough on me and straighten me out. I have absolutely no discipline. I've always gotten away with murder at home."

He went on to say that whenever his parents wanted him to do anything – finish his homework, clean his room, or turn off the TV – he would always just say that he would, and then not do it.

"There were never any consequences. When my brother died my school work went down the toilet. It's a miracle I ever got into B – and even more of a miracle I graduated – barely graduated," he corrected himself.

"Now I'm completely directionless. I haven't got the foggiest clue about what to do with my life."

I noticed that Mark had dropped the "Dr." and that was encouraging. "OK," I said, "I'll sign on. I'll be your drill sergeant."

I got my first opportunity at the very next session, which he spent lamenting the complete lack of sex in his life.

He would go to bars and look at some of the attractive women, sometimes even catching their eye, but then be totally unable to follow through. The idea of undressing in front of a woman was unthinkable, especially when he would look in the mirror at night to check out the state of his psoriasis.

"I can go out with women, talk to them. I can listen to them, I can even be helpful. But there's no way I can have sex with them."

He told me about one young and attractive woman he met who was puzzled by the fact that he didn't even make a pass at her.

"She asked me if I was gay for Christ sake! And then she wondered if I found her unattractive in some way. It broke my heart. I was too embarrassed to explain."

I decided it was time to become Drill Sargent Akeret. "Take off your clothes, Mark."

"What?"

"You heard me – strip! Leave your underpants on, but take off everything else. I want to see how bad this supposedly heart-breaking psoriasis really is."

He hesitated.

"You're kidding, right?" he asked with some apprehension. "*You will do it now, soldier!*" I shouted.

Mark leapt out of his chair and started to undress. Off came his sweater, his shirt, his undershirt, and finally his pants. He was watching me as intently as I was watching him.

"You forgot your socks."

"I always leave my socks on."

I gave him what I hoped was my best drill sargent look.

"Okay, okay," he said as he tore off his socks. "I hope you know what you're doing, Akeret." I hoped I did too.

"You look pretty damn good to me, recruit," I observed when he was finally standing in front of me, naked except for his underpants. "I only see a few spots here and there. What's the big deal? Any woman would be lucky to sleep with you."

I wasn't just trying to cheer him up; it was the literal truth. He looked like a Greek statue. But I could tell as he put his clothes back on that he was unconvinced.

"Don't you believe me?" I asked.

"It comes and goes," he said. "It's just not flaring up right now. When it does, it's horrible. You have no idea what it's like to have a diseased body."

"That's where you're wrong, Mark. Let me tell you about the time I had leprosy."

"I'm not in the mood to joke!" he said angrily. "I'm not joking," I insisted. "Sit down and listen."

"In my first year at boarding school in New England, my roommate looked at my feet one morning and immediately diagnosed what he saw as the beginning stages of leprosy."

"And you believed him?" Mark snorted.

"Of course I did! His father ran the largest leper colony in the world, in Burma."

"So this is a true story?"

"Word of honor," I said, holding up my hand. "He told me he had leprosy too, that it was latent but contagious, and that he'd probably given it to me."

"Wow," Mark said. I had his full attention.

"I remember feeling terrified that I would go blind, that my toes and fingers would begin to rot and fall off. I stopped undressing in the locker room, afraid that someone might see I was a leper."

Mark was silently nodding his head as he listened, letting me know that he understood fully.

"What about girls?" he asked.

"Dating or sex was just out of the question. I felt utterly isolated, unable to tell anyone about my disease for fear that I would be thrown out of school. My roommate checked me daily to see whether the leprosy was spreading."

"Was it?" he asked.

"A few weeks after my roommate's supposed 'diagnosis,' I got the flu and had to go to the school infirmary. The nurse ordered me to undress for a complete physical. When she looked at my feet, I could see she was shocked and disgusted. She said, 'Don't you realize you have [...]?'"

I paused, and told Mark how I'd closed my eyes and braced myself for the official diagnosis of leprosy. "But the nurse finished with: 'you have a very severe case of athletes' foot. Why haven't you been in here to have it treated?' "

"So you didn't have leprosy after all."

"No. And it took me a while to forgive my roommate for the torture he had inflicted on me. But I was so relieved not to have leprosy."

"But Akeret," he said, "that's not the same thing at all. You only *thought* you had leprosy – I really do have a terrible case of psoriasis."

"What's important," I said, "is that I exaggerated how bad it looked and how upset it made me, just as you are with this obviously minor case of psoriasis."

"It's not minor," he insisted somewhat grumpily. I said, "Your parents are coming in next session, correct?" He sighed. "Is that really necessary?"

"I say it is – and who am I, Mark?" "My drill instructor," he said wearily.

"Are you tired of me being your drill instructor?" "No. Not yet, anyway."

"Then we'll see you and your parents on Tuesday."

Every chance I get I like to have parents come in for a session – regardless of the age of the person with whom I'm working. I'm never sure what will happen, but something always does.

The visit with Mark's parents was no exception.

Mark's mother had inherited a great deal of money and they lived on a beautiful country estate outside New York City.

His father had been a schoolteacher and then headmaster of a prestigious prep school. He'd retired in his early fifties and now spent the bulk of his time gardening on the estate alone. Mark told me he avoided conflict of any kind at all costs. He was tall, elegant, and handsome – you could see where Mark got his good looks.

Mark's mother was the dominant emotional force in the household, but her outlook was unrelentingly bleak. She had lost a 2-year-old daughter to heart complications; then, years later, her older son Luke to suicide. She expected nothing but tragedy in her life and seemed almost gratified when something horrible happened to justify her attitude.

She was convinced that Mark would follow in the footsteps of his older brother and end his own life too.

She spoke first.

"I've always known our family is cursed," she said, "and time has proven it. My daughter Lisa, dead at 2. Luke at 20. And now Mark with an incurable, disfiguring disease."

"This is killing me," Mark moaned. I wasn't sure if he meant the psoriasis or his mother's gloomy outlook.

"Why do you talk like that?" she demanded sharply. "Why must you always be so dramatic?"

"I'm just trying to express how I feel," Mark came back. "I'm like the living dead. I have no career, no job, I watch way too much TV, my body is covered in sores. I'm just rotting away."

I wanted Mark's father to say something.

"What do you think?" I asked him. "Is Mark rotting away?"

"I think Mark is potentially very gifted. He has talent, and brains, no doubt about it."

"But [...]?" I prompted.

"But we haven't been very good parents." "Speak for yourself," Mark's mom interjected.

"Face it – we let Luke and Mark do whatever they wanted to do. We set no limits. There were never any consequences for bad behavior."

"So this is all my fault?" she said. "I knew it would come to that." "I'm not saying that; I'm just as guilty as you are," Mark's father replied. "Mark and I had fun together when he was young, and I guess I wanted to continue to be his friend and playmate, not his parent. I certainly didn't want to do to him what my Dad did to me."

He stopped talking and stared at the plants in my office. It appeared that he was holding back tears. The room became very still. For once Mark's mom seemed to know that it was best to keep quiet.

"And what did your father do to you?" I asked as gently as I could. "Ah! He was [...] impossible. Always threatening suicide."

There was a family history of mental problems. Mark and Luke's grandfather had spent time as a patient at Austin Riggs psychiatric hospital in Massachusetts. Mark's uncle – his father's brother – had been diagnosed a schizophrenic.

"He was exceptionally gifted too – just like Luke," Mark's dad went on. "Gifted and crazy – that's the real curse in our family. Fortunately I wasn't nearly so much of either a genius or crazy. But I could see the signs in Luke."

He became more and more animated as he spoke, in contrast to Mark's mother, who expressed nothing but weary despair.

"Luke left a note in the hotel room before he jumped: 'This is my decision.' He could be so precise, so decisive at some moments, so incapable and indecisive at others."

"He spent the entire week before he died agonizing about whether he should stay in his apartment or move into a dorm room with a roommate. He hated the idea of a roommate, but, left to himself, all he did was watch TV and vegetate."

"He was assigned to write his own obituary for a journalism class," Mark's mother cut in. "That could drive anyone to suicide."

I realized the conversation had become entirely about Luke. "How did Luke's suicide affect Mark?" I asked.

Mark's father tried to answer but his mom cut him off.

"He stopped going to class, he didn't finish any of his papers. He stopped caring about prep school and went right downhill."

"You must have been concerned he was going to follow in Luke's path and end his own life too," I said.

"Look," Mark's dad began. "Luke and Mark are very different, Luke [...]."

"Tell him about the lasagna," Mark's mother cut in.

"Oh, come on!" Mark interjected.

I could see that Mark's dad had retreated back into his shell. "What about lasagna?" I asked.

"It was stupid," Mark said. "Tell me anyway," I prompted him.

Mark sighed and began the story of the lasagna.

"Right after Luke died we were having lasagna for dinner. There was one piece left. I asked Dad if he wanted it and he said 'no.' I knew he really did want it, that he was just doing what he always does – backing down from any kind of confrontation, even one as ridiculous as this one.

"I said, 'C'mon, Dad! Be selfish for once. Take the damn last piece of lasagna!' But he kept insisting he didn't want it. And I became really angry and screamed, 'Why can't you cry with me about Luke's death?' "

"I still don't understand what lasagna had to do with Luke's dying," Mark's mother said.

"I couldn't let it go," Mark went on. "And finally Dad got really annoyed and said 'Why do you always have to be so dramatic all the time?' I said, 'You want dramatic?! Here's dramatic!' And I picked up the last piece of lasagna and threw it against the dining-room wall."

"You don't know what it's like for a mother to lose a son," Mark's mother said, as if it had been she who threw the lasagna against the wall.

"Did you clean it up, Mark?" I asked.

"I think the maid did," he said, looking down. He had the grace to be ashamed in front of me, his drill instructor.

"You wanted to say something about the difference between Luke and Mark?" I asked Mark's father.

"I just wanted to say [...]" He began.

"Mark is behaving exactly the same way Luke did before [...]" Mom interrupted.

"Yes, I know," I replied. "But I want to hear what Mark's father has to say." She simmered, but kept quiet.

"I want to point out that Luke lasted all of ten days in college," Mark's dad said. "He couldn't handle it. He immediately began threatening to kill himself unless he was allowed to come home. He was a very disturbed young man and we should have kept him institutionalized or gotten him a different therapist."

"Therapists!" Mark's mother muttered under her breath, but Mark's father wasn't about to be silenced this time.

"Mark, on the other hand – despite his brother's suicide; despite losing his cousin in a car accident; his best friend in a mugging [...]"

I looked at Mark; he hadn't told me about any of that.

"Life is filled with loss," Mark's mom said. His dad ignored her and went on: "Despite all of that, Mark graduated from prep school, went to college, stayed there, and finished."

"With lousy grades," his mom jumped in.

"He finished. That's important. And that's a huge difference from how Luke behaved."

"But I was just acting – performing," Mark said. "Just like Luke. Inside I was dying from all of these things happening, but I put on a good front and acted."

"The important thing is you functioned, Mark," I said. "Your father is right."

"In fact," Mark went on, "I'm thinking I might want to pursue acting as a career."

"Oh, please," his mother said.

"There's a good MFA acting grad program I'm interested in applying to. You have to audition with a monologue in front of a committee, and write an essay on why you want to be an actor."

"And you think you can get in?" his mother asked, "with your grades from Brown?"

"MFA candidates are evaluated on talent," he said. "It's the audition and the essay that count the most."

"And they both require work, Mark. Focus. Exactly what you lack. You're just like your brother."

"I think it's a great idea," I said. "You would," she said.

"And so should you," I insisted. "People who are going to commit suicide don't make plans for the future, or have aspirations. You should welcome this idea."

"Let the boy at least try," Mark's dad said. "I never acted on my dreams and I've lived to regret it," he said, looking once again as if he might weep.

"Mark loved his brother," I said. "He treasured his company and misses him deeply, but he's not going to commit suicide like Luke did."

"And you know this how?" his mother sneered. I leaned forward and lowered my voice.

"I know it because I have a crystal ball locked away in that closet over there."

All three of them turned to look at the closet where I keep copies of the books I've written.

"It allows me to see into the future," I continued. "I gazed into it just before you arrived, and it told me that Mark is going to be just fine."

Mark's dad smiled wanly; his mother looked at me, mouth open, as if I had suddenly grown horns and a tail.

I surprised even myself by saying this nonsense. On reflection, I think I saw a need to shock Mark's family out of their pattern of despair and defeatism. I also wanted to show Mark's mom that humor was an option to leaven even the most serious conversation.

Besides, if Mark's mother was going to revel in tragedy, I was going to take a stand at the other end of that continuum and revel in optimism.

"Well," Mark's mother said finally. "I think we're done here."

"That crystal ball stuff was very cool," Mark said straight away at the beginning of our next session. "My mom thinks you're a total wacko."

"And your dad?" I asked.

"I think he sees what you were trying to do." "And what was that?" I asked. "Do you see it?"

"Show some confidence in me – more confidence than they have in me. Hell! More confidence than I have in me. Do you really think I have a future?"

"I know you do," I said, "with or without a crystal ball. I don't buy into your mom's family curse theory.

"You've had some tragedy in your life, Mark. Almost everyone does at some point or another. But the real tragedy is if you let tragic events color everything else in your life."

Mark talked for the first time in this session about how much he missed his brother, how close and yet competitive they had been. They wrestled a lot, and Luke always won. He teased Mark about reaching puberty late, and told him he'd get leukemia if he masturbated.

"He was very depressed the last time I spoke to him on the phone. He'd just gotten out of a mental hospital. I knew he'd tried to kill himself in the past. I never thought he'd really do it. But he did. He checked into a hotel in Boston and then jumped out of a fourteenth-floor window.

"You're not going to believe this," he went on, "but my parents didn't even have the guts to tell me. The headmaster was an old friend of Dad's and they got him to do it.

"I screamed at the top of my lungs, 'Nooooooooooo. He wouldn't do that!' I couldn't stop crying. I ran all the way to the infirmary, screaming my head off the whole time. I almost ran right through the glass door."

He also talked about the woman he was seeing.

"She's beautiful, but totally messed up. She was raped when she was 14. I listen to her problems and try to help her, but it's hard; she reminds me of my brother.

"She keeps saying she wants to have sex, but she doesn't want to have sex, which is fine with me, since I'm in the same place. I want sex, but I could never undress in front of any woman."

Toward the end of the session I challenged Mark to a round of hand wrestling, the kind where the opponents stand facing each other, grasping each other's hand, each with a foot placed forward and against their opponent's foot.

Neither combatant is allowed to lift or move their feet while each attempts to throw the other off balance. If either foot moves, that opponent loses.

I often suggest this exercise to patients – especially male patients – to get both of us out of our chairs and interacting in a new, more immediately physical way. Whether they are willing to take the challenge or not tells me a lot about who they are.

Mark didn't hesitate for a second. He almost jumped out of his chair and said, "You might want to think twice about this, Akeret; I'm really good at this stuff."

I didn't tell him that I had been beating guys bigger, older, and stronger than I am since I was a child; I used to regularly beat my teenage camp counselors when I was only 10 or 11 years old.

Mark and I were about the same height, but I was probably a few pounds heavier.

"Which way do you want me to throw you?" I asked. "On to the couch or the floor?"

I was intentionally playing big-brother Luke and trying to intimidate him.

"One, two, three – go!" I immediately used the power of Mark's thrust to throw him on to the couch. He was astonished and delighted, and immediately wanted to do it again. This time I tossed him on to the floor.

"You're really good at this, Akeret," he said, rising, 'just like Luke."

"No!" I said. "Not just like Luke. Because, unlike Luke, I'm going to teach you how to do this, so that you can win."

And that's just what I did over the next few sessions. I told him that I wanted to help him realize his true resources and win at life, and that this was exactly what we were doing in our work together.

I realized I had morphed from being Mark's drill sergeant to being his older brother, and that now I was becoming a substitute for the strong father he'd never had.

Mark and I were working together so well that I was very encouraged. And then, suddenly, we weren't.

"You want to see psoriasis, Akeret? *This* is f----ing psoriasis!"

Mark had come storming into my office, raging, taking me completely by surprise.

Without another word he began to rip off his own clothes, tears streaming down his face. I couldn't understand what was making him so angry. Then I looked at his body.

It was horrifying – covered with red, scaly sores and welts, some of them oozing pus. There was barely an inch of normal skin anywhere on his body, except for his face, which still looked like that of a Greek god – an angry Greek god.

"See? *See?*" he demanded. I did.

"Yes," I said. "I see why having an intimate relationship with a woman would be a problem."

"I can't even have 'an intimate relationship' with myself," he gasped, and began to cry.

I felt horrible, remembering how I had ordered him to undress and how I had breezily diagnosed him as "fit for action." I had completely ignored his reality – the fact that psoriasis comes and goes.

I felt even worse when I thought about the "leprosy" story I had told him. That was just a practical joke – and this psoriasis was no joke. He looked ghastly without his clothes on.

I had wanted so much for him to succeed with women, I almost thought I could will it. But in this area my theories about the power of optimism had been misplaced – just plain wrong, in truth.

We were going to have to go back to the beginning and try something else, and I had no idea what.

A few weeks later we were talking about Mark's most pressing fears. He was convinced he'd never become a success, never marry, and never have a family.

"I'm a quitter, like Luke," he said.

"Why?"

"Because no one ever disciplined me while I was growing up. I never had to work for anything, so now I don't know how. I could eat whatever and whenever I wanted, watch TV to all hours. I never had to do a chore. Someone always cleaned up after me."

"Is that what I'm here for," I asked, "to clean up after your mess?"

"I thought so. I thought you were going to be my drill sergeant and make me shape up," he said.

"I played that role temporarily, but the fact is you have to become your own drill sergeant, Mark. No one can really do that for you."

"You sound really serious now," he said. "You're scaring me."

"Good. Therapy isn't just a chat, Mark. It's damned hard work. And it's hardest most on you. It's your work. You have to decide what you want.

"Do you want to live? Do you want to have a life, a career, a mate, a family?"

"Yes. I do," replied Mark, "but [...]"

"No 'buts.' If you want something, you go after it. You said you were thinking about applying to graduate school for acting."

"I still am."

"You still are – *thinking about it!* Do it, Mark. Make a plan. Execute it. You're only a quitter if you quit, not because people made things easy for you when you were a child. You're not a child anymore. You're a grown man."

"But the psoriasis [...]"

"You don't have to audition for the graduate program in the nude, do you?"

"I hope not."

"So what are you waiting for?"

Later, he related a dream he'd had the night after his parents had come to the session with him.

"I was trapped on a dangerous island, the kind where an evil genius has his lair, like in a James Bond movie. I managed to escape, and then realized my parents were still trapped on the island, so I went back to try to rescue them.

"Suddenly, I find myself driving this very fast red sports car convertible down a twisting mountain road. But I'm driving so fast I flip the car over. Then I'm outside the car looking into it, and I see my own decapitated body in the driver's seat."

"How did that make you feel?" I asked.

"Great!" he said. "That's the amazing thing – I felt relieved, happy to be rid of my own head."

Then the dream switched to his home, where the family cat also had no head.

"And the cat is walking around the house with no head urinating on everything."

"Congratulations, Mark," I said. "You did it." "Did what?" he asked.

"You got rid of what's inside your head."

"I still don't get it."

"What is it that's inside your head that you want to get rid of?" I pressed. He was quiet for a moment. He had to figure it out.

"Shit. That's what's inside my head, isn't it? It's full of all that shit my mother spouts about how I'll never be able to succeed at anything. It's full of my own shit about how I'll never have a life because of my psoriasis."

"Bingo," I said. "And what about the cat?"

"I don't know. It was Luke's cat. He hasn't let anyone else touch him since Luke died."

"Go on," I urged.

"Oh, I get it – cat's piss on the rug when they're pissed off! It's just like when I threw the lasagna. My parents thought I was just being dramatic. But I wasn't. I was totally pissed at them, furious, because they're so focused on Luke they can't allow me to be myself."

We were both quiet for a few moments while it sunk in.

"I need a new head with some new thoughts, don't I?"

"Yes, you do," I said.

Mark's dream turned out to be a turning point. He finally finished his application to grad school and brought his essay in for me to look at. It was ostensibly about why he wanted to be an actor, but it was really about why he wanted to live.

I asked him to read it aloud, and this is how it began:

> "We" is a word in my family that is haunted by the ghost of my brother. Once we were four, now we are three. Before Luke killed himself, strong emotions were discouraged in our family; afterwards, we were incapable of feeling any emotion at all. We became numb. The pain of Luke's death has irreparably damaged and scarred the love we had for each other. Still, I loved my older brother perfectly. He was my idol, my teacher.

Mark read the words with great feeling. The essay ended with Mark acknowledging that he had to go out into the world and begin taking care of himself; that he had to become responsible for his own life:

> I have to do my laundry. I have to learn to breathe, to listen, to feel, to pay taxes – to speak iambic pentameter as though it were my mother tongue. Is life complex? Yes. Life is complex – and uncertain; often upsetting and painful. My brother could not handle that and chose to die. But I choose to live – to act, in both senses of that word. I want to dedicate myself to learning and mastering the craft of acting, and I want to pursue theater as a defining act of affirmation in my own life.
>
> I loved my brother. I honor his memory and I respect his decision to leave this life. But I will not be following his example. Not this time.

I was very moved by Mark's essay and told him so.

We had made so much progress in so many areas – except for one: his psoriasis. And that became our focus as we neared the end of our work together.

Mark had become more vigilant in managing his psoriasis as part of his general attitude of taking more responsibility for himself. Cortisone injections provided some relief, and he could control flare-ups by lying in the sun. A trip to the Dead Sea worked wonders, and his psoriasis disappeared completely for a while. But eventually it returned.

We had both hoped our analytic work would have a positive impact on the condition. He had never had psoriasis until a few weeks after Luke's suicide. Its appearance in his life had to be due, at least in part, to a psychosomatic reaction. Mark was certain it did.

"Wouldn't it be a miracle if my psoriasis just disappeared as soon as our work was over?" he asked one day.

"That would certainly be wonderful," I agreed. "But you are doing better at controlling it. That's something."

"It bothers me that I'm so hung up on it," he said, "that I'm so narcissistic. I just stare at myself in the mirror sometimes. I can see I'm very handsome, but what good is it if I can't get a woman to love me as I am?"

"Well, Mark, there's healthy narcissism and unhealthy narcissism," I said. "The healthy kind is when you look in the mirror and like what you see, take some delight in it. The unhealthy kind is when you just keep looking in the mirror all day because there is nothing else you want to look at."

"I think I have some of both," he said. "Tell me about your healthy narcissism," I prompted.

"Well, I know I'm taking better care of myself. I stopped smoking, stopped watching too much TV. I was accepted into the grad program, to my own astonishment. And you know what? I think they're lucky to have me."

"I think they are, too," I offered.

"I just know I can't let my skin condition control my entire life. Psoriasis can't be the sum total of who I am. I think I'm going to start writing, and I'm going to begin with a monologue about my skin condition."

I didn't say anything. I didn't have to. I was in awe of how far he had come. He wasn't just surviving any longer – he was moving forward, seeking new challenges. He was thriving.

But there was still a lot of anger about the psoriasis bubbling under his more optimistic exterior. I never forgot what Mark told me about how he would act as if everything was all right – go through the motions. I had a feeling he was doing some of that with me.

One of the arguments against empathy in the field of psychoanalysis is that if you share too much of your own feelings with a patient – become too empathic, too "buddy-buddy" – the patient will never become angry with you, blocking any useful transference that may arise from those emotions.

I disagreed. I had shared a lot of my own emotional history with Mark: not just the leprosy story – which had turned out to be so insufficient – but stories of my own youthful insecurities about girls and sex.

I had attempted to fulfill the role of a surrogate father for Mark because he so needed a strong father's guidance. But I had to admit that he also filled an emotional need for me.

I have four daughters I adore beyond measure, but there are times when I wonder what it would be like to have a son. Mark became something of a surrogate for me in that regard.

And while I had never had a son, I had been one, and I knew there could be anger in that relationship right alongside of love and good fellowship.

To spark his smoldering anger into flame, I began ticking off all the progress we had made together. I knew if I kept doing that, taking self-satisfied credit for what he had achieved, his anger would come out eventually. And it did.

One day toward the very end of our work together, just as we were finishing the session, he exploded as I was once again enumerating all of the ways in which I had helped him.

"You've helped me with so many things, Akeret, sure – *but not my f---ing psoriasis!* That's the reason I came to you in the first place. Admit it: you're just as much in the dark about it as everyone else. Right?"

"What's going on, Mark?" I asked. "You're angry."

"Of course I'm angry. I came to you looking for help with my condition, and you've dealt with everything but!"

"But what's different today that you've suddenly become so angry? Any new dreams?"

"I did have a very upsetting dream lately. But I don't want to talk about it."

"If it was upsetting, I think you have to talk about it," I countered. He paused and took a deep breath. Then began.

"Well, I was back home, watching TV instead of writing a paper. It was past due. I heard someone pacing back and forth outside my door, and that made me feel guilty about not working harder on the paper.

"Later I was actually at college, looking for my philosophy professor so I could tell him my paper was going to be late. I was writing about change, about whether anger was more important than love in bringing about change."

That was interesting, I thought.

"Then I saw my professor, but he wasn't a professor anymore. He was a student, sitting in the front row of the classroom, and so bored he was actually falling asleep. The lecturer yelled at him to wake up and pay attention, and that's when I woke up."

That was even more interesting.

"So who's falling asleep, Mark?" I asked.

"I don't know. A student. But it's not me. I know that much. I'm wide awake. And pissed!"

"Then who's left?"

He was quiet for a moment.

"You, Akeret. It's you. You're the student. You're the one falling asleep when you should be helping cure my skin condition.

"What's going to cure it, Akeret? C'mon! You're so smart, with all the answers? What's the answer to my psoriasis? What's your 'theory' about that? I'll bet you don't even have one, do you?"

I had never seen Mark so angry. I knew I had to give him something real, something truly helpful – and right this second – or all our work could go right down the drain.

I looked around my office for inspiration and saw one of my orchids near the French doors.

"You're like an orchid, Mark." I said. "Huh?" he asked. "A flower?"

"Yes. A rare, tropical flower. Beautiful but damaged. You haven't been well taken care of. You've been stressed beyond your capacity to deal. Your brother's suicide, the unhealthy atmosphere in your home. An orchid can't bloom when it's diseased and you can't bloom as long as you are so stressed. So we have to continue un-stressing you."

He didn't say anything, but at least he wasn't yelling.

"Your psoriasis didn't start yesterday; you struggled with it for five years before we ever saw each other. So it will take time to cure the condition completely. But we will. You have to admit, your condition has gotten better. Our goal now has to be to completely *rebloom you!*"

He was still silent. Then he said, "You always pull a rabbit out of your hat somehow, don't you, Akeret?"

"It's not a magic trick, Mark. It's the truth."

"So I'm a rare orchid? Okay. I'll buy that. I'd rather be a diseased and healing flower than Mr. Psoriasis – the Greek god who can't make it with women.

"You know, Akeret, I'm starting to actually believe there's a lot more to me than my psoriasis."

"I know there is, Mark."

There are no happy endings in therapy the way there are in fiction, and certainly none in the sense that the patient goes forward with all of his or her problems solved forever. Life continues to throw us curved balls.

All you can hope for as a therapist is that the patient is more vitally involved in life, and more resourceful when it comes to handling the difficulties life sends our way.

Mark's story would qualify as a happy ending if it had ended right there. But it didn't. One night, years after we had stopped working together, Mark called me up very late at night in crisis.

"I need to see you right away, Akeret. I'm totally messed up, worse than before."

"Your psoriasis?" I ventured.

"No, no, that's pretty much under control. It's just that [...] everything has gone wrong with Sarah, the woman I've been living with. She wants to leave me, and I don't know what to do.

"It all started when Emily died. She was my best friend in grad school, and here's what's horrible – she died from a misdiagnosed illness. And I wasn't there for her. I should have been there. I should have made sure she went to a better hospital, had better care.

"I wasn't there for Luke. I wasn't there for Emily. Now I'm losing Sarah. Everything is shit.

"I'm totally depressed. I'm not sleeping, not eating. I've never been like this before. I can't get out of bed. I watch TV all day and think about Luke. It's not like I'm considering suicide. It just seems so inviting sometimes, to be gone, to not have to feel anything at all."

I really didn't like the way this was sounding. "Why didn't you call before, Mark?"

"I don't know. I thought I could handle it. Can I come in right now?"

"I don't think I'd be very good this late, Mark. Can you come tomorrow morning early, before I start my regular hours. Let's say 8 a.m."

"Are you kidding? I can't even get out of bed before noon."

"It will have to be at the end of the day then. 7 p.m. Okay? Don't do anything stupid, Mark. Do you hear me?"

"I hear you," he said. "See you at 7."

The second he hung up I had the urge to call him back and tell him to come over right now. His comment about not wanting to feel anything at all had unsettled me. But I didn't. I was afraid it would send the wrong message, and maybe even put the idea of suicide into his head more strongly.

As the night went on I regretted more and more not telling him to come right over, and I slept less and less.

I worried about him all the next day during my sessions. Cell phones had become popular over the previous few years and I knew he had one, but I'd never gotten the number. I reproached myself for that, too. Yes, it had been late when he called. Yes, I was tired from working all day. But none of that was any excuse.

And if he ended up following in his brother's footsteps [...]?

I didn't even want to think about that and put it out of my mind. Or tried to.

At the end of the day, after the last patient had left, I walked into the waiting room to find it empty. No Mark.

As I walked back to my office I had a sudden, sharp memory of the time I had looked into my "crystal ball" and predicted that Mark would never kill himself. How could I have been so arrogant?

I sat behind my desk and waited. And waited. I watched the time go by on the clock. Ten minutes. Fifteen minutes. Twenty. Mark had never once been late for a session in all the time we had worked together.

I could feel the anxiety surging within me. Shit! Why hadn't I insisted he come right away last night?

I thought about Audrey, the actress, and how I had failed her. She had jumped out of a window too, just as Luke had. If Mark went the same way, I'd never be able to forgive myself. I didn't even know if I'd be able to practice anymore.

Mark was now half an hour late, and I had given up all hope. I could feel despair and panic rising in my chest when suddenly I heard the elevator stop on our floor.

I ran to the door and almost pulled Mark off balance when I flung open the door as he was opening it.

"Where were you? Are you okay?"

"Damn it, Akeret, you look worse than I do! Yes, I'm fine. I got stuck in the subway. Damn cell phones don't work down there. What's the matter with you, anyway?"

"Come on in. I think I need to tell you something."

Usually, I never share details of one patient with another. But this case was different. I told Mark about my experience with Audrey, about how she had written to me to say how depressed she was, how much she hated her new therapist. I told him how I had done nothing to help her, and she had killed herself the same way Luke had, by jumping out of a window from many stories up while her new therapist was in the next room.

"I should have driven out there and insisted she be given a new therapist. But I didn't. I let professional courtesy and boundaries and all that stupid crap stop me. And the result is that a beautiful, beautiful young woman took her life. I've lived with the guilt of that ever since." He could see how genuinely upset I was.

"It's not your fault, Akeret," he said, taking on the role of my therapist.

"I know. But knowing that doesn't stop the feelings of regret, of intense guilt, does it?"

"No," he agreed. "It doesn't."

He was quiet and I said nothing, letting him figure it out. "Luke's death isn't my fault either, is it? Or Emily's?" "No," I agreed.

Mark reached over and picked up the little brass elephant that rests on the side table next to the patient chair in my office. He had often done that during times of deep reflection.

"I went to see my mom at her place in the city last night after talking to you. I ended up staying there."

Mark's dad had died during the intervening years, and Mark's mother now had an apartment in the City, in addition to the country estate.

"Was that helpful?" I asked, doubting whether it would be, given his mom's gloomy outlook on life, and wondering how many floors up from the street her apartment was.

"Actually, yeah, it was. She's changed since my dad died. I'm not sure what it is. She has a more positive attitude, and I think she genuinely wants to help me through this. She said I should come and spend some time with her in the country, and I think I'm going to do it."

We talked for the next hour.

"You lost Emily, Mark. You lost Luke, your Dad, and perhaps you're losing Sarah. That's a lot of losses for someone as young as you are."

"How could he have jumped?" he asked, suddenly talking only about Luke. "He didn't have psoriasis or anything like that. I still miss him after all these years. I was telling my mom that today and she was really amazing; supportive, not in the least judgmental or pessimistic.

"I told her, I think Emily's death finally put my psoriasis into perspective for me. It just doesn't seem like all that big a deal anymore."

Mark did go to the country and we kept in phone contact. He spent a lot of time with the family dog, going for long walks. His mom left him alone, asking only to have dinner with him every night.

"I asked her what happened to change her attitude," Mark told me in one phone call, "and she said it was the progress I had made with you.

"She said watching me grow from being a totally dysfunctional slacker into someone with purpose and a real life, with a viable acting and directing career: it made her see life – and therapy – differently.

"Change is possible, she thinks now. And therapy can be good for some people."

His depression lifted completely after about four weeks in the country. He called to tell me he was feeling fine and actively seeking work as a director in theater, with several promising leads out on the West Coast.

And that was the last I heard from him until I went looking for him.

Thirteen years later I contacted Mark through his alumni association to ask if I could tell his story. He was living in Oakland, California, where he had been the past ten years, directing and acting regularly in plays and films.

He was delighted I wanted to include him in my book.

"I remember reading *Tales from a Traveling Couch* in Italian," he said. He had been living in Italy with a woman called Bianca, acting over there and studying Italian, and having an incredible time.

"The sex with Bianca was fantastic. You'll be happy to know my psoriasis is almost completely gone. Your orchid theory seems to have worked."

"It sounds like you are blooming," I said.

"I am. And I'll be coming East for a visit in a few months. I'm hoping we can get together. There's something I want to tell you in person."

We met at Le Pain Quotidian, a French-themed Upper West Side restaurant that offers soups, salads, and delicious desserts.

Mark seemed taller to me when he strode into the restaurant, brimming with confidence. Could he have really grown so tall, or had I shrunk with age?

We gave each other a hug and sat down. "You look great," I said.

"Your orchid theory was right on the money, Akeret. I spent a long time learning how to un-stress and bloom again. And it paid off. Not only is my psoriasis under control, it's virtually disappeared.

"And for the first time in my life I'm in love with a woman who is not a basket case. I don't have to spend all of my time holding her hand and being her therapist. We help each other. We started out as friends and gradually discovered that we loved each other."

"Is that what you wanted to tell me about in person?" I asked.

"That [...] and this: I'm changing careers, Akeret. I've enjoyed working in the theater but I've gone about as far as I can go there. I'm going to enter graduate school again this fall – only this time to study clinical psychology.

"I want to become a therapist and help people, the way you do. What do you think, Akeret? Do I have the right stuff for your profession?"

I was filled with pride, and thought, "This must be what it feels like to have a son decide to follow in your footsteps."

But to Mark I said, "I think you'll make an excellent therapist, Mark. It's a splendid idea, and I'll do everything I can to help."

References

Husserl, E. (1970). *The Crisis of European Sciences and Transcendental Phenomenology: An Introduction of Phenomenological Philosophy*, trans. D. Carr. Evanston, IL: Northwestern University Press (original work published in 1954).

Krishnamurti, J. (1998). *You Are the World.* Hampshire: Krishnamurti Foundation (original work published in 1972).

Commentary on Akeret's case

Empathy, therapist need, and the muddy in-between

Eric J. Dammann

A good case history should engage the reader, get us thinking, and generate plenty to discuss, debate, and learn from. Furthermore, the author should be willing to expose the good, bad, and ugly of their work, and try to offer honest assessments of what went well and what didn't – to expose themselves as well as their patients. Based on these requirements, Dr. Akeret's chapter succeeds, which should come as no surprise to those familiar with his work (e.g., Akeret, 1995). Dr. Akeret was trained as a psychoanalyst in the interpersonal tradition, and follows clearly in the footsteps of Alexander and his concept of the "corrective emotional experience" (Alexander, 1946), as well as Kohut's emphasis on the therapist's empathy as a crucial curative factor (Kohut, 1984). He also, for good measure (and I would guess proudly), follows in the footsteps of radical analysts sometimes accused of conducting "wild analysis," which typically signified (to detractors) a treatment in which the "rule book" had been thrown out and the analyst's countertransference was running amok. The fascinating case presented here demonstrates all three, and ultimately hinges on a few pivotal moments when significant ruptures in the therapeutic alliance take place. In the comments that follow, I will try to explicate what I see as some possible reasons for these ruptures, and focus on three main areas: the use (and misuse) of empathy, potential problems with the "corrective emotional experience," and how countertransference may have impacted both of these.

Dr. Akeret's patient, Mark, is a young man who has experienced a number of traumatic losses. Furthermore, due to his father's passivity and conflict avoidance, and his mother's narcissism and depressive tendencies, he has not had a supportive environment to help him work through these losses. This has left him depressed, guarded, and fearful of fully engaging the world as an adult, and he has recently lost his older brother, with whom he had a loving but competitive relationship. It is into this mix that Dr. Akeret enters Mark's life.

Regarding Dr. Akeret's therapeutic stance, clearly his main goal is that the patient should have an experience, not just "insight" or learning. Furthermore, he is explicit about wanting to create a corrective emotional experience by sometimes acting consciously in a way different from Mark's parents. Thus, for example, he states that "if Mark's mother was going to revel in tragedy, I was going to take a stand at the other end of that continuum and revel in optimism," and later he notes that "I had attempted to fulfill the role of a surrogate father for Mark because he so needed a strong father's guidance."

Much has been written about the "corrective emotional experience," and I think most current analysts believe that in any successful treatment there are some meaningful corrective emotional experiences that occur. What remains controversial, however, is the analyst's intentionally acting in a way so as to be a "better" version of some past relationship (Alexander, 1950). As Christopher and colleagues note:

> The contemporary relational perspective is thus very much in harmony with Alexander's emphasis on the relational and experiential aspect of treatment. Where it differs, however, is in its sense of (a) whether the therapist is capable of determining in advance what type of relational stance on his or her part might be desirable and (b) whether it is desirable to intentionally play a certain role with the client, even if it were possible.
>
> (Christopher et al., 2012, pp. 59–60)

Furthermore, they suggest that such a purposeful therapeutic strategy would "inevitably taint the therapist's responses to the client with an element of disingenuousness. For relationalists and interpersonalists, it was critical that the therapist's response to the client not be deliberate or staged" (p. 60). While some might debate this point, I believe it is relevant to the current case history in terms of countertransference issues that may have led to some of the empathic misattunements that occurred. For example, although clearly multi-determined (more on this below), I wonder if it was, in part, his effort to be different from Mark's mother – the optimist to her pessimist – that led to the somewhat shocking (especially due to its occurring in the second session, before a good working alliance had been established) command that Mark take his clothes off. Consciously, Dr. Akeret is attempting to show Mark that the psoriasis is "no big deal" – to minimize it rather than maximize it as his mother does. This recurs later when he tells Mark about his own "leprosy." Again, I think this is partially motivated by his wish to be different from Mark's mom's gloom-and-doom view, but it also leads to a rupture because Mark rightly feels that this minimizes his experience of an actual disease.

In a related vein, Mark is a young man who hasn't been "seen" – neither by his preoccupied mother, nor by the other women in his life to whom he is ashamed to "expose" himself. In Dr. Akeret's wish to be different from these other people in Mark's life, it seems that he may be trying too hard to forcefully "see" Mark (again leading to the command that Mark "expose" himself and be seen). Paradoxically, the effort to be different and "see" Mark may have actually made him unable to see him (by minimizing the pain and extent of the condition). His effort to see, in other words, made him temporarily blind. Dr. Akeret's quip about having a "crystal ball" is also interesting in this light, as a crystal ball is used to supposedly "see" things that are not visible otherwise, but of course it often reflects back what we ourselves want to see. In summary, then, why did Dr. Akeret need to see Mark's symptom as "no big deal?" Is it possible that the effort to provide a corrective emotional experience led to rupture – in other words, in trying to be different from Mark's "gloomy" mom he becomes equally mis-attuned on the other end of the scale, by minimizing the level of trauma associated with the symptom? Perhaps the enactment here is that Mark is again feeling "unseen" by an "other" temporarily blinded by his or her own needs.

Another example in which I wondered whether Dr. Akeret's stated aim of being different from past relationships may have caused a closing down of exploration concerning Mark's conflicted masculinity. As noted above, Dr. Akeret often focuses on action rather than on insight in the therapeutic setting, and therefore Dr. Akeret addressed this issue by challenging Mark to a hand-wrestling match. His conscious intention was to get a first-hand sense of how Mark dealt with this, as well as to offer a corrective experience of male competition as a positive force (he was going to teach Mark how to do it rather than just beat him, as Mark's brother had done). While I think this likely had a positive effect, I wondered if it may have also closed down an exploration of Mark's conflicts about masculinity. For example, Dr. Akeret (rightly, I believe) connects the psoriasis to his brother's suicide, but another important meaning in the symptom seems to be that it allowed him to avoid sexuality. In fact, Mark makes it explicit that he "can't" have sex with women because of it. In exploring his dream of the car crash and decapitation, they discuss the imagery as connected to the need for him to get rid of the "shit" in his head, as well as being about his anger. While I think this is correct, I again felt that the conflicts about masculinity and sexuality were missed. One doesn't have to be a dyed-in-the-wool Freudian to wonder about Mark's not being able to handle the sleek sports car, and that he gets his head cut off after trying to drive it. And the fact that this happens immediately following his escaping the "dangerous island" where the "evil genius" has his parents trapped is also significant. Furthermore, Mark reports this dream immediately following their discussion about his passivity. Earlier in the session, when Dr. Akeret is addressing this issue, Mark again turns to the psoriasis as an out: Dr. Akeret says, "You're not a kid anymore. You're a grown man," to which Mark responds, "But the psoriasis [...]"

Of note, the psoriasis was the one area where there had not been much progress well into the treatment. And while the link between his brother's death and the psoriasis being about "joining him in a kind of living death" seems plausible, I again wonder if something about conflicts around masculinity and competition were missed. Perhaps Mark's real fear was that if the psoriasis went away and he could be a fully realized adult male, he would have defeated his beloved older brother, who was never able to achieve this objective. For this reason I wondered about another level of enactment taking place in that fateful second session. Is it possible that aside from what I described above, this session was also enacting

Mark's passivity in the face of strong men, and Dr. Akeret was emasculating him in his role as drill sergeant: "*You will do it now, soldier!*" Why didn't he just ask Mark to show him the psoriasis? Later in the treatment, Dr. Akeret seems to grasp the problem with his earlier stance, when Mark is again wishing for a strong male figure to take over his life, and Dr. Akeret responds: "The fact is you have to become your own drill sergeant." This, to me, may have been the most important intervention of the session.

Finally, if, like the headless cat in the dream, Mark is only able to express anger to strong males by passively "pissing" on them, what better way to "defeat" Dr. Akeret than by keeping the symptom that brought him to treatment? In the session where Mark explodes about the psoriasis still being a problem, he relates a dream in which Dr. Akeret, the supposed professor, is actually a mere student, and a sleeping one at that! The fact that Dr. Akeret was able to see the meaning in this, and own it with Mark, seemed pivotal – Mark's anger toward a strong man could indeed be accepted and "heard." This leads to the metaphor of the orchid, and a move from anger to love as an important curative force. Interestingly, when they meet all those years later, Dr. Akeret notes that Mark seems taller and brimming with confidence – that he had, in fact, become a man.

Efforts to create a corrective experience for our patients can also go awry if we get too invested in the "cure" – what has sometimes been called "therapeutic zeal." This may seem paradoxical, since of course we want to help the patient, but at times during the case I felt that Dr. Akeret was rushing in too quickly, leading to other moments of empathic mis-attunement. Analysts since Freud (1912/1958) have warned about the dangers of being too invested in a certain outcome, and from a more current perspective Greenberg (1986, p. 81) notes:

> [T]herapeutic "zeal" is detrimental to the analytic process because it encourages the dissociation of crucial aspects of the patient's personality – aspects that may be regressive, masochistic, destructive or rebellious. If the analyst clearly values a particular sort of change, the patient can come to feel that acceptance by the analyst is contingent upon the patient being collaborative and making progress, an atmosphere in which critical aspects of the transference can become irreparably lost.

In the first few minutes of their work together, when Mark asks how Dr. Akeret knows he won't be the same after treatment, Dr. Akeret responds by saying, "because I won't let that happen." In this same session he also says, "it will be an experience you'll never forget." The problem here is that both statements are potentially untrue: there is no way we can know in a first session much of anything about what will happen. So what led Dr. Akeret to make such bold predictions? In the first session he also dives into an interpretation, asking Mark why he "gave" himself psoriasis. Again, why so quick? When Dr. Akeret follows his interpretation with "I guess you didn't see that one coming – maybe not all therapists are as predictable as you think," I felt that his own need to be seen as different and provocative was to the fore. Some of the early interventions felt to me at least partially like a premature wish to cure that was interfering in his letting the material unfold in its own time.

I would now like to turn to the role of empathy in treatment. Empathy is a tricky thing, because we can never fully know how much we are seeing the other, or ourselves. In other words, it is sometimes difficult to tell the difference between empathy and projection. Furthermore, what feels like empathy may also sometimes be a narcissistic identification, or may be used defensively – perhaps out of our "wish to know," or a wish to cure that is premature (see Moses (1988) for a good discussion of the potential misuses of empathy). Finally, I believe that trying to be "empathic" can lead us to assume that we understand something, when often we don't. This can lead to a premature closing down of exploration.

At times in this case I felt that Dr. Akeret was trying too hard to be empathic. In the first session Mark tells Dr. Akeret, "You can't possibly imagine what it's like to live with all those sores and pus." Dr. Akeret's response, "Maybe I can; I have a pretty good imagination," felt a little like forced empathy, and didn't allow for an exploration of Mark's subjective experience of it. Similarly, in a later session Mark says, "You have no idea what it's like to have a diseased body," and Dr. Akeret responds with "That's where you're wrong, Mark. Let me tell you about the time I had leprosy." Again, this led to a rupture as Mark felt unheard, and I wonder whether Dr. Akeret's wish to be "empathic" got in the way of his taking what would likely have been a more empathic route, by saying something along the lines of "Tell me what it's like, Mark." Similarly, in the emergency session in which Mark is distraught over another loss, Dr. Akeret greets him at the door and immediately discloses his own traumatic experience with a patient's suicide, all before hearing anything from Mark about his own experience.

Having discussed some potential countertransference issues that led to ruptures, I should clarify that these issues by no means make this a "failed" treatment. All treatments involve empathic failures and ruptures, and it's clear that Mark made significant improvements and that the treatment was pivotal in helping him get moving in his life. So, what worked? Paradoxically, I wonder whether the very things that led to some of the countertransference errors may have also aided in the positive changes that occurred. For example, while I believe that Dr. Akeret's wish (need?) to be the "optimistic opposite" of Mark's mother led to some empathic ruptures, I think it is equally true that this optimism brought a breath of fresh air into an otherwise stale and deadened system (both familial and internal). In addition, while Dr. Akeret's wish (need?) to "see" Mark led to some ruptures as well, it is clear that at times Mark did feel genuinely "seen" by Dr. Akeret, as well as accepted for who he was, and, more importantly, who he could be. Furthermore, Mark had a felt sense of Dr. Akeret's willingness to push himself out of the status quo comfort zone, and affectively, Mark was able to push himself into uncomfortable territory as well. This is most evident in his moving and compelling essay for the MFA program. All of this helped Mark make significant progress resolving his conflicts around agency and relatedness.

Another significant reason for the success of their work was Dr. Akeret's ability to become aware of some of his empathic failures, most notably during the pivotal moment when Mark's psoriasis flares up and he comes to the session in a rage. This rage jolted Dr. Akeret into waking from his countertransference slumber, and allowed him to see some of the empathic failures – as he correctly puts it: "The empathic experience I thought would help me relate to him most deeply turned out to be only skin deep." Furthermore, he is able to see how he had "completely ignored his reality." And finally, he is then able to see how his therapeutic zeal led him astray: "I had wanted so much for him to succeed with a woman, I almost thought I could will it." This session was clearly a critical moment in the therapy, and I wish Dr. Akeret had spelled out more how these ruptures were repaired. Did Dr. Akeret share his feelings about what had happened, or his understanding of why it had happened? Why or why not? Or did his new awareness simply allow him to change his approach? My guess is that part of the repair came from Dr. Akeret's being able to respond non-defensively to Mark's anger. Finally, I'm curious if the countertransference issues noted above were related to something specific in this dyad. If so, how does Dr. Akeret understand this?

To conclude where I started: I would like to thank Dr. Akeret for his case presentation which will, I'm quite sure, lead to spirited discussion, as well as opportunities to think about some critical issues in psychotherapy. In a paper about the therapeutic power of empathy, Dr. Akeret is also offering us a word of caution about its misuse, and the need for mindfulness when we are convinced that we understand the other and their experience. We can never truly "see" another, but if our own needs aren't distorting the picture (or, more accurately, when we are able to become aware of when they inevitably do), we can make an effort that is often profoundly curative. Perhaps the *effort* to empathize is what is ultimately felt by the patient, especially if we are able to navigate those moments when we miss.

References

Akeret, R. (1995). *Tales from a Traveling Couch.* New York: Norton.

Alexander, F. (1946). Individual psychotherapy. *Psychosomatic Medicine, 8,* 110–115.

Alexander, F. (1950). Analysis of the therapeutic factors in psychoanalytic treatment. *The Psychoanalytic Quarterly, 19,* 482–500.

Christopher, C., Safran, J., & Muran, J. C. (2012). The corrective emotional experience: A relational perspective and critique. In Castonguay, L. & Hill, C. (Eds.), *Transformation in Psychotherapy: Corrective Experiences across Cognitive Behavioral, Humanistic, and Psychodynamic Approaches.* Washington, DC: American Psychological Association.

Freud, S. (1912/1958). Recommendations to physicians practicing psychoanalysis. *Standard Edition, 7,* 109–120. London: Hogarth Press.

Greenberg, J. (1986). The problem of analytic neutrality. *Contemporary Psychoanalysis*, *22*, 76–86.

Kohut, H. (1984). *How Does Analysis Cure?*, (Eds.) A. Goldberg & P. Stepansky. Chicago, IL: University of Chicago Press.

Moses, I. (1988). The misuse of empathy in psychoanalysis, *Contemporary Psychoanalysis*, *24*, 577–594.

Chapter 2

A change in sexual orientation

A case of pseudo-relatedness

Nicholas Samstag

Introduction and identifying features

Art presented for treatment in 1997 as a 30-year-old heterosexual, white Jewish male with a significant history of depression, severe family tensions, and concerns regarding his sexuality. He was not in any romantic relationships, and while acknowledging prior interest in and sexual involvement with men, complained of not being able to find "the right girl." Art had also experienced several professional setbacks, and suffered from "feeling stalled" in his chosen career.

A former patient, with whom I had terminated several years before, referred Art to me. Our work began as a one-session-per-week psychoanalytic psychotherapy, lasting for two months, and then extended to twice a week in response to Art's significant anxiety and depression. In September 2000, three years into our work, I suggested to Art that he begin an analysis of three times a week, to which he agreed. We terminated the analysis in 2008.

In reflecting on my early impressions of work with Art prior to starting the analysis, what stands out most in my mind is how mechanical, rigid, and controlling I found him to be, as well as how oblivious he was to the effect he was having on others. He reminded me of the Swiss soldier Captain Bluntschli in Shaw's "Arms and the Man"; a failed ideologue whose bravado is transformed into an authentic character after facing death and acknowledging his humanity. As will be noted, Art and I used literature and drama to connect with one another as well as to distance ourselves from aspects of the analytic experience.

Art was handsome, six feet tall, with an athletic physique of which he was proud. A strong forehead and a dimpled chin completed the picture of a leading man type. He was typically dressed in loose-fitting sports clothes, and often appeared younger than his stated age. I recall that as Art was telling me why he was seeking treatment, I found myself feeling that he was expecting me to do something to him, or for him, that would take his pain away. Art was accustomed to hiring people, and although he treated me with respect, there was something impersonal in his attitude. The transference initially suggested that he viewed me as his most recent employee, and I was not so much a person as a collection of professional functions that he expected I would harness on his behalf. Art told his narrative of unrequited love, lack of professional advancement, and chronic depression in a mechanical, emotionally distanced way. I was aware of feeling empathy for him, as well as being put off by his lack of connectedness. My countertransference early on consisted of judging him, at times, as an entitled spoiled brat who externalized his difficulties in living. I was also aware that there were many aspects of Art's story that were similar to my own, and of my tendency to compare myself to him in both flattering and unflattering ways.

Patient history

Art was born in the mid-1960s in the southern United States, where his father was stationed during the Vietnam War. Art's birth was induced, with no further complications. A heart murmur was detected when Art was 2 years old, but was no longer in evidence, nor was there any indication of physical disease.

In 1967 the family moved to Westchester, and Art's father completed his medical residency and surgical training. The family stayed there for a year, and then moved to Connecticut in the early 1970s. About 15 years later, the family moved to another part of Connecticut when Art graduated from high school. He was a good student, excelling at what interested him and not working particularly hard at what didn't. Art initially enrolled in a small, undistinguished liberal arts college, and had a difficult time fitting in and making friends. He would pack his academic schedule with numerous design projects, and showed no interest in fitting in with other students. He dressed in conservative suits, or sweater vests, and pressed slacks. Art said that he "could have walked out of a Bloomingdale's window display." He transferred to a more competitive liberal arts college, and graduated in 1989. Art went directly into an Ivy League MFA program for Architectural Design, and graduated with honors in 1992.

After graduate school, although he had received some good reviews for his projects, Art was not able to support himself. His father, who was a successful doctor, consequently supported him financially.

Art's early professional architecture career was notable for his unbending interpersonal style. He was fired more than once for not being able to get along well with his colleagues and clients, and failed to get jobs in spite of his talent because he was not "a team player." As a partial consequence of his regular unemployment, Art had time to design projects for which he was the only contributor. He was disciplined and hard-working, keeping to a strenuous work schedule that continued throughout our time together. Unlike working with clients and colleagues on contracted projects, Art had had some notable critical success with his designs which he submitted to various design contests, and which involved only himself.

Art had turned his social isolation into something productive, if not happy. Other examples included a sophisticated online creative design business, where he and a friend created custom-made graphics honoring people for special occasions. His reason for doing this was twofold; if he couldn't make it as a top-tier architect or designer, he still wanted to be involved in something creative. He also figured he might be able to support himself financially and get his mother and his sisters off his back about taking money from his father. Art had several customers, all of whom were impressed and pleased by the work he created, but which never amounted to anything financially significant.

One way of understanding why people found Art difficult to connect with was that he seemed more engaged with abstract principles and constructs than with people. For example, in describing why a friendship never got off the ground, he would tell me that *he* knew what it meant to be "a true friend" and that the other person didn't. "I know how to put other people first. I go out of my way for them. And they don't. They don't know what it takes." Or, in describing why the beginning of a sexual relationship ended abruptly, Art would have no idea what his contribution might have been. He would become despondent and wonder how the other person, male or female, could be so lacking in romantic protocol. He would say things like, "So we had really good sex, and I put him in a cab. We agreed that we would talk the next day. I called him, and no response. It's been over a week, and still not a word. These people just don't get how this works."

I began to feel that Art's primary relationships were with ideas. Or, to say this in another way, *Art was more narcissistically invested in his intellectualizations than he was interpersonally connected.* He seemed to function as an acolyte for abstract causes, claiming often that he was "a perfectionist" who would not compromise his standards to win "popularity contests." This attitude, needless to say, did not endear him to others. The most devastating example of this was when Art was fired as the theatrical designer of a popular off-Broadway play in 1996. This took him completely by surprise, and he demanded that the artistic director tell him the reason. When he was told that it was because he disrespected the director and producers by acting "like a drill sergeant," and showed "contempt" for his colleagues by not taking their input seriously, Art was incredulous. Art nursed this failure, experiencing a deep sense of narcissistic injury that was slow to heal.

To summarize, Art had a painful lifelong history of unrequited relationships. With both friends and lovers, he would portray himself as the "real deal, the loyal one," the one who would "go the distance for someone [he] cares about." Art saw his relationship failures as the fault of others, who were not committed, smart, or aware enough to know what they were missing in him, and because he felt he wasn't better looking.

Developmental and family history

Art described a lonely and sad childhood in which he fought intensely with his mother and longed for his father who was mostly absent. Art idolized his two sisters, who are five and four years older, whose approval and support he actively sought in vain. Having no friends, and little comfort from his family, Art turned to movies and television for escape, especially the television series *Star Trek*. Inspired by Leonard Nimoy's character, "Mr. Spock," who, as a half human, half alien, did not feel much of any emotion, Art often tried to re-create Spock's "neck pinch" on his mother in a spirited attempt to knock her unconscious.

In reaction to his social isolation, Art withdrew into his head. He said that he began to "think of what it would be like to be dead" from around the age of 6. He regularly entertained what his parents would say at his funeral, and rejoiced in the idea that they would be emotionally distraught and racked with guilt. Art had no chums, in the Sullivanian sense, and very few friends. He would spend protracted periods of time in the basement, pursuing one TV- or movie-inspired design or another, often experiencing bodily sensations that unnerved and sometimes excited him. For example, he would describe "frissons" where he would become acutely aware of his spine touching the back of the couch, or of how his underwear felt against his body. Art associated these experiences almost exclusively with the triumphs, adventures, successes, and relationships on screen that eluded him in his real life.

Art described his voluntary exile as "out of sight, out of mind." Art used intellectualization as a primary defense against the anxiety provoked by interpersonal aggression. Examples of this included a large vocabulary, cultivated in childhood, which he would use to impress adults and defend himself against his contemporaries who sought to tease or bully him. (Upon inquiry, it became clear that Art seemed unaware that he was often teased and bullied as a direct consequence of these behaviors.) Similarly, Art had established ideals of ethics and morality that he regularly espoused and to which he rigidly adhered in order to control the interpersonal space. He promoted himself as an erudite and principled person, leading with his head, not with his heart, and was mystified as to why this put a lot of people off.

As a result of being dismissed or shouted down by his sisters and his mother, and consistent with his tendency to intellectualize, Art had the habit in conversation of quoting TV, plays, and movies in lieu of his own voice. This allowed him ready-made scripts by which to navigate relationships, and to test how much threat or goodwill was there. My sense was that Art lived at a great distance from himself as well as from others, and that I needed to both respect that distance, while at the same time help to bridge it.

Art's earliest memories of his mother paint a picture of her as cold, rejecting, psychologically unaware, and obsessed with money. Art recounts that his paternal grandfather would say that his mother would "fill up the bucket of love and then kick it over." Art's mother was outwardly hostile to her husband, and would put him down repeatedly in front of the children. She would typically harp on how much money he was spending on Art and his sisters, and how much he should be giving to her. Art claimed that his mother would routinely say hurtful and inappropriate things to all members of the family, and then be mystified by their angry or hurt reactions.

Art's mother sought treatment after she discovered her husband was having an affair. Art claims that his mother learned from her therapist "to say whatever was on her mind," and embraced this advice with gusto. Art described numerous examples of his mother's bull-in-a-china-shop style, including the time one of her grandchildren was hospitalized with a serious illness. Art's mother told her daughter she couldn't accompany her to see him because she didn't want to miss her bridge game, and the pot she might win.

Art describes his father as a benign, hard-working man, who never understood, but always supported, his unhappy son. Art was deeply disappointed in him. On one occasion when Art's father became incensed that Art was watching and enjoying *All in the Family*, he blustered that it was "racist and disgusting," missing its satirical focus entirely. Both parents routinely missed the subtleties and nuances of interpersonal communication. Having failed to connect with him directly, Art attempted for several years to try to get his father to understand him through theater, movies, and TV. He finally gave up, saying that his father "just doesn't get me. He doesn't understand people." Art's father would say in response to Art's exasperated attempts at connecting with him, "I just don't go that deep." The picture of Art's father which I built up over several years was of a kind, hard-working, and masochistic man who invested himself almost entirely in his work as an escape from a family that either dismissed or criticized him.

A central focus of Art's treatment was to understand how his father's largess both helped and hindered Art's development. Art's father would typically respond to his son's unhappiness by giving him money, to "compensate for his not being there." He sent Art to an expensive arts camp after Art demanded at the age of 10 to come home from another camp he hated due to "unbearable bullying." He also established a trust fund for Art before he graduated from college, and paid for his graduate education. In addition, he contributed significantly to Art's projects, as well as raising money from his wealthy friends. Significantly, Art's father paid for his treatment with me as well.

In contrast to Art's mother's image as a volatile and nasty person, Art's father had an idealized image, both in the family and in the town where they lived. People often compared him to "Marcus Welby, MD," the unimpeachable and courageous TV doctor of the late 1960s and early 1970s.

History of prior treatments and surrounding circumstances

Art had been in some sort of clinical treatment since the age of 8, and had subsequently seen "at least six therapists." He didn't remember whether they were psychologists, psychiatrists, or social workers, and stated that he had gotten "something, but not a lot" from the collective experience. I was not optimistic, initially, that our work together would be any different. It was also clear to me that Art was the identified patient; that at an early age he became the repository of the family's unrecognized pathology, and, as is often the case, would develop far greater awareness and insight than any of his relatives.

Art's presenting problems remained the same: depression, social isolation, deep lack of self-worth, and an increasing unease about his sexual orientation. By the time he sought treatment with me at the age of 30, he had been profoundly disappointed by both love and work, and his primary defenses of intellectualization, denial, and projection were very much still intact.

Art's first therapy at age 8 lasted for approximately 11 months. His father was mostly working away from home, his sisters excluded him, and Art and his mother were physically antagonistic toward one another. Art was trying to "neck pinch" her, and she was beginning to shove him around. Art claims that he was "fine with therapy until it got in the way of my Star Trek watching, and then I asked to stop." Art's father complied, and Art withdrew more deeply into his basement experience.

Art's second treatment was in the tenth grade, and lasted through the end of high school. In addition to his continued social isolation and family stress, it was revealed that his father was having an affair with a woman in their community. Honesty, integrity, morality, and duty were among the virtues extolled by Art's father, and which he attempted to inculcate in his son. Art assaulted this woman verbally on the day following the discovery of the affair, feeling personally betrayed and narcissistically wounded. Art claims that this was the point when his suicidal thoughts hit their peak. He denied ever having a specific plan, but did spend considerable time fantasizing about a building falling on him, or jumping out of a window, and, as mentioned above, how his family would feel at his funeral. This theme of vengeful suicide and the familial reaction to it constituted a core aspect of Art's emotional and fantasy life, as well as related narratives in which he was mourned and missed by friends who had treated him badly, or who did not return his affections.

The family was in particular turmoil during this time, collectively blaming Art's father. It is notable that Art's father had no explanation or insight as to why he had the affair. At his wits' end, he suggested that they all seek family counseling, to which the other family members reluctantly consented. Art recalls not liking the family therapist, and they stopped going after a few sessions.

Diagnostic impressions

From an early age, Art was emotionally abandoned by his father and sisters, and hated by his mother. As a consequence he felt like an alien in his own family, as well as in the majority of social contexts. This considerable emotional neglect and abuse contributed to a spectrum of significant psychological difficulties, including autistic–contiguous, paranoid/schizoid, depressive, and narcissistic disorders.

The self that Art saw reflected back to him in his attempts at establishing interpersonal connectedness was unrecognizable. Unable to consider that he was contributing to this dissonance, Art assumed that the fault lay with the other.

Ogden's concept of the autistic–contiguous position is helpful here in understanding how profound Art's isolation could become in those moments when everything dissolved for him apart from the most basic physical sensations. Following Klein (1948), the paranoid/schizoid and depressive positions reflected the broadest range of Art's experience. At the start of our work together, Art was more solidly in the paranoid/schizoid camp, often experiencing an emotional remove whereby he would lose himself in plays, movies, and literature, and commune with intellectualized notions of what it means to be human. As this energized him, he would attempt to connect with people and typically feel unrecognized and alone, both helpless to change anything for the better, and hopeless that anything would improve. This then would force Art to withdraw into his basement room, both literally and metaphorically, where he escaped into plays, TV, and movies, and the cycle would begin again.

The resulting narcissistic defense prompted Art to construct an armored idealized character that felt superior and invulnerable to his hostile and indifferent family, as well as to his peers who mostly taunted or ignored him. Art projected an unattainable ideal that validated his unrealistic sense of self and protected him from the pitfalls of actual human interaction. The clinical challenge was how to alternately both recognize and challenge his false sense of self, while connecting with undefended aspects of the real self as they emerged. This defensive style was established by an early age, whereby Art would chastise his friends and acquaintances, saying that they were not behaving as they should, according to Art's standards of friendship and fair play.

By understanding depression as aggression turned inward, as a retreat both from external impingements and internal persecutions, I was moved to invite Art out of his basement existence. I could also relate to what it means to be depressed, and felt a personal resonance in hearing Art's narrative.

I cannot say that I especially liked Art at the start of our work together, nor did I think that this would be a particularly rewarding treatment for either of us. However, as we continued working, Art seemed slowly but steadily able to look at himself more closely, and to become an active participant in the process. He let down his guard, became curious about who I was as a person, and progressed from splitting himself off into schizoid withdrawal, to actively engaging in the mixed bag of interpersonal relatedness. He also discovered a greater sense of personal agency that allowed him to translate insight into action.

Course of treatment

For the purposes of clarity and organization, I will divide my analysis of Art into four phases: Transition (September 2000 to February 2001), Beginning (March 2001 to December 2003), Middle (January 2004 to January 2007), and Termination (February 2007 to January 2008). Admittedly, this is a somewhat arbitrary division, but it will hopefully provide a structure through which to assess both the dominant content and processes of the work.

Phase one: transition

Prior to beginning our analysis, Art and I discussed the fee. I said that I wanted to charge him the same per hourly rate, and he agreed. I asked him whether he had any feelings about the increased bill, and he said that his father "owes it to me. He messed me up, he can pay to fix me." I pressed a bit further, and inquired whether he thought his analysis was a way to hurt his father. He thought for a moment and said, "It hurts him that I'm in treatment, period. The extra money will bother my mother."

Art began our three-time-per-week analysis sitting in a chair, and after a month or so expressed interest in lying on the couch. After two months he became very dissatisfied, claiming he did not find the couch productive, saying it "felt weird and superficial." We talked about his unease at relinquishing control, and not being able to see my reactions to him. Art and I had established a positive therapeutic alliance, and Art's dislike of using the couch prompted a productive and engaged dialogue. The increased frequency and exposure, from once to three times a week, however, initially had the effect of making Art feel self-conscious and more resistant than he had been before. The following excerpt comes from the third week of the analysis:

ART: [Sitting down and waving a yellow sticky note] So, I have this dream. [Pause] Do you want to hear it? [Pause]

NICK: What do you think?

ART: That you're waiting for me to jump right in. Right? [Pause]

NICK: I get the sense I'm not following the script. That you know what you want me to say, and I'm not saying it. I feel you're putting words in my mouth that aren't what I want to say. If I want to say anything. [With an edge to my voice]

I was clearly frustrated by Art's seeming discomfort with our new arrangement, primarily because it didn't seem genuine. On the contrary, I felt that he resented gratifying me by becoming an analytic patient. I was also aware that we had more of these chess-game-like sessions in which we willfully struggled rather than related to one another. With this awareness, I sought to find ways of using my frustration to connect to Art and his experience. The following example is taken from the third month, revealing Art's discomfort, and my attempts at transitioning us from a therapy into an analysis. What is also notable here is Art's articulation of a new transference to me.

ART: Hi.

NICK: Hi.

[Silence]

ART: [Shifting in his chair] Well, this feels uncomfortable! [Strained laugh]

[Silence]

NICK: How so?

ART: I don't know what to say, and you're staring at me, and not saying anything.

NICK: What's that like for you?

ART: It feels creepy.

[Long silence]

NICK: What feels creepy? [Edge to my voice]

ART: It doesn't feel natural, it's like we now have to perform in this analysis play, that we are watching at the same time we are performing. It reminds me of Stoppard's *The Real Inspector Hound.*

[Short pause]

NICK: You think we're watching a set-up for a murder we're participating in? Who's the victim?

ART: Bravo. Very good. I don't know. I am, we are. Maybe it's the analysis. I don't know.

NICK: Bravo?

ART: You sound pissed.

NICK: I'm aware of that. I'm also aware of wanting to join you in these literary references, but when I do we lose our own words.

[Silence]

ART: [After considerable shifting in his chair, and much sighing] I don't know what to say.

[Silence]

ART: I thought of another Stoppard quote, but I know you don't approve.

NICK: [Sighing] How do you know that?

ART: [Sighing] Because "it's not my own voice," blah, blah, blah.

NICK: So I'm the critic? [In reference to *The Real Inspector Hound*] There I go again! I want to say "You made me do it!" What is this like for you employing me to reject your own voice?

ART: I feel you're judging me. Yeah, I guess that's right. It feels shitty. And yes, yes, it feels like my mother.

NICK: You see me as your mother?

ART: No, no, no. I actually see you as *House.*

NICK: *House*? The cranky drug-addicted doctor?

ART: Yeah. Who goes after the disease and doesn't give a shit about anything else.

NICK: Ouch!

ART: No, no, it's not that I think you're insensitive, but you are committed to getting the facts, finding the cause, the root of my issues, and you're not worried about my reactions.

NICK: Like when I point out that you often don't use your own voice?

ART: [Sighs] Yeah. This is not a personality contest for you.

NICK: What is this like for you?

ART: It's like I have a smart doctor in my corner who won't rest until he cracks the case.

NICK: A drug-addicted doctor?

ART: Hmm [...] I don't think you're a drug addict.

NICK: Well, you do in your association to me.

ART: Yeah, I guess so. Well, maybe it's that you seem driven like he does. That nothing will get in your way to find the answers you're looking for.

NICK: What does that feel like to you?

ART: It feels [...] good. And sometimes a little scary.

NICK: How do I scare you?

ART: [Pause] Maybe by knowing things about me that I don't know myself.

NICK: It seems in seeing me as *House* you assume my primary concern is with your "disease" not with you as a person.

ART: [Long pause] I think that makes me feel safer than if I consider you might be caring for me.

NICK: I think that's something you should consider.

ART: OK. [Smiles, and looks away]

NICK: I think you might also consider that *House* suggests a composite of your mother, your father, and yourself. He's a bull-in-a-china-shop like your mother, he's an MD like your father, and he connects primarily to ideas, like you do.

ART: Wow!

NICK: Wow?

ART: You listen to me!

During sessions such as these I found myself divided; on the one hand, I wanted to join with Art where he was in the content of the session, in this case the reference to Stoppard and to *House*. On the process level, on the other hand, I was aware that Art used plays, movies, TV, and literature as a defense against accessing and revealing his own voice, and that this had a painful history for him in his family where he never felt that his own words were worth anything. Art prided himself on his ability to make literary references that elucidated, and distanced, his interpersonal experience, and bested his interlocutors. He felt protected that way, and often superior. Quoting from various scripts afforded him an authority he otherwise lacked. This almost always felt distancing and competitive, yet it also afforded potential entry into his subjective experience. It was clear to me that although Art knew this intellectually, he didn't feel safe to expose his feelings.

In the analysis of the transference, it seemed clear that Art was idealizing me and minimizing how in my attempt to understand him I was scaring him. I felt both flattered and alarmed at Art's transference to me as *House*. I had seen the show, and liked it, but was put off by the distanced, intellectualized manner of the central character. I was also aware of a tendency on my part to get too wrapped up with intellectual matters, and felt stung by, yet grateful for, Art's perception. I would try, I told myself, to be more "experience-near."

It is no wonder that *Star Trek* became a kind of lodestone for Art, in which the central theme was the attempted integration of disparate peoples and worlds.

I believe *Star Trek* represented Art's fantasy of an integrated family. Similarly, Art's transference to me as *House* encapsulated himself and his two parents into a symbol for domestic union. And the character of *House* was similar to many aliens on *Star Trek*, who were often cool and exotic, and sought after as examples of powerful and valuable otherness. This was especially the case with the half-human, half-alien Mr. Spock whom Art internalized. Mr. Spock, in essence, became Art's ego ideal. It was his deepest desire that someone would be attracted to him and find him valuable, as an exotic alien who could only be captured with love and understanding.

Phase two: the beginning of analysis

One of the central themes of our work together was Art's deep anxiety over his sexual orientation. At the beginning of the analysis, Art was still in denial concerning his attraction to men, despite the fact that he had had only one short-lived sexual relationship with a woman, lasting for five months, when he was 18. Art had lost his virginity with this young woman at a summer camp when they were both senior campers, and whom he described as "the hottest girl, bar none," and told me how skilled he was at making her climax. This was, however, a summer romance that didn't last. Once camp was over Art became disinterested. Art had a long history of finding something wrong with every girl he met. After what seemed to be promising dates, he would sigh and say that the woman had an "unbearable voice," or "was a Republican," or "wasn't well read." The ones he claimed to want were either married, in relationships, or didn't want him.

Art had encounters with boys starting at age 6. These were non-invasive, "you-show-me-yours-and-I'll-show-you-mine" experiences in which there was mutual fondling. During adolescence Art had multiple, short-lived sexual relationships with men. These later relationships primarily involved mutual ejaculation, sexual petting, oral sex, and on rare occasions anal intercourse where Art was always dominant. He would say he was lonely and responded to men because they went after him, but he would vastly prefer to sleep with women.

Art was embarrassed by these sexual encounters, and had great difficulty talking about them. Being Gay to Art was "the nail in the coffin" of any chance he had to be happy. Attesting to Art's denial, he didn't believe that he appeared to be Gay and assumed that those around him viewed him as straight. Among the many notable examples of this was a costume party Art attended during this time, dressed in a professional Superman costume. He had custom-made cards that read "Clark Kent" with his phone number, and used one to try to pick up a "great-looking" woman at this party. The woman took the card and, looking at him incredulously, said, "Very funny. You're Gay, right?" This mystified Art. When I wondered gently whether he might be homophobic he would become incredulous, and say, without any irony, that some of his best friends were Gay.

The following exchange is taken from a session within the second year of the analysis, and would prove to be a turning point. Art came in on this particular day looking quite depressed and anxious. He had trouble maintaining eye contact, and sighed frequently.

ART: [After three or four minutes of silence] So, I don't feel so hot. I had a shitty day and night. [Pause]
NICK: It would seem so.
ART: Yeah. You know, I try, I really do, but my life is one big rut. I go to the gym, I spend most of my time in darkened rooms looking at plays or movies. I can't get any directing jobs. No love life. What's the point?
[Silence]
NICK: Why don't you tell me about it?
[Pause]
ART: So I had this totally shitty day where in spite of all my mailings, schmoozing, cold calling, I have no jobs, now or pending. I was turned down or just not responded to, by every design firm and project manager I contacted. Ever since my rejection from the International Design Competition (not the real name) I haven't been able to recover.
NICK: That's the project you were fired from?
ART: Yes, which totally messed me up thanks to that asshole creative director and his flunkies. Anyway, so I came home after my fourth protein shake of the day. [Long pause] [In a very soft voice] He finally left, and I cleaned up and went to bed.
[Pause]
NICK: He?
[Long pause]
ART: What?
NICK: You said "he finally left." Who's he?
ART: Oh, God, oh God. I guess I have to tell you, right?
NICK: Well, this seems to be where we are in the story.
ART: [Sighs] I called up a guy online for sex. He came over. I had told him what I would and wouldn't do. We got off. He left.
NICK: I'm glad I asked.
[Pause]
ART: Do you think this means I'm Gay?
NICK: What do you think?
ART: I really don't think I am. I do this because I'm lonely. I don't feel anything afterward. I can't wait for them to leave. It's like it never happened.
NICK: Them?
ART: Yeah.
NICK: How often do you have internet sex?
ART: A few times a month.
NICK: Always with men?
ART: Yes. I'd never do this with a woman.
NICK: Why is that?

ART: It's degrading.

NICK: Sex?

ART: Internet sex.

NICK: But not degrading for you or for the men you're with?

ART: It's different. We just get each other off. Like guys.

NICK: What kind of sex do you have?

ART: Do we really have to talk about this, Nick?

NICK: No, we don't, but it seems relevant to why you are here. I am aware that you feel uncomfortable, and I wonder why that is?

ART: Isn't it obvious? I don't want to be Gay! I don't want you to think of me that way.

NICK: What way is that?

ART: Having sex with men.

NICK: What sort of sex do you have?

ART: Really? Do I really have to tell you? [Pause] OK, OK. [Sighs] I have a routine. I find them online. Different sites. I tell them I will only fuck; I will never be the bottom. I tell them I will only have safe sex, and that I am HIV – and they have to be, too. Is that enough?

NICK: What's it like telling me this?

ART: [Sighs] Well, it's not great, but it feels better getting it out. I can't help thinking that you're judging me, though.

NICK: What gives you that sense?

ART: It's nothing you're doing. It's just what I think.

NICK: So you think there is something wrong with being Gay?

ART: Do you think I'm really Gay?

NICK: What do you think?

ART: I think I'm lonely, and kind of desperate for attention. But I still think I just haven't found the right woman.

NICK: Rather than labeling, it seems fair to say that you enjoy having sex with men. Would you agree?

ART: [Long pause] Well, yeah, otherwise I wouldn't do it. But I really want to be straight. I don't want to be that lonely Gay guy.

NICK: Why would you assume that you would be lonely?

ART: Oh, come on, being Gay is like a curse.

NICK: Do you ever find yourself attracted to me?

ART: Oh God, really? Come on! No! I mean [...] no. I really like you, I trust you, but I don't see you that way.

NICK: Which way is that?

ART: You're just not my type.

NICK: What type is that?

ART: A California pretty boy.

Although Art and I formed a deep emotional connection with one another which we both enjoyed and acknowledged, there didn't seem to be any sexual tension between us. A partial explanation for this is that Art's sexuality was compartmentalized, and thus unavailable to him in situations and with people he had not designated as sexually viable. Although not Gay myself, I have been aware of sexual tension in treating Gay men over the years. I believe the difference is that in the latter case the integration of sexuality within the therapeutic relationship has at times felt intimate and exciting. With Art, however, it mostly felt that we were conferring on a part of himself that he was finally able to talk about, but was not yet ready to bring into the consulting room. I considered at the time being more insistent in my enquiry of Art's potential sexual attraction to me, but decided that I had opened the door sufficiently. To press this further without any evidence that this is what Art was feeling seemed unwarranted.

However, we did explore a great deal about how his transference to me combined aspects of himself, his rejecting mother, and his idealized father. As far as my countertransference to Art was concerned, I was aware of feeling frustrated by his defensiveness, and also at times envious of his wealth. I tried to be aware of when these feelings threatened to distract me from what was going on with Art, and attempted to find ways of using these perceptions to connect more effectively with him. I was pleased to note that what had essentially developed over time was a solid trust between us where we were united in trying to uncover why Art seemed so hard to love, and to love in return.

Over the following months, Art struggled openly with having sex with men and going on dates with women. While insisting he "felt nothing" for his male partners other than feeling glad to "get off," Art claimed repeatedly how satisfied he was in his ability to sexually please women, saying that sex with women was "the ultimate." This seemed overvalued and defensive, while his statement of having no feeling with men seemed steeped in denial. In both cases his sexuality was split off from his emotional experience. Furthermore, regardless of their gender, it seemed extremely difficult for people to attach to Art. Or, to put this another way, Art had a talent for putting people off, for slipping away, as if he was made of Teflon. This was confusing, because while Art did have some off-putting personality features, there was nothing so toxic about him that would seem to explain why no one was interested in becoming his friend or lover.

Throughout this time, Art maintained that if he were just better looking women would flock to him. Specifically, he was extremely distraught by the fact that he would never look like Brad Pitt. Art had a very clear belief of which body type was "better" than others. California-type blond men with visible cheekbones, "six-pack" abs, powerful chests, and "pretty" faces were all essential to this ideal. In Art's estimation he was passable in all of these areas apart from his face; he believed it just wasn't appealing enough. All my attempts to question this assumption seemed to have little impact. Art saw himself primarily as a substandard physical object, with little belief that he had sufficient internal substance to attract desirable people of either gender. "If I was only better looking," Art would say again and again, "then I would have a chance. But I'm clearly not, and so no one gives me the time of day."

The following clinical vignette occurred several months later. Art had just told Holly, a woman with whom he was romantically involved for four months, that he was also interested in men. Art said he had to tell her because he didn't want to be her boyfriend, and felt he was leading her on. "I feel like she's me. I'm the one who's always hoping to get into a relationship with someone, and devastated when they don't want me." This session, and the analysis of the dream within it, proved to be another crucial point in the treatment.

ART: So I had "the talk" with Holly. Told her about everything, except the part about my paying for it sometimes.

NICK: When did you have the talk?

ART: Last night.

NICK: How did it go?

ART: [Long pause] Well, after I admitted to enjoying sex with guys she said she would "have to sit on it." I thought that was a funny way of putting it, but Holly has no sense of irony. She said she had to find a way to trust me again.

NICK: What was that like for you?

ART: You know, it felt shitty, but OK. I felt relieved. I can't continue to be with her in a romantic way anymore. She's sweet but way too girly.

NICK: Girly?

ART: Her whole room is done in pink and lace. Looks like a 10-year-old's room. But I have a dream I want to tell you.

NICK: Please.

ART: This was last night, after the talk. In the dream, my father took a manuscript I was working on and destroyed it. In it, I made him feel that he ruined my life.

NICK: What was the manuscript about?

ART: It was a story about a guy who failed to get women, became Gay, and failed to get a real boyfriend. He was just not good enough in any area. And then he killed himself.

[Long pause]

NICK: So you destroy your father by destroying yourself.

ART: Yes. And in the manuscript I had written that I liked penetrating men, hurting them. And I knew that would get to him.

NICK: You were punishing your father by hurting these men.

ART: Yes.

NICK: I wonder if the dream is also suggesting that at some imaginative level you think a solution to your problem would be if your father kills you, or kills that Gay part of you depicted in the manuscript.

ART: [Pause] Yes, that's true.

NICK: And that this character is also the *man you script*; your image of who you should be, have to be, in order to seek your vengeance on those who have hurt you.

ART: [Long pause. Begins to weep] I wanted him to tear up the script, to see me. Do you think I've written a part for myself that I confuse with who I actually am?

NICK: I think that you want to be noticed, but are afraid to be known. You want your father to know you, but if he does, you fear he may not love you.

[Long pause. Weeping more heavily now]

ART: Well, yes and no. [Laughs] I had just told Holly that night I sleep with men. On some level I suppose I assume now that the heterosexual life is no longer a possibility. I do blame my father for this. His marriage to my mother was a nightmare. Of course I don't want that. I can't be straight and I can't stand to be Gay. There's no other way out. I want him to see how I suffer.

Within this same time period, Art had the following dream:

ART: I'm on the way to a hot date with a girl, and the building I'm in has a lot of construction going on. I'm wearing a really bizarre three-piece suit of pastel colors. I want to change into a white shirt and jeans, and I know I've got a little time.

It's like a really nice, elegant hotel. Luxurious but not stuffy. There's scaffolding everywhere, drop cloths, paint cans. I'm confused about how to get to the thirtieth floor, where my date and I agreed to meet. There are four elevators, and none of them go directly to 30. I take one of the elevators to 14 and find out that I have to walk the rest of the way. I go into the stairwell where it's really hot, and start to climb. I notice that all the doors are locked leading out of the stairwell. I continue to climb and find an open door that lets me out on the twenty-fifth floor. I find a porter and ask him to tell me how to get to 30, and he says I just passed it. I become exasperated, I'm sweating and irritated, and the porter says, "Sir, you passed 30 long ago." "But I just got out on 25!" I say, screaming. The porter just looks at me and I dash back into the stairwell. Who would do this? I think to myself, I'm going to be late. I can't call her because I left her number on my desk in the room. I keep going up and down the stairs, but the doors are all locked except at the twenty-fifth floor which I now think is actually above the thirtieth. I finally sit on the stairs and start to cry because I know I'm going to be late, and then I decide to forget trying because I'll just look like an idiot. There was too much reconstruction going on.

NICK: Reconstruction? You want to be 30 again? Weren't you 30 when we started our work together?

ART: Construction, I mean construction. Yeah, maybe I want to start again. I want a big do-over. With you, with my life. To get it right this time. It felt like the outside walls were being redone or done in another way. Made to look better.

NICK: Like a face-lift?

ART: Oh my god, yes, yes. In giving myself a pretty new face I missed getting the girl.
NICK: Maybe missing getting the girl is the point.
ART: [Pause] Yeah. Maybe that is the point.

During the following months, Art gradually stopped dating women and began seeing men exclusively. At first it was only to have sex, but then Art became tired of that and claimed that now he was ready to find a boyfriend. He began to tell the few friends he had that he was Gay, and what I had discussed with him on multiple occasions turned out to be the case; none were surprised and all were supportive. Then, with great trepidation and anxiety, Art told his sisters and his parents. Again, none were surprised, and his mother was even kind. So Art embarked on an openly Gay life, feeling both relief not to be hiding this essential part of who he was, and fearful that he would never find a partner.

Phase three: the middle of the analysis

Of all the many playwrights and songwriters Art referenced and quoted in our sessions, Stephen Sondheim was his favorite. There were many occasions when I found that Sondheim's presence more than filled the space between us. The following dream, taken from the fourth year of the analysis, heralded a shift in Art's awareness of how he used Sondheim to dampen his own voice and protect himself against his fear of being unlovable:

ART: This was a couple of nights ago. Sondheim had just written a new show. I was blown away.
NICK: What was the show?
ART: I don't recall the specifics, but in the dream I remember that I thought it was better than *Night Music* and even *Into the Woods*, which as you know is my favorite. Anyhow, I sent him four or five telegrams telling him how much I enjoyed it.
NICK: Why so many?
ART: They were mock reviews that referenced his other shows, using the actual language of each of those shows. Each one was complemented by the one that followed, so all together he had a review of his entire Opus, plus a rave review of his most recent production.
NICK: Let me get this straight: You used his words to honor his words. Where were your words?
ART: Wait, there's more. So the next scene I'm watching him being interviewed on a talk show, and he's telling the interviewer that he got these five telegrams hailing all of his work in the midst of one rave review of the latest one. And then he mentions me by name and says if I'm watching to please call him so he can thank me in person. The scene changes again, and I'm at

XYZW [an elite musical theater design group] and the whole group is blown away that Sondheim wants to see me.

NICK: That's your second "blown-away reference." What do you make of that?

ART: Blown away, blown away. [...] Well there's the sexual meaning, but that doesn't feel right. There's the way you blow something off your hand [makes a blowing sound] that's insignificant. Then I guess there's the death meaning, like being destroyed.

[Long pause]

NICK: If you don't have your own words, you don't really exist?

ART: Yeah, yeah, yeah, you're right. I know, I know, we've been talking about this for so long. I feel I can't stand on my own without others speaking for me. [Pause] In the dream I so want his respect.

NICK: Who's Sondheim?

ART: The Master. You. A successful man who doesn't give a shit. It's who I want to be.

NICK: I wonder if the dream also suggests that you want to credit me for your greater sense of awareness?

ART: [Getting teary] It feels desperate. Like I'm Cyrano and I need a Christian de Neuvillette.

NICK: I feel it's getting crowded in here.

ART: Shit, I'm doing it again!

NICK: Try to tell me, in your own words, what does this feel like to you, Art, not to anyone else.

ART: [Crying] Like I really don't have my own language, my own voice. That all this quoting masks the fact that I don't feel worthy, that I feel empty inside. You know it just occurred to me that to be loved for my words, which are so often others' words, is to be erased.

NICK: It seems to me you are in touch with what you feel now, and that this is new for you.

ART: Yes, it's strange. I just feel terrible, but it feels good to feel that.

Phase four: the final months

My analysis with Art thus far was notable for Art's enhanced capacity to accept his attraction to men, and to reflect on the distance he kept from himself, as seen most strikingly in his tendency to forfeit his own voice in the co-opting of others' language. Art found substantially more of his own voice by acknowledging his feelings, especially in regard to how empty, alone, and deficient he felt. Paradoxically, and in stark contrast to his lifelong tendency to feel narcissistically wounded, Art had now gained strength in acknowledging his vulnerability. This was a positive sign that he was able to avail himself of insight. Similarly, Art was also able to relate to me more authentically, and to use our relationship increasingly as a guide to help him connect to others in his world.

In the first few months of our penultimate year in the analysis, Art decided to get a dog. This was something he had deliberated about for a long time. On the one hand, he felt that having a dog would provide him with a loyal companion and, given the daily walks required, would also force him to get out of his apartment and into the world where he might meet people. On the other hand, he was intimidated by the image of a Gay man walking a small dog. Although Art felt more and more accepting of who he was, he was still unhappy at times about how he appeared. He had had Cairn terriers as a boy, and vividly remembered the solace he felt with them. And so, after making several visits to an exclusive upstate breeder, Rufus came into Art's life and into our analysis.

Our sessions on Rufus, in addition to focusing on how he was a response to Art's loneliness, also gave us an opportunity to further explore how money had and did play a determining role in Art's life. The following clinical vignette is from the first session after Art brought Rufus home:

ART: So, he's home. Well, he's in his cage, but he's home.

[Pause]

NICK: It's not clear to me what you are feeling right now.

ART: [Sighs] He was expensive.

NICK: How much was he?

ART: I'm embarrassed to say.

NICK: Why is that?

ART: Because it's my Dad's money, not mine. And I'd never be able to afford him. Or, for that matter, much of what I do now.

NICK: What else are you thinking of?

ART: [Pause] Well, this, my analysis. Yeah. They are related, I guess. I mean I couldn't afford this or him.

NICK: You're assuming, I guess, that you wouldn't be able to make any money?

ART: Well, I guess I am. I mean I haven't. Not really.

NICK: You haven't had to.

ART: Yes, I know that, and I feel fed up about it. I mean, it's my father's money, but he wants to give it to me. And it makes my life much easier.

NICK: In some ways. In some ways it seems it makes it harder.

[Long pause]

ART: He cost $2800. That's not including training which will be another few hundred, or a thousand. Thank you, Dad, for messing me up and paying for it.

NICK: You feel angry that he owes it to you, and angry that you end up feeling you owe him.

ART: [Pause] It's what he can do, I get that. We've talked about this so much, I know, and at times I'm OK with it, but at other times it feels bad.

NICK: Like now?

ART: Yeah. My Dad is buying me my best friend. But you know what? At least I now have one.

Over the course of the analysis, Art and I had discussed how his father's money had both helped and hindered him. Art was helped, in that he could continue to pursue professional design jobs while also indulging in his passion for movies and theater. He was hindered in being deprived of the character strength gained from having to do things one doesn't want to do, and the subsequent sense of agency that often results. Art's low frustration tolerance was one of the most debilitating consequences of his father's largess.

As Rufus grew, Art did also. Art's greater acceptance of who he was allowed him to get Rufus, who, in a sense, led him out into the world. Art became more and more comfortable identifying as Gay, and on many occasions met both men and women on walks with Rufus who became good acquaintances or friends, and, with some men, lovers. Rufus became a transitional object, allowing Art to bring his deeply personal feelings and fantasies into full view. He ceased to be an ideologue, and entered the world as a human among humans.

Unlike human friends and lovers, who have their own egos and otherness, an animal companion largely reflects one's own projections. As such, one has relationships primarily with oneself through them. Rufus was always excited to see Art, always happy to be scratched, and fed, and played with. He always leapt up from wherever he was sleeping to race toward Art when he came home. Rufus was thus a constant, loving, and devoted interpreter of the best self which Art imagined. Rufus was the bridge between isolation and relatedness. As Art and Rufus became more and more devoted to one another, Art was more able to find his own voice, especially when his attachment to Rufus was threatened. This occurred frequently, and most poignantly, when Rufus became ill.

Rufus contracted an intestinal virus that required numerous emergency visits to the vet. The following vignette is taken from a session after Art had had a conversation with his mother regarding Rufus' condition:

ART: [Looking haggard, very sad] Rufus is back in the hospital. He was doing better, but then he started vomiting again and had diarrhea.

NICK: I'm sorry to hear that.

ART: Yeah, thanks. [Tears up] My mother called. I told her what was going on with him, how this is very serious. She said, "Well, just don't let him suffer." I knew just what she meant, but I played dumb. I said, "What do you mean?" She said, "You know when the time comes, it comes."

NICK: What was that like for you?

ART: Familiar and awful. Like she wants me to put him to sleep. That she wants to kill me. Instead of yelling at her, or eviscerating her verbally which I usually do at times like this, I said, "You know, Mom, I love him. And I am going to keep him alive whatever it costs. [Weeping] I'm worth him. I'm worth this.

[Pause]

NICK: What did she say?

ART: She didn't get it, of course. She sputtered something about how much money I was spending on him, and how it wasn't fair to him. What she meant was she can't stand that my father gives me all this money. I just hung up the phone.

NICK: What was that like for you?

ART: It felt like I know who I am now, and I know who she is. I've been scarred, and I've been privileged. She's a sad, spiteful person, and has been a terrible mother. And I'm going to do whatever it takes to save my dog.

NICK: It sounds like some things have come together.

ART: Thanks to you.

NICK: I appreciate that, but I think it's more accurate to say thanks to us.

ART: [Crying] Thank you for helping me help myself.

In connecting with Rufus as deeply as he did, Art validated his capacity to love by having the best parts of himself reflected back to him with unconditional love in return. I think of Fonagy's statement that the infant gets the greatest sense of connection to the mother by seeing the glint of recognition in the mother's eyes, and of Sullivan's (1953) concept that personality consists in the reflected appraisals of others. Art got from Rufus what his mother couldn't or wouldn't give him. As a consequence of this, his self became fortified, and Art became a more related person.

Art began dating Jerry shortly after this session. It was the first time he had been interested or able to pursue a romantic relationship with a man. Art and Jerry embarked on what would evolve to be a loving and romantic partnership. It was not without problems. Jerry was a recovered alcoholic, who was prone to spiritual discourse that put Art off. Jerry was displeased on occasion by Art's tendency to be controlling. But they became a couple and together saw Rufus through his illness.

It was shortly after this that Art wondered if we should stop the analysis. For several sessions he had spoken about his relationship with Jerry, his design projects, and continued pursuit of steady work in an engaged and upbeat way. He had no signs of depression, and he felt like a very different person. One day he said, "You know I've been thinking, should we stop? I mean I love coming here, but I'm not sure I need this anymore." I had been feeling similarly, and that although there was more to do, we had accomplished much. We agreed to set a two-month termination date, and in that time discussed what we had done, and what we might have missed. Among the latter was a sense we both had of not exploring Art's anger and violent fantasy life as much as we might have. Art acknowledged that he still felt distanced from that aspect of himself at times, and I wondered whether we were both intimidated by what we would encounter if we had explored more deeply. So, having come thus far, we agreed that it was a reasonable time to stop the analysis.

Concluding thoughts

This chapter has described Art's journey from a life apart to a life among. To think in Kleinian terms, Art's development during the analysis represented a transition from the paranoid/schizoid to the depressive position. Art had spent the bulk of his life relating to ideas and social structures in lieu of people. He claimed to want a girlfriend because he thought he should be heterosexual, and was devastated when women would reject him. It wasn't the particular women he wanted, but what they represented in terms of social norms. With potential friends, as well, Art was eager to ask people out socially, only to be offended and hurt when they declined, or accepted and then failed to reciprocate. He wanted to be *seen* as having friends, and to experience the closeness and love he believed to exist in friendships, but similarly, *he didn't particularly like the people whom he chose.* Professionally, Art wanted to design structural and aesthetic relatedness in architectural projects, but was unable to relate to his colleagues and clients in the process. Art had been socially rejected beginning at an early age, and continued to feel alienated from and to alienate others. He was unaware of how he participated in this mutual alienation, and despaired that he would never find fulfillment. As far as Art's sexuality was concerned, when we began our analysis he wasn't able to distinguish between his personal need for control and his sexual desire. With both men and women, his sexuality was split off from his personality, and was a major contributor to his inability to form attachments.

By the end of our time together, Art had joined with me in being able to examine and deconstruct much of his defenses and resistances. He was less prone to narcissistic injury, and had developed a far sturdier character that was able to acknowledge loss and pain without withdrawing into anger and depression. His tolerance for frustration was far greater than it had been, and Art was able to sit with displeasure rather than distracting himself. Art's attachment to Rufus was a consequence of his growing capacity to love, and a significant outcome of our work together. With Rufus, Art was able to love an actual being, an animal, that prepared him to find Jerry. Art found his own voice, and in his own words was able to embrace both the joy and sorrows attendant on being human. For my part, I lost sight of Captain Bluntschli, and discovered an integrated person, Art, whom I had helped reclaim, or perhaps claim for the very first time, a voice that had long eluded him.

References

Klein, M. (1948). A contribution to the theory of anxiety and guilt. *International Journal of Psycho-Analysis, 29*, 114–123.

Sullivan, H. S. (1953). *The Interpersonal Theory of Psychiatry.* New York: W. W. Norton & Company.

Commentary on Samstag's case

The presentation of "Art"

Robert Watson

First impressions: I am pleased that Dr. Samstag chose to present his work with such a challenging patient. The case clearly demonstrates his ability to engage with a patient who has great difficulty in relating to any other person. I also believe that it clearly demonstrates how interpersonal psychoanalytic treatment can be very powerful in helping patients who have such interpersonal difficulties. I believe that no other form of treatment would have been as effective. To present such long-term work, it is essential to present the analytic work in specific segments, or "eras," of the treatment. I do wish, however, that Dr. Samstag had presented more material on the transitions between these "eras." The use of dreams with an unrelated patient is essential and I was glad to see the amount of dream material presented in the case. I have certain differences in what I would have focused on in the work with some of the material, but overall there was a productive use of the dreams. The patient showed enormous progress in his ability to relate to others, which was the most important change in his life. I do wonder about the lack of progress in his professional life and if more analytic work could have been focused on this aspect. Was it not addressed because of the father's financing the treatment and therefore was there a hesitancy in both patient and analyst about examining this issue in more depth?

Specific issues in the case study: I noted that Dr. Samstag presented some of his countertransference issues early on in his presentation of the case. He was clear in much of what he felt about Art, but I am curious as to what he found similar to himself and how he then used this to aid the treatment. Identifying that Art was at times in Ogden's (1992) autistic–contiguous position was important in understanding his difficulties in relating. I thought that more could have been explored about his bodily issues, such as his "frisson" of the spine in adolescence. I also wondered about his heart murmur at age 2, especially how it was dealt with in the family. Certainly Art spent most of his time in the schizoid or depressed positions, but what influence did his experiences in the autistic–contiguous position have on his self-system and his interactions with others?

Having parents pay for treatment for any adult patient is always a difficult issue. I don't believe I would have demanded that Art pay for his own treatment, since it did not appear that he could pay for it from his own income. I'm not clear on what contributions he did make. Given the family's issues around money, and especially Art's mother's reactions, I would have liked to have known more about how this issue was explored in the treatment. How was the fee discussed, and what was Dr. Samstag's reaction to accepting the fee? I would have linked the financial dependency with Art's difficulty in establishing a professional career for himself. Was Art a "winner" over his mother by having the father pay for his lifestyle? Art's professional difficulties were certainly a product of his difficulty in relating to others, but I wonder whether he ended the treatment when he did, not wanting to look at issues involving his dependency, fear, and how money was used in the family.

Dr. Samstag did excellent work on Art's false sense of self and his hostile defense style in his interactions. He was able to help Art recognize and challenge these self-issues, and helped build a sense of self which Art could use to interact with others. He also helped Art think about himself and his interactions in a thoughtful and constructive manner which led him to be much more psychoanalytically minded. I thought their interchange about the *House* comment was especially telling in the changes Art was able to make in his interactions with Dr. Samstag and in thinking more flexibly about himself. I believe I would have thought more about the transference aspects of House being arrogant and unable to work well with others and not focus on the drug use. It is also possible that House is a representation of Art's dysfunctional self in his professional life and not simply a representation of Dr. Samstag.

Again I was very pleased to see Dr. Samstag's use of dreams, which I feel is critical with a patient like Art. I believe I would have considered some of the dream material with a different focus. In the dream about the manuscript and his father I think Dr. Samstag rushed to an interpretation when he said, "So you destroy your father by destroying yourself." This is usually a red flag that the analyst is anxious about some aspect of the dream. In this case it may be a transferential issue about Dr. Samstag and the treatment. Their work with this dream did, nevertheless, prove helpful in that Art developed new ways of thinking of himself and led to a freeing up of some of his fears around being Gay.

With both the "Sondheim" and "Reconstruction" dreams, Dr. Samstag did an excellent job of picking up on words in the dreams and helping Art "play" with them, creating a clearer understanding of his self-system. One area that could have been explored more was Art's emotional reactions in the dreams and how they could be tied to his experiences in and out of the consulting room. Overall, the work with dreams appears very important in the patient's accepting his self-systems and helped him present himself to his family in this new way.

Art's great improvement is evident in his getting and being attached to Rufus and then being able to begin and sustain a relationship with Jerry. This is the kind of change I believe we are hoping for in many of our patients. It is interesting to note that Art said, "My Dad is buying me my best friend," referring to Rufus. One could also consider the implication of this statement possibly applying to Dr. Samstag, since his father paid for the treatment. Again, I would have liked to see more exploration of this payment aspect of the treatment.

Overall, this is an excellent presentation of a very difficult case. Now that Art has become able to relate to others in a much more productive fashion, it would be very interesting to explore his lack of professional success and how it may relate to money and his family dynamic.

Reference

Ogden, T. H. (1992). *The Primitive Edge of Experience*. Northvale, NJ: Jason Aronson.

Chapter 3

The curative power of an interpersonal approach in the treatment of a patient whose father killed his mother

Helen Quinones

> Caminante, son tus huellas, el camino y nada más;
> Caminante, no hay camino, se hace el camino al andar.
> Al andar se hace camino y al volver la vista
> atrás se ve la senda que nunca se ha de volver pisar.
> Sino estelas en la mar.
>
> (*Caminante*, Antonio Monchado, 1912)

> Traveler, it is your footsteps that render the road visible and nothing else;
> Traveler there is no road, as it is made as you journey.
> As you journey you forge the road and as you turn to look behind,
> you see the path that never will be tread again.
> It is but a wake of a boat cutting across the ocean surface.
>
> (English translation by Helen Quinones)

As is reflected in this poem, there is no one truth that pre-exists and guides us as we walk the road toward wisdom. Wisdom is a road that is made by the very steps one takes, steps that can only be glimpsed at momentarily when we glance behind us. Interpersonal, relational psychoanalysis is such a road, a road that is paved by clinical moments whose importance we don't fully recognize until we glance from whence we came.

The theory which commenced my journey as a relational psychoanalyst was that posited by Harry Stack Sullivan, who widened the field of psychoanalytic inquiry from the individual psychic of the patient to the interpersonal dynamics of both patients and analysts. In a two-person model of psychoanalysis where the analyst is both participant and observer, every interaction between patient and analyst replays patterns of relatedness which fend off aspects of the self that were forbidden, and therefore remain unseen, unfelt, unintegrated. It is this shift in the field of psychoanalytic inquiry that recasts (without replacing) the understanding of transference/countertransference as a relational dynamic that contains the personal histories, defenses, and fantasies of both patient and analyst. Transferential distortions are forged not only by the power of the patient's history as is postulated by the classical concept of the repetition compulsion but also by the analyst's own defenses. In relational psychoanalysis one strives to recognize how the analyst contributes to the patient's transference. It is only by seeing how each influences the other that one can begin to construct an interpretation which can unlock the relational stronghold of a transferential impasse. The ubiquity of this mutual influence is captured in the following:

> The paradigm changes, in my view, only when the idea of the analyst's personal involvement is wedded to a constructivist or perspectivist epistemological position. Only in effecting that integration is the idea of the analyst's participation in the process taken fully into account. *By this I mean very specifically that the personal participation of the analyst in the process is considered to have a continuous effect on what he or she understands about himself or herself and about the patient in the interaction.*
>
> (Hoffman, 1991, p. 76, emphasis added)

If one is to abide by this social constructivist approach it is assumed that therapeutic growth is a result of first seeing and then freeing up the defensive dyadic structure which maintains conflicts out of awareness for both patient and analyst. In this relational paradigm insight emerges once the analyst can loosen the interlocking grip of defenses, both for the patient and for him/herself. It is a cycle of continuous growth for both patient and analyst.

The praxis of relational psychoanalysis is therefore relatively complex. It contains the inherent challenge of recognizing and using one's own subjectivity to further the patient's understanding. It requires that one face the ambiguity of the spaces created as the defensive structures of both patient and analyst become less powerful. In keeping with psychoanalytic practice it also requires recognition of the unseen, preconscious, and unconscious dynamics that do indeed motivate behavior.

How a relational psychoanalyst faces these challenges – namely recognizing mutual influences of defenses, capturing the preconscious or unconscious dynamics, and allowing for the ambiguity of widening relational spaces – has been addressed by such renowned contemporary psychoanalysts as Edgar Levenson, Donnel Stern, and Phillip Bromberg. This chapter was written in answer to these challenges. In its writing I have attempted to capture my development as a psychoanalyst who strives to integrate a relational approach with psychoanalytic principles of unconscious motivation. It is with some uncertainty that I attempt to hold both the primary tenets of classical psychoanalysis with those of relational psychoanalysis.

This integration will probably be a lifelong journey of uncertain steps. But for this moment in time I will be discussing a patient who was initially presented to the William Alanson White Institute as a graduate case. It is a patient who has facilitated an emerging psychoanalytic stance based on the general principle of facilitating "an enrichment of the self, the person [...] becoming more present, more defined, closer to an aware personality understood" (Levenson, 1989,

p. 550). The case will be divided into three sections, each representing: shifts in the patient's self-perception, defenses, and shifts in my capacity to use my subjective experience to understand key clinical moments. The first section will focus on an enactment of a pivotal transference–countertransference impasse whose resolution shifted the patient's perception of himself and mine; the second section will focus on the use of visual images that contain preconscious, subjective experiences, and the third section clarifies the concept of state sharing that continues to guide my work to date. The chapter contains two interactions illustrated by dialogues from taped sessions. Given the personal and intimate focus of the chapter, permission was obtained from the patient and all demographics have been disguised. The patient also requested to exclude all materials related to his sexual development. The absence of his mother in the case material is not due to a purposeful exclusion. It is an absence, a lacuna, that has existed throughout the treatment.

Introduction to the case

JR was in his mid-thirties when he commenced treatment six years ago. At that time he was troubled by his withdrawal from friends, extended family, and his sister whom he wouldn't see for months. He recognized this as a pattern that was part of a depression he had fought since the family tragedy that befell him in the late 1990s when he was in his mid-twenties. The family tragedy was the beating to death of his mother by his father who had long suffered from untreated mental illness and alcoholism. Prior to the family tragedy he had lived a life circumscribed by the strong familial loyalty that protected the secrecy of domestic violence. It was these boundaries of secrecy that led to a solitary life in high school and his first suicidal depression. At that time his depression was intensified by the increased frequency of his father's alcoholic, violent outbursts and adolescent angst. He was never treated professionally, as his father did not comply with the high school counselor's recommendation. Following his mother's death he did seek and received two courses of trauma-based treatment that alleviated the depression. Several years later he completed his undergraduate studies. Following graduation he was gainfully employed in his field. He also traveled, found his own apartment, and developed friendships with colleagues. This reprieve from depression was short lived, as he re-experienced a devastating disappointment when a relationship he had hoped would be his first fruitful romance ended. It was at this time that he remembered feeling so emotionally numb that he started sky-diving "just to feel alive again." Once again he sought and began intensive treatment that commenced in 2009.

The following excerpt from the original case presentation describes my first impressions:

> What I recall of my initial encounter is that JR was aware of the impact on another when speaking about the murder of his mother and subsequent

> incarceration of his father. I imagine he noticed the same look of shock in my face that this fact had probably elicited repeatedly in others. He attempted to reassure me that he had been in treatment twice "for the post-traumatic syndrome" and had worked out much of his feelings about the murder in his previous therapy so that we didn't have "to go into it." Initially I heard this as a warning – stay away from the trauma – but placing it into an interpersonal context it was a plea not to think less of him. I tried to maintain an open mind, in other words, not just search for the pathological ramifications of the trauma but also see his strengths. What remained engraved in my memory was the lack of emotional depth and genuineness when describing his failed intimacy with women.

I also recall being very cautious, as there seemed to be so little palpable affect. I felt danger, but was it the danger of the extent of his depression or was it the muted concerns contained in the question [...] Is there potential for a pathological transference during which he would "really" play out an erotic fantasy? How much did he identify himself with his father's brutality?

Despite these anticipated clinical challenges I accepted him as a patient. He commenced treatment in September 2009, and with the exception of illnesses and vacations he attended all sessions which were initially scheduled at a frequency of twice a week and then increased to three times a week.

During the first year I resisted entering an intimate interpersonal space, with the exception of confronting his ambivalence about psychiatric treatment, and, reconstructing a historical narrative from his electronic diary, I allowed his defenses to hold the interpersonal anxiety that existed between us. Rather than recognizing how difficult it was for him to face a female, I lost my analytic self by remaining curious about the lyrics of his favorite songs (he is an avid music fan [...] so there were endless songs to talk about) or the newest electronic gadgets. He became the entertainer and I the entertained. There were session fragments that sounded like parlor conversation, such as describing his favorite foods. We were both feigning being present – the patient by focusing on trivial topics and I by defensively maintaining a non-directive therapeutic stance.

As I prepared myself to present the case to the Institute, a visual image emerged. It is an image of my walking the perimeter of a wall which surrounds an open space with JR in the center. It is the wall that imprisons him in his loneliness; it is the wall of solitary confinement. It is this image that gave me the first hint of an empathic understanding. I didn't know then what became subsequently revealed – that it was shame, fear, and rage which served as the mortar for this solid wall. A wall that kept him encapsulated in a loneliness that "produces the sad conviction that nobody else has experienced or ever will sense what they are experiencing or have experienced" (Fromm-Reichman, 1990, p. 313).

It was not until the end of the first year that I was able to don the mask of neutrality which hid my own insecurities and fears. At that time, the economic crisis of 2010 hit his professional field; consequently he lost his job within a year of commencing his treatment. He had begun psychiatric treatment for an affective disorder but it didn't buffer him, as the job loss collided with a severe seasonal depression. This pushed him into a state of existential despair. He questioned the importance or reason for his life. With indifference, no remorse, or guilt, he fantasized about committing suicide and minimized the impact his death would have on the lives of others. I became angry and aggressive in my interaction. I told him that suicide was equivalent to homicide, something I was sure he would not want to repeat given his family history. I explained that, in essence, he would be killing off the very people who care about him – listing them, his surrogate family, sister, niece, and best friends. [...] And I added, "if you think you can get away with committing suicide without feeling guilt [...] it won't work. I will follow you past the grave to make sure you feel the guilt of killing off those who care about you." A ludicrous threat, this phantom superego, but it conveyed the fact that there was yet one more human being who cared about him.

My shift to a more personal interaction helped him through the suicidal crisis. It was the first step into his courtyard of solitude. He sought friends again, forced himself to go on a first ski trip, and was hired as a seasonal worker on time-limited projects. He manifested a renewed belief in himself in a session where he described the lyrics of a song in which the singer, like himself, rallied against daunting forces.

The enactment

It was not until the second year of the treatment that I found myself once again distancing myself, in essence closing my analytic eyes. At that time he reported the worst dream of his life which occurred when he ended his first course of treatment following the death of his mother. I recall silently transcribing the dream, making minimal inquiries. Rather than addressing and interpreting the dream, I withdrew into the facile interaction characteristic of our first few months. However, as both Freud and relational analysts would have it, what is not seen or interpreted becomes enacted – played out – more directly between patient and analyst.

By the third year, empowered by my own analysis and relational psychoanalytic supervision, I did recognize and eventually confront the sadism that imbued his fantasy life reflected in the dream. This confrontation occurred in conjunction with the phase of treatment in which he was describing forensic photos of his mother's severely bruised, dead body; sharing song lyrics of depraved criminal acts, and finally re-reporting the dream. It was the juxtaposition of all of these elements that led me to feel the difference between witnessing, along with the patient, the father's brutality from being beaten down by it; that is, enacting it. The following are excerpts from two consecutive sessions in which I confronted JR:

JR: Oh, let me turn off my phone. [I had asked him a week before to turn off the email option on his cell phone, as each time he received one there would be an uncomfortable sound] I know you don't like the sound it makes, you know others have commented on the sound as also irritating, but I like it exactly for that since it gets people's attention.
HQ: So what others find irritating you enjoy.
JR: Yeah, I don't like it when people download popular rhythmic songs [...] it isn't effective [...] I downloaded this from a video game soundtrack. Of course, I could have downloaded the music from other songs I listen to.
HQ: The ones you have shared with me that deal with hopelessness, suicide.
JR: There are other bands. These write songs, such as, "F. [...] Knife," "H. [...] Face." [At this point he goes on to tell me the content of the songs]
HQ: Why so many details; what are you trying to say?
JR: Perhaps that there is an ugly side of life.
HQ: Do you feel that we have avoided the ugly side of life? [There is a transition that I cannot recall, following which he proceeds]
JR: I remember in March 2001 having the worst dream of my life. [...]

The dream: I met someone new, ordered drinks, and while the woman went to the restroom, the bartender gave me a pill and suggested putting it in her drink. She came back, drank it, and started passing out. The scene changes to somebody's house. There was a sex orgy taking place, with people all over the room. I proceeded to have sex with her, penetrating her anally. Her stomach was turned toward the floor. I wanted to check if she was unconscious and turned her head too much. I snapped her neck and killed her in the process. Her eyes were open with a look of horror that may have happened during the rape. I continued having sex; I don't remember having an orgasm. I dressed her up and carried her, trying to make it look as if she was drunk. Then I put her body in a dumpster. Looked around to see if somebody saw me. Walked past the house that had become a video store. I walked in and a salesperson told me the price of a CD.

Whatever happened that night just completely disappeared. He reported waking up feeling guilty, sick, and ashamed.

HQ: What do you make of the dream?
JR: Certain bad decisions can lead to evil – in the dream I gave her the pill without thinking.
HQ: What about bad decisions in your real life?
JR: Shortly after my mother's death, when not living at home I worked in an asset-reclaiming agency, which meant working with estates, wills, and death certificates. It was a constant reminder of my mother's death. [...] That was a wrong decision.
HQ: What about when you were living at home?

JR: Every morning I awakened at home I thought to myself – what are you going to do today and I never did anything. [Referring to the beatings] I felt a sense of guilt that I believe has metastasized into feeling emasculated.

HQ: You did try to do something on more than one occasion, such as taking your mother and sister to a hotel for refuge three months before her death, and attempting to call the police on the night of the final beating, only to find that the telephone had been disconnected.

JR: Not enough. I just remember being demoralized, any effort became fruitless, things would go back to the way they were.

In the subsequent sessions JR continued recounting the scenes he witnessed of his father's brutal assaults. As he recounted them he would cover his face so as not to witness my reactions or show his own. Once he asked if I thought he was a bad person. I answered genuinely that I didn't. As he described these scenes I again began feeling beaten down, demoralized, hopeless, and subsequently recognized this is how a child feels when eroded by chronic domestic violence. I was empathic, yet knew that I had not yet fully addressed the murderous aggressiveness contained in the dream. So I proceeded in a subsequent session:

JR: I am feeling better.

HQ: How so?

JR: I am not thinking of my family life.

HQ: Did you ever share the details of your family life with another person?

JR: Yes, I have shared them as "anecdotes."

HQ: What made you share it with me?

JR: I thought you were asking for details.

HQ: So I opened the door.

JR: Yeah.

HQ: What impact do you think it had on me?

JR: I don't know. I figured you are a professional and have heard this many times before. [...] Like sky-divers who jump many times.

HQ: In my experience – which is quite a bit – I have never heard of such "anecdotes" of family life – they were really anecdotes of brutality.

JR: Were you really upset?

HQ: I felt as though we acted out the beatings of your mother. Hearing the words of your songs, sharing the forensic images was like being punched.

JR: But I thought this is something you would be used to.

HQ: What about the dream? How did you think I felt listening to it?

JR: Well, I thought it was over the top when I said it was a previous therapist.

HQ: It was a dream that encompassed every single way that a woman can be attacked – rape, sodomy, necrophilia – it was pure rage against a woman. What brought up that rage?

JR: It was a dream I had a long time ago.

HQ: But you bring it into the present context. Is there something that triggered the rage against me? *Did you feel I was holding you responsible for something you couldn't be held responsible for, or guilty of something you couldn't control?*

JR: No, I feel that way every time something bad happens to me and I don't have control over it.

HQ: Is there something bad happening now?

JR: Just that I often wonder how I would be if my parents weren't like that – what capacities I would have developed, who else I could be.

HQ: Do you feel that therapy is failing in the same way?

JR: No, for the record it has been the best in the last couple of weeks. [He pauses] How did that dream come up again?

HQ: Irritating sounds.

JR: Oh, I was talking about rock-n-roll bands. [...] It reminds me of a song by Slayer called 213 in which one of the band members was trying to understand the workings of the mind of the serial killer, Dahmer. [...] [In a trance-like state he begins to repeat the lyrics, describing Dahmer raping a dead woman, then he glances at me] Oh, look at your face[...]

HQ: If you need someone to listen to these details it can't be me, maybe another therapist.

JR: For the record I am happy with the therapist I have chosen – you're sensitive.

HQ: But you are attacking that very sensitivity [...] Slayer was trying to understand the workings of a serial killer. Whose mind are you trying to understand?

JR: In general, necrophiliacs.

HQ: Not in particular, like your father's mind.

JR: Not in that dream, I was worse than my father. I did it all in one day.

HQ: Yes, he did it over years. [...] While you're trying to get into the mind of your father, you're living out again your father's brutality.

JR left the session genuinely surprised, and commented that he had not thought of it in that way. In subsequent sessions we considered a referral to another therapist but decided to continue.

Enactment discussion

The dissolution of this impasse may have been facilitated if I had then captured earlier what I eventually captured in the interpretation. In the grip of the sadomasochistic hold, I was silently understanding the transference as imbedded in his identification with the aggressor, namely his father. In this transference/countertransference conceptualization he was the father, symbolically beating the mother with the brutality contained in song lyrics and the dream. I was like the terrified, silent, screaming mother. It reflected the split in the transference

– he the perpetrator and I the victim. Seeing this as just his distortion and projection did not enable me to break away from my subjective experience of sadomasochism. Essentially what was being talked about was "simultaneously being enacted between patient and analyst" (Levenson, 1993, p. 383). The trigger to his rage was an inquiry I had made about why he had not taken any action on the night of his mother's final beating. This inquiry was meant to have been neutral but instead implicitly contained an accusation of guilt. I revisited the aforementioned image of the courtyard in more detail and saw with my mind's eye that he was not at the center of an enclosed Spanish garden but in a sparse prison yard. In the enactment I was both the accuser, sending him to prison, and the passive, intimidated victim. It was this view of myself as both the victim and the perpetrator that helped me construct the interpretation, "Did you feel I was holding you responsible for something you couldn't be held responsible for [his mother's death] or guilty for something you couldn't control [the beatings]?" It is through the interpretation that I recognized that the culpability of the fatal assault does indeed rest in the hands of his father, not his.

Once freed from the sadomasochistic enactment I was then able to enter the prison yard with him. It enabled me to share the state of being frozen by terror and dread. It was through sharing his affective state that I was able to understand that repeated childhood trauma erodes one somatically and affectively via demoralizations and hopelessness. It was through feeling this in my very body and soul that I understood the submission and lonely futility which is at the core of domestic violence.

Following this enactment I recall shifting from an uneasy, distant, therapeutic stance to one from which I could see him more clearly. He was distinguishable in my mind from the image of a father who had psychologically beaten down the mother to a state of fatal submission. I felt emboldened within the enactment – but by what? I believe it was being given the permission initially by my supervisor to listen to and respect my internal voice that said "enough." It was holding myself in mind; that is, not losing my own presence. It empowered me to join him affectively in his experience of the original trauma by not losing sight of my own subjectivity (essentially accepting my own limitations). It is this capacity to see and respect both subjectivities that is critical in working through a sadomasochistic relational dynamic.

Interpersonally, I had stepped into the relational field where both of our subjectivities collided. I had asked JR to recognize my experience, thereby introducing an "other" whose perspective and experience differed from his. By doing this I witnessed the dissociation that anesthetized him from the brutality contained in the song lyrics and his dream. In subsequent sessions I recognized that the enactment loosened the power of the dissociation, enabling us to negotiate a relational stance that was protected from repeated abuse. It was within the security of this relational stance that JR continued speaking of his rage without it being mutated or contaminated by an induced identification with his father. He spoke of his rage in high school leading to fantasies of shooting faceless people in school or entering his chemistry classroom to drink a fatal concoction. He spoke about the split he feels between his own sensitivity and his hatred against the world.

To date, we continue to return repeatedly to the night of the final beating in an effort to understand what had immobilized him. Each time he painfully relives that night we have tried to understand why he didn't take further action – was it a passivity that comes from years of futile silence? Was it the paralysis and desensitization of repeated trauma, or the emotional distance of rage that led him to dehumanize another? Each time he revisits a time in his life when his own will and outrage was immobilized, he emerges more strongly motivated to exist outside the shadow of his parents.

Transitional phase

Although I had learned the importance of maintaining an analytic presence that was as aware of myself as of JR, I was ashamed at not knowing how to adapt this stance to the work that was not so readily recognizable by a major impasse. How do I know my subjectivity, see his, and develop an understanding that encompasses both? In answer to these questions I understood that the analyst's subjectivity, like that of the patient, is contained in his or her internal dialogues, fantasies, reactions, and memories. The task, then, is to use one's own spontaneously generated, preconscious psychic events to further one's understanding of the patient's experience. It was at this time that I became aware that aspects of my subjectivity were contained in visual images which would emerge during the course of a session. The following two vignettes will exemplify how visual images that occurred during moments of impatience and disappointment helped me see what perhaps couldn't be readily recognized consciously.

Visual image 1: riding the river current

By the fourth year there were still many sessions filled with descriptions of JR's everyday activities. He would describe the food he ate, his exercise regime, etc. I grew internally impatient with his obsessively ruminating about his daily activities. Then came the day when there occurred a spontaneous silence. It was like a silence heard when in the middle of the eye of a storm – the bustling, breaking noise of the wind and rain suddenly stops. He was speechless and appeared frightened; I was silent and confused. It was then that I recalled the following personal event:

> I was white-water rafting with a group of friends, sitting comfortably on the back of the raft. Within seconds I was thrown from the raft into the water that was running swiftly. Initially, I found myself with no fear, enjoying the swiftness of moving with the river's current. Then I reached a juncture of white water that required that I closely time my breathing with the rhythm of the rapidly breaking waves. I remember becoming panicked until I heard my friends who were close at hand.

Once I turned my attention back to JR he was still silent, and I asked what was on his mind. He responded that there were many "directions" he was going in his mind and couldn't decide which to take. I reassured him that sometimes it is hard to put into words all that comes to mind and added that sometimes it isn't necessary to put it into words straight away.

In this way I wanted to protect the space that had opened up without filling it immediately with words. It was also sharing with him the freedom from anxiety that may be experienced when one recognizes that some experiences cannot be controlled or put into words. It is surrendering to something that is more powerful than oneself. I am not sure how many sessions transpired before JR reported his own dreams of riding a raft in the river. (It is important to note that I had not disclosed my memory.) In his dream he rode the raft with his sister beside him but then decided to get off the raft to see a TV show. His sister continued on the raft and went over the waterfall. He was unaware of what had happened to his sister, paying close attention to his TV show.

This synchronization of my image with his dream led to my recognizing his need to control the intensity of his emotions via the obsessive details of his daily activities. I had to match my rhythmic breathing (as I did in the memory) with his. It is this rhythm of regulating affective states that is at the foundation of defences – defenses that can allow for the experience of affect without being flooded or over-stimulated.

In subsequent sessions I understood his need to regulate his affective experience that he described as intense, yet maintained my own need to not be flooded with verbiage. We had an unstated negotiation to not allow the obsessional defenses to run away with our capacity to mentalize that which he spoke about. At times, I pointed out to him when he lost me in his associations and at other times he, himself, recognized when he was derailing the train of thought. It became important that we didn't lose each other in the details of moment-to-moment descriptions – in essence riding the currents of a river without necessarily leaving one behind as he had done in his dream and I in my memory fragment.

Visual image 2: the rose is just a rose – or is it?

At one point JR came to the session with a rose. It had partly withered during travel so he stood holding a petal together with the rest of the flower. He described in vivid detail how difficult it had been to keep the rose alive before he presented it to me. I expressed my appreciation and was momentarily carried away with the gift, equating it to the story of the rose in *The Little Prince*. Once I had found a vase, JR let me know that the rose was bought by contributions from a group of friends (costing him little); originally he had bought it for another friend (not meant for me) but had forgotten to bring it to their meeting. As I felt the warmth of the moment dissipate I saw in my mind the color of the rose change from a vibrant red to gray.

I did feel disappointment as the warmth of the momentary recognition of the attachment dissipated. I made no comment at the time; just waited. It was several sessions later that he recounted a memory of his father that provided the contextual understanding of my visual image. The memory of his father was one that related to his wish for recognition. He remembered being in a bowling game with a group of his grammar school friends. He was enthusiastically anticipating some victory, as he had proven to be a worthy bowling opponent. His father decided to join the game himself, competitively beating him in front of his friends. It was as if the father had taken the bowling ball and used it as a wrecking ball, robbing JR of the yearned-for recognition. It was after he told me of this memory that I spoke about the relational dynamics of his giving me the rose. I postulated that perhaps he had killed the moment in order to prevent his being robbed by my own narcissistic need to be recognized as a significant figure in his life. However, he subsequently corrected this interpretation. His actions were instead motivated by his not wanting the gift to be misperceived as an improper expression of romance. This was especially critical given his past history.

However, in our cautiousness we both failed to understand the relational significance of the rose. His vivid description of his struggle to maintain the petals attached to the stem and keeping it alive until it reached my office induces an image of a young boy's romance with his mother. Within this context it is in line with the image of the Little Prince who represents the child's capacity to recognize the uniqueness of his rose in a field of so many others.

Discussion of visual images

It was through my private reverie consisting of a memory and a simple visual image of the fading color that I was able to capture my own subjectivity. The feeling of freedom from anxiety that I subsequently relived in the quietness of my study helped me understand the importance of succumbing to processes that are more powerful than oneself. It is the earliest form of a self that can succumb to all its passions and pain in the presence of another. It is the capacity to be alone without isolation (Winnicott, 1986). He can succumb to his feelings in my presence as I could in the presence of others. It was with this renewed psychoanalytic confidence that the trust lost during the enactment was regained. I felt that I had the capacity to deal with "what dreams may come" as I, too, was in the presence of others.

Here and now

Over this past year JR has made significant gains in his life. He has sustained his emotional connections with his friends and has become increasingly involved with his sister and nieces. He is more spontaneous, allowing himself to explore freely new ventures like stand-up comedy, photography, and guitar playing. He is cautiously planning a career change.

He has also discovered aspects of himself that had been frozen in time by the trauma. For example, he recognizes the childlike playfulness of "his 5-year-old," the awkward, runaway sexuality of his 15-year-old (who he keeps "on a leash") and the 85-year-old who "can still hate the world." The tempo of the clinical process has shifted. He generally commences the sessions with details of the week and then shifts to a more reflective mode. He can be silent, then he finds a way to share the images and thoughts that emerge during his silence.

Yet there continues to be the challenge of sustaining an empathic stance based on knowing him from within myself, as it is this shared internal presence that helps decrease his loneliness and gives him the courage to take on new challenges.

A recent session exemplified for me that empathy is not only based on a cognitive recognition of affect but also on a joint experience of the feeling itself. It is by sharing the feeling itself that the correct words are used to communicate an experience. Sullivan (1953, p. 183) refers to this as the syntaxic mode of experience in which

> [W]ords have been consensually validated (that is), a consensus has been reached when the infant or child has learned the precisely right word for a situation, a word which means not only what it is thought to mean by the mothering one, but also means that to the infant.

The following dialogue exemplifies the attempt to share the meaning of the word *awe*:

JR: I was reading a magazine article on awe [...] it could be a lot of things [...] for me, I am someone who gets excited over little things. [...] For example, I saw an open bag of Ghirardelli chocolates. [By the enclave in front of the office bathroom] Since the bag was open it looked like it was ready to be served to people who walk by and I begin to think: Can this be public domain [...] the label says share it with someone (so I get even more excited). Then I also noticed the texture of the wrapping [...] and finally I popped it into my mouth.

[Laughing at the humorously told details I informed him that I wasn't sure whether it was public domain, as it didn't belong to me, but I would ask my office mate]

JR: [He continued] I hope it is [...] that is a recent example, but my day can be filled with that sort of thing. This past week when I went to leave for work [...] I leave early enough to see dawn so there is a little sun but not that much, so I can see how the sky changes color [...] a little orange just over the horizon and above that dark blue [...] there is a line of buildings with an active smoke stack that spews a column of gray smoke. The whole scene is in silhouette.

HQ: It is a nice awakening.

JR: It is a good way to start the commute [...] I wish I had a camera [...] so I spend a lot of time alternately looking at the road and at the sunrise.

HQ: So you are enjoying dawn's early light.

JR: There we go. [Pauses but then continues, giving other examples of finding joy in small things [...] the sumptuousness of eating a yogurt or a turkey provolone sandwich when you are very hungry]

HQ: [An image came to mind of a child's session during which I was in awe of what the child was doing [...] I didn't share the image. Instead I stated] So these are all examples of your capacity to be awestruck.

JR: I guess I never looked at it as awe [...] maybe [...] yes.

HQ: It is almost as though you are seeing things for the very first time, the way a child does.

JR: I call it childlike wonder [...] I have that a lot. I never realized that is what I had until last year. I realize it is a part of me, and I want to keep it. I heard a podcast on Freakonomics radio about thinking like a child and what goes with that and how an adult thinks – the benefits of thinking like a child – and I realize I have certain elements of that. It helped me out in a way because a child won't think "I can't do this," whereas, an adult would. That helped with the guitar playing. I did not realize that is what I was doing until I heard the podcast. I basically just fool around with the guitar. That is how I was when I was young. I wasn't really thinking about how good I can be. I just enjoy doing it for the sake of doing something. [He then describes other moments that exemplify this childlike quality becoming increasingly emphatic] On Monday when I go to your Riverdale office I am going to find the article and will come to the door, magazine in hand [gesturing that he will point to it] and I will say "you see!"

HQ: I do see. [...] [I then shared the fragment of the child's session that I had thought of earlier in the session] I have worked with young children of 3 to 5 years of age who were language delayed. They didn't have enough language or play to tell me about what was going on. So I had to try to understand them without words. And I remember one child that was absolutely awestruck with a toy. He took that toy and looked at it from the top, from the bottom, all around, as if he was discovering something new to him. It was more than curiosity – it was a discovery.

JR: That does sound like me. Remember the collapsible numbers cube you have in your Riverdale office? I was looking at it from inside and out. I think the playful, childlike wonder has helped me out a lot.

HQ: It has certainly helped you come through dark times.

JR: The article mentioned that a sense of awe is helpful in maintaining positive emotion. It helps stave off depression. So if I didn't have this [...] my depression would be a lot worse.

HQ: It is almost life giving. [...] It has given you life when you have felt at a loss.

JR: Yes.

HQ: Are you feeling at a loss right now?

JR: I think I am having more of an interest in picking up dating again; not sure how I am going to make that work. I was thinking that this past year I have gotten closer to my sister and her family. I feel like I am more capable of handling things like that. I find I am more interested in things like that. I guess New Year's Eve reminded me of how new I feel when the ball drops. I was thinking about how I have been a new person the past five years and I am rediscovering or unearthing aspects of myself that I hadn't taken note of before [...] I have been working to try to rebuild myself so I have come to terms with how bad I was off socially. I didn't get the help at a young age and I had to pay the price for it. I feel I have fixed parts of myself. Even if I haven't fixed up those parts completely, I have fixed enough to get me going. I feel I need to take that approach with dating. For me a human connection that I got a taste of when I was dating Mary [...] I am wondering if I am capable of that again. So if there is a loss it's that I don't have that human connection.

Discussion of clinical session 2

In this session, JR's emphatically gesturing how he was going to show me the article triggered a shift in the way in which I was present in the session. It was a shift that awakened me to an enactment – he was trying to communicate something important to him and I was only partially listening. He was speaking about awe, self-discovery, and I was trying to understand it from the intellectual distance of an adult rather than from the visceral immediacy of a child. I had attempted to capture the understanding of his feeling state when he described his excitement at seeing dawn by using metaphors, such as "enjoying dawn's early light, an awakening." Although these metaphors captured the beauty of dawn, it didn't capture the feeling of awe. I was the adult while he was trying to capture as closely as possible a child's experience. It was not until I was able to share my awe at a young child's sense of discovery that my affect resonated with his. It is this capacity to succumb to the moment-by-moment sense of rediscovery (reflected in the child's play and in JR's numerous examples) that enabled me to understand what JR meant by childlike wonder.

My recognition of this intrinsic capacity enabled me to see not only awe as a defense against depression but as a life-sustaining, adaptive, coping mechanism. It is a capacity that I believe has prevented JR from entering the darkened waters of a depression which is characterized by an inability to suckle life from the environment.

Although the session on awe may also represent a countertransference reaction to the aggressiveness described at the beginning of the treatment, I would argue that it is not. Awe and rage represent seemingly discrepant aspects of his personality, each needing to be recognized as they interact in the relational context. Neither can be denied. The innocence of a child can soothe the aspects of the personality that attack joy, tenderness, and vulnerability with the ruthless impunity of an introjected, primitive aggressor.

Conclusion

The steps of this psychoanalytic journey are seen more clearly now that the fog of emotional distance has lifted and moved away. It was through an enactment that I heard my own voice of protest, it was through the sights and sounds contained in visual images that I saw my own subjectivity, and it was through state sharing that I feel attuned to him. In this journey JR is discovering a self that is emerging from the shadows of human cruelty. It is with the hope of engendering growth which engenders further growth that I hold onto the following words:

> As this take place, each reenactment permits a negotiated degree of intersubjectivity to develop, which is what makes the nonlinearity of reenactment not simply a process of repetitions. As the nonlinear cycles of collision and negotiation continue, a patient's (and I believe the analyst's) capacity for intersubjectivity slowly increases in those areas from which it had been foreclosed or compromised.
>
> (Bromberg, 2011, p. 27)

Acknowledgments

Submitted with grateful thanks to "los cuatro cabelleros" [the four gentlemen]: Edgar Levenson, MD, Supervisor; Philip Bromberg, PhD, Mentor, and Gilead Nachmani, PhD, Analyst, and to my patient whose trust I cherish.

References

Bromberg, P. (2011). *The shadow of the tsunami*, New York/London: Routledge.

Fromm-Reichman, F. (1990). Loneliness. *Contemporary Psychoanalysis*, *26*, 305–329.

Hoffman, I. (1991). Discussion: Toward a social-constructivist view of psychoanalytic situation. *Psychoanalytic Dialogues*, *1*, 74–105.

Levenson, E. (1989). Whatever happened to the cat? *Interpersonal Perspectives on the Self*, *25*, 537–553.

Levenson, E. (1993). Shoot the messenger – Interpersonal aspects of the analyst's interpretations. *Contemporary Psychoanalysis*, *29*, 383–396.

Monchado, A. (1912). *Campos de Castilla*. Madrid: Renacimiento.

Sullivan, H. (1953). *The Interpersonal Theory of Psychiatry*. New York: W. W. Norton & Co.

Winnicott, D. W. (1986). *The Maturational Processes and the Facilitating Environment.* New York: International Universities Press.

Commentary on Quinones' case

Going where we need to go

Suzanne Little

Dr. Quinones' analytic journey with a young man in the aftershock of his mother's death due to beating brings to mind Ghent's (1990) seminal paper on the confusion between submission and surrender, and the dread of yielding to something larger than oneself.

The patient, now in his thirties, is imprisoned in a "caretaker" self. Identified with a sadistic father whose murderous act he witnessed and passively condoned, JR finds intimacy toxic. He is anesthetized to need. In a counter-phobic move to spoil his one real connection, he objectifies his analyst. More crucially, he dissociates the shame of internalized victimization encapsulated in the horror of that final fatal moment. Bromberg (2003) calls this affective haunting – a traumatic memory that lives, unprocessed, in the present, fated to be re-enacted, until new perceptual reality is created. Dr. Quinones, sensitive to but also besieged by her patient's torment, struggles to know him without being defensive, abandoning, or unduly abject.

Like Monchado's travelers who forge their path while living it, analyst and patient move in and out of dissociated states. We wake to sleep, the poet Theodore Roethke (1991) tells us, but we must take this waking slowly. We learn by going where we have to go. Roethke captures a paradoxical awakening in the circularity of life and death, a yielding to awareness that is non-awareness (sleep, death). It resonates with a contemporary view of an unconscious process in which knowing the mind and experiencing fragmented mental states is as crucial as finding what's in the mind and uncovering repressed contents. In relational praxis, analysts inhabit co-created intersubjective fields. We meet our patients in intense moments of interpersonal exchange on the edges of cognitive understanding. Creative surrender, as I read Ghent, entails an acceptance of uncertainty, an openness to transitional experience, a yielding to rhythms, resonances, and synchronies when thoughts are not yet thinkable, and acts of shared spontaneity are potentially more transformative than insight gained from working through.

JR began analysis depressed following a failed romance. He takes up skydiving, he tells Dr. Quinones, "just to feel alive again." It's a desperate act, and an improbable form of rescue, like self-imposed CPR. Estranged from family, isolated from friends, JR fills the sessions with obsessive ruminations, perverse lyrics, and misogynistic fantasies. Dr. Quinones, alternately bored and repelled, colludes in the facile banter. As she puts it, "We were both feigning being present." With analyst and patient at a defensive stand-off, enactments become the default mode of connection.

We see in Dr. Quinones' writing elements of her interpersonal training – Levenson's therapeutic transformations (2017), Bromberg's dreaming aesthetic (2006), and Stern's field constructivism (2010). It is a participatory epistemology leavened with ego psychology ideas of unconscious motivation and defense. Uncomfortable with abstinence but wary of being too directive, Dr. Quinones weighs the merits of disclosure. She has an approach–avoidance relation to self-revelation. In one exchange, she discards an oppressively neutral stance to castigate JR's suicidal thoughts as selfish. In another enactment, as he batters her with gory details from the mother's forensic photos and then a rape-sodomy dream (apparently performed on "another therapist'), she balks at the assault. JR's sadistic subjugation is aggression gone awry, a perversion of object usage designed to upend the clinical asymmetry. But we also see his helplessness, the loss of agency that comes from habituating to impingements which Ghent (1990) links with masochistic submission.

At times, Dr. Quinones' mode of questioning could be seen as another impingement, of imposing morality rather than being receptive to where the patient is. When she asks JR about the dream, he refers to the "evil" act of drugging his victim. Ignoring the symbolism, she fires back: "What about bad decisions in your real life?" By shifting away from the dream, she avoids a deeper anxiety – JR's inability to grasp and represent what has happened to him. I wonder: Does he revisit his dream to plunge to reality, to face the consequences of his emotional free-fall? Or does he wake "to sleep," as in Roethke's poem, yielding to the power of dissociation and the dreaming unconscious?

In a subsequent session, when she questions his need to inundate her with aggressive sexual material, we again see JR's deflecting, dissociative preoccupation: "I don't know," he responds. "I figured you are a professional and have heard this many times before. [...] Like sky divers who jump many times."

There is a risk, of course, in treating the analyst as veteran jumper. If she's inured to the shock of falling, she won't feel the violent impact. This would bind analyst and patient, like father and son, in a dehumanizing desensitization. As Bromberg observes: "the meaning of the struggle between patient and analyst that we call enactment entails an externalization of the war within the patient's internal object world" (2006, p. 33). Clinical enactment is the unsymbolized conflict lived in the interpersonal relationship. Dr. Quinone's interpretation of a re-enacted parental drama, in which she and the patient play interchanging sadomasochistic roles, feels clinically right. He knows intuitively what is most likely to hook his analyst and trip her up. JR's fantasies of embodied connection reveal an entanglement of destruction and desire. Raping an unconscious woman and then copulating with her corpse is a deadened, pseudo-intimate, autistic act, like having auto-sex. I see in JR's assaultive imagery a defense against psychic rape, a terror of being prised open and mentally invaded. In such a scenario, "fatal submission" means catastrophic ego loss. At the same time, if he can embalm (get rid of) his false self in the analyst-cadaver, he is spared the therapeutic work of making associations, linking fragments of experience, piecing himself back together, which in his most desperate moments he feels he can only do alone. As their parallel (not yet mutual) discovery unfolds, we are reminded that therapeutic recognition is a surrendering, a being-with-other (Benjamin, 2004), that can only be based, as Quinones puts it, "on knowing him from within myself." The rose incident is significant not simply for JR's undoing (taking back the flower), or even his fear that the analyst will misconstrue romantic longings. Its real intersubjective meaning as a symbolic love gesture hinges on Quinones surrendering to her disappointment and being able to communicate and use the experience creatively in the treatment.

We see a similar emotional receptivity when JR uncharacteristically stops speaking during a session and Dr. Quinones sits calmly in the "spontaneous silence" and resists the temptation to fill the space with words. In previous work I have described quiet (Little, 2015) as a transitional space between language and silence, akin to Benjamin's energetic third, in which analyst and patient make contact through affective resonances. I distinguish silence, as a communication, from quiet, as an active experience, an inward listening. Silence, used judiciously or spontaneously felt, is often very powerful of course, but also constraining as a form of analytic refusal. Moreover, for the patient, it can be compelled and coerced in a way that quiet never can, as when JR had to succumb to family pressure, upholding an unspoken pledge to keep his father's brutality secret.

Quiet, in contrast, is a developmental capacity, in which contact is neither sought nor imposed. It originates in a primary aloneness (Winnicott, 1965), an "area of faith" that Eigen (1981) describes as an experience which the infant lives through "prior to a clear realization of self–other differences" (p. 413). For patient and analyst, quiet can be the basis for experiencing states of deep communion (Little, 2015).

During JR's "silent session," Dr. Quinones recalls a memory of whitewater rafting and being pitched into raging rapids. She reaches a "juncture" in the river when she must proactively time her breathing to the rushing rhythm. About to panic, she realizes that friends are "close at hand." Some weeks later – Quinones explicitly points out that she had not disclosed her river memory – JR recounts a dream of rafting with his sister. In the dream he leaves to watch TV, unaware that his sister tumbles over a waterfall. Their parallel experiences (her memory, his dream) suggest a relational unconscious at work (Gerson, 2004; Bromberg, 2009), but also expose stark disparities between them. Can JR, like his analyst, learn to ride the turbulence? Can he understand and trust that he can use the help which is "close at hand?" For Quinones, the memory–dream "synchronization" illuminated, in the most visceral way, JR's obsessive management of emotional urgency in daily life. "I had to match my rhythmic breathing (as I did in memory) with his," she writes. "It is this rhythm of regulating affective states that is at the foundation of defenses."

Protecting the wordless dimension in treatment, as Quinones was able to do, does not replace the need to work through conflict. But it offers a container for the inexpressible at those times when another's presence is developmentally needed or when we cannot negotiate difference through speech. In time, I suspect, a co-created resonant matching between Dr. Quinones and JR will emerge as a more explicit verbalized part of their therapeutic interaction.

As analyst and patient journey, so we create the road. Looking back, we realize the impossibility of return. We go where we need to go. When Dr. Quinones imagines JR in various walled enclosures – cells, yards, garden – she traces his movement from psychic confinement to expansive possibility. She takes up Loewald's (1960) empathic parental function of envisioning the child's future. Thus, we arrive at JR's wondrous moment in the treatment. It's a simple discovery, really. He marvels at the joy of seeing changing colors – "a little orange, that dark blue" – in a pre-dawn sky. But Dr. Quinones, in her "adult" mindset, doesn't initially grasp the meaning of the surrender. In a healing reversal of roles, the patient's awe, freely felt, openly shared, reanimates the analyst's imagination. This is the rose he offers. The road traveled is forged anew.

References

Benjamin, J. (2004). Beyond doer and done to: An intersubjective view of thirdness. *The Psychoanalytic Quarterly, LCCIII*, 5–46.

Bromberg, P. M. (2003). One need not be a house to be haunted: On enactment, dissociation, and the dread of "not-me" – A case study. *Psychoanalytic Dialogues, 13*(5), 689–709.

Bromberg, P. M. (2006). *Awakening the Dreamer: Clinical Journeys*. Hillsdale, NJ: Analytic Press.

Bromberg, P. M. (2009). Truth, human relatedness, and the analytic process: An interpersonal/relational perspective. *International Journal of Psycho-Analysis, 90*(2), 347–361.

Eigen, M. (1981). The area of faith in Winnicott, Lacan and Bion. *International Journal of Psycho-Analysis, 62*, 413–433.

Gerson, S. (2004). The relational unconscious. *Psychoanalytic Quarterly, 73*, 63–98.

Ghent, E. (1990). Masochism, submission, and surrender: Masochism as a perversion of surrender. *Contemporary Psychoanalysis, 26*, 108–136.

Levenson, E. A. (2017). *The Purloined Self: Interpersonal Perspectives in Psychoanalysis*. New York: Routledge.

Little, S. (2015). Between silence and words: The therapeutic dimension of quiet. *Contemporary Psychoanalysis, 51*(1), 31–50.

Loewald, H. W. (1960). On the therapeutic action of psycho-analysis. *International Journal of Psycho-Analysis, 41*, 16–33.

Roethke, T. (1991). *The Collected Poems of Theodore Roethke*. New York: Anchor Books/Random House, 1991. (Originally published 1953.)

Stern, D. B. (2010). *Partners in Thought. Unformulated Experience, Dissociation, and Enactment.* Hillsdale, NJ: Analytic Press.

Winnicott, D. W. (1965). The capacity to be alone. In *The Maturational Processes and the Facilitating Environment.* New York: International Universities Press.

Commentary on Quinones' case

A view from a second interpersonal frame

John O'Leary

Dr. Quinones presents a startling case describing a treatment of an adult child whose father murdered his mother. This highly ambitious paper is doing more than the title of her chapter conveys. She gives us a sense of how interpersonal theory works best, i.e., when it employs a perspectivist epistemological position. She also sees herself as an integrator ("I attempt to hold both the primary tenets of classical psychoanalysis with those of relational psychoanalysis").

Her main purpose, however, is to work through certain complex enactments and to illustrate their benefits for patient and therapist alike. In addition, she is interested in the use of certain visual images that can trigger a deeper awareness of patient subjectivity. Finally, she wants to show how this deeper awareness can be sustained by "state sharing." The latter is a way of getting a more profound sense of who the patient is by noting those moments when one is experiencing a very similar, frequently overwhelming affect that the patient has also reported experiencing. Interpersonalists as a group can resonate to these themes. Indeed, I believe many non-interpersonal practitioners can as well.

My task is to track her work, noting its twists and turns, to see where she is executing her stated purposes and to indicate how another interpersonally trained therapist might differ. If we value the multi-perspectivism that Dr. Quinones prioritizes, my efforts should reflect that. Through this analysis I will reveal my own point of view.

The primary way in which Dr. Quinones has chosen to demonstrate her thesis is through case material borrowed from a very traumatized young man in his mid-thirties. He has been in treatment with her for six years. This man is the older of two children (he has a younger sister). The patient witnessed on a continuous basis beatings that his alcoholic, enraged father inflicted upon his mother. After many years, during one of these more violent episodes, the father actually killed the mother. From these data alone, we, her readers, know that Dr. Quinones is in for a very tough time. Our empathy is with her, and also with the young man who witnessed these catastrophic events.

It comes as no surprise that the patient has a documented history of post-traumatic stress as well as clinical depression from early adolescence. Importantly, the patient attended all sessions and was soon coming three times a week.

My impression throughout is that this patient both admired and respected Dr. Quinones. We have no idea of this man's profession apart from knowing that he is immediately recognizable. My inference based on the many references to music is that he is either a rock singer or a song writer, but this is largely guesswork. She has done a good job of preserving confidentiality.

Dr. Quinones describes a few highly dramatic engagements where she gets justifiably angry, for example, when the patient cavalierly discusses suicide. She chides him assertively that "I will follow you past the grave to make sure you feel the guilt of killing off those who care about you." This intervention is clever, attuned to the patient, and appears to work.

A second instance is where the patient reports a harrowing dream wherein he gets a girl drunk, gives her a knock-out pill, takes her back to his room, has anal sex with her, and ends by twisting her head so violently that he kills her. He then puts her body in a dumpster. A few sessions later with more stories of his father's history of assaults, the therapist, now exhausted and depleted, finally exclaims: "Why are you sharing all of this with me"? – strongly hinting that he, like his father, must be getting vicarious thrills by observing the therapist's pain. Dr. Quinones says to him: "In all my experience I have never heard of such anecdotes of family life." The patient asks whether she was really upset. Then the therapist goes after his reporting of the dream. The therapist says it was a dream that encompassed every single way in which a woman can be attacked: rape, sodomy, and necrophilia. It was "pure rage against a woman." What brought up that rage? The patient says defensively that he was reporting a dream he had a long time ago. He says he brought it up with many other therapists. She says, "But you bring it up in the present context. Is there something that triggered that *rage against me* [emphasis added]"? Sometime later she says to him, "If you need someone to listen to these details it can't be me, maybe another therapist." Fortunately, in subsequent sessions she backs away from this threat of abandonment.

The therapist is able to see that an earlier question she had put to the patient was likely to have provoked the alleged rage. Her pivotal question centered on the lack of action the patient took as he witnessed the beatings by his father. She was subsequently able to see that the patient might be extremely sensitive around this issue. He is indeed very guilt ridden regarding his own passivity in the face of such violence. The therapist sees her own interrogation as the beginning of a rage enactment which she later acknowledges and tries to analyze.

In the end we are left with the idea that "standing up for herself" made a difference for both the therapist and the patient. The patient is able to see that he has a real person of feelings in the room with him and that he should act accordingly with far greater empathy for the listener. He also sees a model of a strong woman who can speak out against horror.

What is troublesome for me derives from how we define enactment and how much territory it is supposed to cover. My own understanding of "enactment" is close to that of Owen Renik (1999), who sees it as an unconscious phenomenon, part of the transference–countertransference matrix where both parties experience it as a consequence of certain behavior of the other. It is always retrospective because up to the point of recognition the analyst is unaware of it. Renik goes on to note that for an analysis to proceed, the interaction between patient and analyst has to be such that analysts must be able to recognize their own pathology – which, in turn, presumes a deep emotional involvement with the patient. Dr. Quinones spends a lot of time on the value of the enactment material to the treatment and so I will not discuss other notions she develops in this chapter.

For me, this therapist gets herself into trouble by never fully defining the limits of the enactment. We don't know where it begins and ends. Does it start with her query as to what the patient did while the father acted out these horrors? Does it include her threatening to abandon the patient (terminate therapy)? Does it include her powerful and unrelenting interpretation that he, the patient, has identified with the aggressive and sadistic part of his father? Does it include her strong reaction to the horrific material he is presenting in the song lyrics? Is she personalizing the reporting of dreams too much and seeing in the dreamer a lurking sadist, or all of the above? Because I had trouble with her understanding of enactment versus my own, I did something that may be unfair to her. I threw out the notion of enactment and reread the case as an interpersonal treatment that contained a series of judgment calls, some of which seemed more or less conscious and deliberate, and others that felt more or less transferential.

Approaching things through this lens allowed a few things to stand out. One is clinical style, and how we make (offer?) interpretations. I saw a strong danger here of evolving to a judgmental attitude and sense of certainty. Remember: this therapist places a high value on uncertainty and perspectivism, calling it the hallmark of interpersonal theory. Yet the therapist believes with conviction that the patient identifies with his aggressor father and also agrees with the patient that in some ways he is worse than his father. She concurs that in the dream he, the patient, kills the person in one day. By contrast, the father took many years to kill his wife. The therapist says to the patient, "You are living out your father's brutality." Surely we can agree that the dream is more than the manifest content and that the dream is not always the dreamer. We do not want to confuse the dream content with the real qualities of the dreamer. Are there alternative readings? Is the woman in the dream another, perhaps softer, version of himself that he is trying to choke off and destroy? It's anyone's guess. Having a sadistic dream is not the same thing as being a sadist. Remember: the patient is already doing this to himself, i.e., wedding himself to the manifest content of this dream. For the patient, one bad decision (e.g., putting the drug in the girl's drink) casts him into becoming an evil person, a murderer. Surely we would want to countervail against that.

I may be being too tough on this analyst regarding the exchanges around the dream. Perhaps one has to be a woman to detect the full horror and malicious intent of this dream and how and when it is reported. Nonetheless, these verbal exchanges with the patient are occurring against the backdrop of a severe mood disorder. There is a strong likelihood that the patient is severely depressed. Dr. Quinones gives several examples of recurring depression since his twenties, including suicidal ideation. She speaks of a wall that imprisons him in his loneliness. He has profound issues of low self-esteem. The signs are evident throughout this treatment. I believe there are grounds for proceeding more cautiously. I would not want to convey to this highly vulnerable patient that he is another version of his father.

On the other hand, what is one to do when one feels overwhelmed by the patient's negativity and penchant for discussing painful and sometimes disgusting things? Are we to simply tolerate long forays into this material? Dr. Quinones did the right thing by interrupting the patient in order to bring back her thinking and analytic mind. Dr. Quinones tells us that in the early part of the treatment she had lost herself to the patient's trivia. Little was going on as to real analysis. Where things go awry in this treatment is when Dr. Quinones entertains the idea that the patient has identified with some of the worst aspects of the father and includes that idea in their exchanges.

Things are rarely so black and white. For much of this work Dr. Quinones is trying to regain her analytic perspective – while at the same time maintaining a deeply emotional experience. I am glad she hung in there with this difficult patient.

Reference

Renik, O. (1999). Response to a discussion of enactment. *Journal of Clinical Psychoanalysis*, 8, 595–597.

Chapter 4

Defying destiny

Genetically doomed?

Olga Cheselka

In order to protect the confidentiality of the people with whom I work, I use clinical examples that are composites of various people, although I believe that the description of the analytic work is a good reflection of what has transpired in the therapy.

Introduction to Michael

How do we overcome the obstacles of heredity, of problematic inherited character and personality genes? And what about upbringing? What if there is a lack of nurturance and stability, or even traumatic events in our early lives? Are we doomed to live out unhappy lives filled with disappointment and failure? How do we come to terms with the entanglements of past feelings of obligation, love, dependency, guilt, anger, and resentment? And then how do we deal with our own impulses, our bad character traits, our personal vices? Are we destined to repeat the defeats, downfalls, and deterioration of our family background? Do we all have a tragic flaw that is part of our psychological endowment? These are the questions which formed the background of the work that I did with Michael.

Early session excerpt

MICHAEL: It's my birthday. And one good thing is, I didn't have to schedule rehearsal. I had to talk to my mother, though, a bitch fest. She said, "I'll die soon and no one will care." Like other people in my family, she complains all the time. People like to complain. But I don't want the negativity. My mother – why didn't she make the phone call good for my birthday? There's no encouragement for me, I'm genetically doomed.

OLGA: People can be very different from their parents.

MICHAEL: It's my whole family. One uncle, the mayor of his town, embezzled money, and now is dead from alcoholism. My other uncle committed suicide. My mother's brother was accused of raping someone so he had to run away. My father's a drunk. But I'm interested in how I could change all of this. I'm talking here – will it change me? Or will I still be like my

> mother? Do I purge myself by talking about anger, or do I make the anger worse? Do I make myself what I talk about? Am I using analysis as a bitch fest? Will I feel better after I bitch? I'm still stuck in bitching. I'm not saying anything new. I don't know how to take it someplace else.

Michael was 30 years old when I met him, of slender build and an appearance that was both unremarkable and noticeable at the same time. He had an attractive presentation, which was underplayed by a style of dress that was somber and nondescript. But two things stood out: his hair, which was streaked with blue coloring, and a piercing gaze that was direct and engaging. He both called attention to himself and rebuffed it at the same time, presenting himself in a way that stirred a response of intrigue about this appealing and yet shy and modest-appearing person.

When I first met him, Michael had already distinguished himself as an extremely gifted singer, song writer, and musician. As a child he had been seen as having a true natural proficiency in music. In addition, he applied himself to studying the field of music in all genres, so that he had a deep and broad background. As an adolescent and young adult, he had opportunities to perform in venues that showcased him, and he had received high critical acclaim. He had already worked in the music field for almost 15 years, having started performing in his teens. It was clear that he was passionate about his art, and he continued to study music seriously throughout his life. He had already acquired quite a following in his style of performing and musicianship, and this was perpetuated by an aura of curiosity and fascination around him, as an unconventional artist who flouted bourgeois mores. His lifestyle resulted in gossip and notoriety, as he lived with two women and frequently invited his friends to his home to have sex parties.

Michael's story started in an ordinary enough way. His parents knew each other in high school, and were both in the "popular crowd." His father was an all-round successful student and athlete, and came from a family who were well known in their town because they held positions as politicians. His mother came from a family that were held in high regard for their conspicuous financial successes. Unfortunately, his mother, although known for her beauty, was also known for her sexual promiscuousness, at a time and in a place which held that type of behavior to be disgraceful. Although Michael's parents had not been dating, and had not been seen as a "couple," in their last year of school they went to a dance together and had an impulsive sexual liaison. When his mother found out that she was pregnant, the couple were told by their families that they had to marry.

Even at the beginning, in the most hopeful stage of their marriage, the young couple did not get along, both of them feeling trapped and burdened. Michael's father was not interested in involving himself in politics as most of the family had done, because he was more interested in the arts and had musical talent. He was invited to study at a prestigious music school, which necessitated a move to a large city. Although he graduated, he struggled with depression and was drinking quite heavily. From all accounts of family members he was reputed to be a gifted musician who had the talent to advance to an outstanding career. He also had what was described as a magnetic personality. But his shortcomings became more prominent; he became more and more unreliable, and started using heroin. Shortly after graduation from music school, when Michael was just a baby, his father was told he had to leave the band with which he was affiliated. This led to a brief stint in a rehab program which helped him refrain from most substance use, except for alcohol. He then began working as an agent for other musicians, and started his own agency. After a while he began to earn a tremendous amount of money and enjoyed a prestigious reputation. Unfortunately, as time went on, his abuse of alcohol increased, leading to a decline in his representation of higher level musicians, and a decrease in income.

Michael's mother was a homemaker who had no skills and no ambition to have any kind of career. She felt unloved and unappreciated. Because the family had to move around quite a lot for the father's career, she lost the support network of her family of origin, however limited that may have been. She resented being left alone, and felt deprived of attention. She stayed home smoking cigarettes, waiting for her husband's return in the hope that he would provide comfort and nurturance and entertainment. Instead, he rarely came home when he said he would. It was clear that he had been drinking a lot, and she became increasingly concerned that he might be seeing other women. So she questioned him, and complained about his absences. When he responded angrily and told her to stop nagging, she would resort to tears, accusations, and temper tantrums. He would storm out and stay away for longer periods of time. She pleaded for help from her family. They resoundingly said that divorce was not an option, and that perhaps having more children would bring the couple closer together. So, when Michael was 5 years old, a younger brother was born.

Michael has two early memories. One is of being around 2 or 3 years old and hearing his parents having a vicious fight. He heard his mother say she was going to kill herself, and she grabbed a knife from the kitchen. The father rushed over to her and managed to take the knife away without anyone being hurt. The other memory is of a further fight. Michael was about 4 years old, and this time the father was threatening to leave and never come back. The mother yelled and cursed, put Michael in the car, and announced that she was leaving. She drove to a shopping mall and left him in his stroller as she shopped in various stores. A neighbor who knew them well happened to be at the mall and saw Michael alone, crying softly. So she took him with her until she found his mother. Although perhaps in today's world someone would have reported his mother to Child Protective Services, his mother acted in a contrite fashion toward the neighbor, and there were no consequences following this incident.

Throughout this time Michael's father was drinking more and more. His father's family of origin did not want to help him, so his only sense of support and connection came from the very ambivalent relationship he had with

Michael's mother, and with Michael himself. Very often his father would return home in a drunken stupor and bang on the door. His mother would have barricaded the door and told him not to come in. His father would continue to knock until Michael would let him in. The fact that another child was born into the family did not change any of this cyclical behavior. Although Michael's father's career had started out as very promising, over time his success became more sporadic. At the beginning, his career was marked by periods of intense work, when he was completely involved with attending to his clients. He had significant skills and impressive instincts in regard to representing his clients, which resulted in remarkable gains for the people with whom he worked. At these times Michael's father was ebullient and jaunty, and there was more than enough money for the family to enjoy the luxuries of large purchases and expensive vacations. This changed over time, so that increasingly, as Michael was growing up, his father would lose clients and the family would be forced to move to another location in a new community. Even so, Michael's father was able to continuously forge new relationships with people who were eager to work with him. In light of his erratic work history, it is something of a mystery as to how he was able to repeatedly attract new people who wanted to work with him. An explanation that Michael heard from family and friends was that his father had charisma. That is, he could be charming, engaging, and enthusiastic, in addition to being fully present with someone. He projected a feeling of confidence and expansiveness that was quite compelling. Unfortunately these attractive qualities became less and less accessible as he struggled with depression, anxiety, and substance abuse.

Until he was in high school Michael tried to manage the hostilities between his parents. Michael remembers that when he went to bed at night he would wait to hear the footsteps of his father returning home. He tried to sharpen his senses, his hearing and sense of smell, so that he would always know what was going on. When he smelled his father lighting up a cigarette he knew that his father was beginning to drink, and that the way to avoid a fight between his parents was for him to go into the living room with his father and listen to his rambling stories. When the father fell asleep it was safe for Michael to go to sleep. His father liked Michael's company, especially as Michael got older, and he was proud of Michael's musical ability.

When Michael was only 3 years old he was urged by his father to start learning to play the guitar. It became clear that Michael had unusual ability and talent, and that he was something of a prodigy. His father became increasingly forceful about Michael having a career in music. However, as he entered high school, Michael felt that he wanted to concentrate his efforts on becoming a singer and song writer, as well as a musician. He found a highly regarded school for the arts, which would allow him to study singing, writing, and music, and was accepted there. This school was in a city at some distance from his parents' home. As it happened, Michael had an aunt living in that city, who was pleased to have him live with her while he attended high school. He recalls being happy about the thought of being able to leave his family and live in a large city, where he would have access to hearing musicians and singers who were experimenting with stretching the boundaries of conventional music. He started school, found it to be a stimulating and creative place, and was enjoying this new phase of his life. However, as luck would have it, his father lost a few clients around this time, and the family decided to move to the city where Michael was living. They insisted that he move back in with them, but he refused. His father threatened to cut him off financially and emotionally. Fortunately for Michael (as he saw it), the family's attention starting shifting to Michael's younger brother George, as his brother was also developing quite a reputation as a musician, winning several national contests. George's musical genre was different from Michael's, so they were not in direct competition. As time went on and George's success continued, the parents were much more involved with his brother, and told Michael they could no longer give him any money. Michael remembers this time as being difficult, but ascribes this to his financial woes, not to the disenfranchisement with his family. But he became less confident in general and more anxious about his performances, and he began to drink. He stopped working on his music for a while, and went on to college. However, he became depressed, and at the age of 19 he dropped out of college. He had the feeling that he might never return.

His life during that time was not easy. He had to find work, and ended up doing repair work and carpentry, even though he was not particularly skilled in this work and felt like a fraud as he pretended to know more than he did. He had very few friends, and actually lost some of those relationships as he became more reclusive and depressed. He found himself crying himself to sleep every night, in despair and in a depression that previously he had never allowed himself to feel. Yet at the same time he started making friends with some of the people that he hung out with at the bars he frequented. One of these people was a professional who was financially well-off. He took a liking to Michael, and seems to have had an interest in helping someone who was in dire straits. He encouraged Michael to go back to college, and said he would give him some help in paying for the first year, and together with financial aid Michael was able to stay in school. Over the years Michael has remained friends with this man who helped him. Their friendship seems to have been a mutually respectful, non-exploitative relationship.

As Michael went through college his life improved considerably. He started therapy at the counseling center, and found this very helpful. He met a woman, Jane, who was interested in the same area of music that was compelling to him, and they became constant companions. They eventually married and worked on their art together. Michael reports having a satisfying and rewarding relationship with his wife. They were good friends right from the beginning of their relationship, and they maintained a positive, supportive liaison throughout the time that I worked with Michael. With all the struggles that Michael was having, along with his background issues that were resulting in depressive episodes, he clearly wanted meaningful connections, and was able to find them at pivotal points in his life.

However, even though he and Jane were both performing and enjoying some success, payment for their work was minimal, and they made barely enough to live on. They became increasingly discouraged about their difficulty in making money. They were especially disheartened by the demands of the people who hired them, who refused to increase their pay, even as Michael's band was drawing in larger and larger crowds of people. After a few years, feeling drained and dejected, they decided to pursue music only on a part-time basis, on evenings and weekends. That would allow them to look for day jobs to make some money for their living expenses. However, they could only find low-level jobs, and realized these jobs depleted them, so that they were too tired to continue with their artistic pursuits. Michael was getting increasingly depressed and pessimistic, and Jane encouraged him to start therapy again. He reached out to his college counselor who was in a different city, and she gave him some referrals to people in New York. That is how I met Michael.

The treatment

Michael was struggling in his life, but he had actually achieved a respectable amount of critical recognition and acclaim in music. He began the treatment by saying he was afraid that he would not be able to fulfill his potential, that his family background of unhappiness, substance abuse, and dysfunction "doomed" him.

In our first session, Michael stated that he had difficulty working consistently, even though he felt that his career was immensely gratifying. He felt he could "truly express" himself and "fully reinvent" himself in his chosen field. In addition, he wanted to find relief from the stress he experienced because he was having an affair, having to keep two women (his wife and his girlfriend) satisfied. He talked about the guilt he felt about the relationship, even though he and his wife had an agreement that they would have an "open relationship," where each one would be free to have a sexual relationship with someone else, but not a "loving relationship." As far as he knew, his wife had not followed through on this. But he said he needed the "liveliness and the excitement" of the situation to prevent him from getting depressed. Within a few weeks, however, it became clear that Michael was feeling that he wanted to extricate himself from the relationship with the girlfriend but just didn't know how to do it, and was very concerned about hurting her feelings. This concern was customary for him in all his relationships. It took several more months before he was able to tell her, in a somewhat roundabout way, that their affair was over. It seemed that she was also ready to leave the relationship, and it ended without acrimony.

For several weeks Michael focused on these two issues. One other major precipitant for starting therapy emerged in our third session. Michael brought up the fact that one of his uncles (his father's brother), had committed suicide several months prior to Michael beginning therapy. Michael said he hadn't talked about this sooner because he didn't realize how much it had been bothering him.

He also revealed other information about scandals in his father's and mother's family; how one uncle had been convicted of embezzlement, and had to go to jail, and another uncle had fled the country when he had been accused of rape.

When I first introduced the idea of psychoanalysis and the use of the couch (about six months after we first started working together), Michael was enthusiastic about having the opportunity to explore his issues in more depth. Some of his comments, though, reflected the concerns that were repeated throughout the course of our work together: that people thought he wanted too much, and would be a person who would exploit others, and that he feared confronting certain deep-seated issues. In one session he recounted a dream that demonstrated these issues, which went as follows:

> He owned a beautiful, tranquil house on the ocean, where the sound of the waves hitting the shore was soothing and comfortable. He was arranging for people to rent the place for three weeks for a considerable amount of money. However, he was aware of something that he didn't tell them; that within a few days there would be a major construction job going on that would be noisy and totally ruin the tranquility of the place. Later on Michael realized, with some embarrassment, that the renters would be aware that he must have known about this, and that he cheated them.

This came up in the first session after we had agreed to work analytically, three times a week, using the couch. Our contract included the agreement that I would accept a reduced fee which would make it possible for Michael to afford his treatment. If his financial circumstances changed, we would renegotiate the fee. It seems that at some level he felt that he was asking too much and exploiting the situation. He was also fearful that being in analysis would mean upsetting whatever psychic equilibrium he had established.

The cycles of thought that were predominant in our early sessions were as follows. Michael felt there was so much in his personality and background that doomed him to ultimate failure; he was afraid of burn-out or alcoholism; and his worries about the envy and jealousy of those around him. In addition, his defensive style of grandiosity appeared; that he had the right to ask for more for himself, and he had so many strengths which would overcome these problems that he would be victorious in the end. He also brought up the issue of aggression, which would usually (as it did in the following excerpt) lead to defenses of denial and undoing. For my part, I attempted to use the inquiry to stir up questions about underlying feelings of despair and shame and greediness. I wanted to deconstruct some of his rigidified ways of thinking in order to allow him access to the dissociated material around emptiness. I felt, in addition, that this would ultimately enable him to access a sense of aliveness and vitality. The following excerpt demonstrates how these issues arose.

A session excerpt

MICHAEL: I'm waiting to hear from my manager and agents to know if our next concert will be financed. I want to write a groveling letter, asking for help, but I stop myself. I'm driving myself crazy, trying to be more creative, to keep moving forward, or I'll feel like I'm dried up and have no more career. In five years I may be washed up or alcoholic. I can't relax. I have to work. I fear my genetics. Family history is inescapable. I want to be somebody, and make good music, but how long can I last?

OLGA: You feel you've used up your potential, and that you're doomed to be like your father?

[I was trying to access his deeper feelings of insecurity, emptiness, and despair]

MICHAEL: Yes, but there's touring ahead for this year. I'm not doomed yet. And I can get more from the concert producers. You know, I'm the artist, I'm the one the people are coming to see, the one who's bringing the crowds in. I have what they need. They aren't artists, they're producers and have money. I should feel I deserve it, but instead I feel a pull to apologize and ask for less money.

[Here he uses defenses that are typical for him – an undoing of the negative thoughts, changing feeling doomed into feeling special]

OLGA: Maybe you're talking about whether you ask too much in general.

MICHAEL: The issue is I feel I won't last too long. People are doing me a favor. I have survived by pleasing other people. I'm 100 percent dependent on others. I have to impress. I have to convince people to give me work. And something in that is not healthy.

[He is making a correction to my interpretation. He is saying that he has to depend on others (which he doesn't like), and get in their good graces – not that he's asking too much]

MICHAEL: And my friends, and other people I know, when they hear how well I'm doing they get jealous. They say I've been lucky, that I just got in the good graces of people who have some power. I've paid my dues and gone through many rejections. It upsets me that people think I don't deserve what I get.

OLGA: There's a conflict. You don't want to depend on people who have helped you, but you need them. And you don't want to care what people think, but you're afraid they are saying you don't have the real stuff, you've just charmed people.

MICHAEL: Yes, that's where courage comes in, you have to ignore some things. Everything is now set in motion with my career. But I don't want to pander. Sometimes I go so far out of my way to be contrary, to make my point. Sometimes I think I'll say, "Screw you, and forget about all this." I panic that things will suddenly go away. But I haven't messed up *so* much in my life.

[Here Michael enlarges upon the idea of conflict, by bringing up another conflict: that of fear of his contrariness or underlying aggression. However, he resorts once again to a defensive position, saying that he does well, rather than sticking with the uncomfortable feeling]

Thus, in the first phase of our work together, Michael described himself as depressed, worried, and obsessive. He talked quite a lot about the difficulties of his work (a subject that was continued throughout the treatment), and the problems of managing financially with very meager resources. In addition, he spoke about his anxieties that interfered with his ability to be creative; his fear of failure, the idea that he was stretched too thin because other people leaned on him too much, and his concern about finding the energy to be consistently productive. The transference themes that came up seemed to center around a need to impress me with how needy yet hard-working and deserving he was. My countertransferential reaction was to be supportive and encouraging, because I felt admiring of the difficulties he had endured, and how persistent he was in overcoming his problems. In retrospect, I think I was responding to his neediness by being a nurturing "mother figure," trying to alleviate the depression and sidestepping the aggression. Thus, we maintained a positive working alliance. This transference/countertransference matrix probably replayed Michael's relationship with his father. It seems that Michael's feelings and attitudes, stated above, echoed the sentiments of his father, and my reactions were similar to the ways in which Michael reacted to his father.

As time went on, the issues we talked about continued the themes of his depression: the stress he experienced to keep performing and not be "all washed up," questions about how to keep creativity flowing, and difficulties in avoiding living or working to "please other people." In addition several new themes emerged. He talked about wishing he wasn't so ambitious so that he could just be playful and creative. He didn't want to get caught in a cycle of feeling that he "needed success," and that the experience of a "big commercial hit" would act like a drug, in that he would become addicted to it (a reference to the analysis?). Then he felt he would lose his originality and innovativeness. Along these lines he reiterated how he had so much trouble regulating his moods. He was always fearing and avoiding the underlying depression. He realized he felt depressed even after several concerts that had been huge successes. He questioned how he could find something new and exciting to revitalize himself. He said, "Wanting love [referring to his desire for approval from people] is my biggest enemy." This was an indication of one of the major conflicts he had experienced between dependency and agency. To me it seemed that his depression was driven by opposing forces. He felt as though he had to take care of and please other people, not transcend them, but wanted to fully develop and expand himself.

Many times Michael talked about how he was afraid that he would end up like his father or his uncle who, as mentioned, had committed suicide some months before Michael began analytic work. In addition, he talked about the deprivation he felt because he had never been appropriately parented. He was also angry about the amount of "parenting" he had to do with his band members, and was envious of the easy comforts they received from their families. At times he felt overwhelmed by discouragement and shame, and struggled with what he considered his "weak personality," because of the need to replenish himself in ways that he felt would be self-sabotaging in the long run (such as drinking, smoking, having sexual affairs outside of his marriage). It was difficult for him to find the inner vigor in his personality because he was so conflicted about separateness/aggression and dependency/relatedness.

Yet, as the analytic work continued, several goals were attained that were important to Michael. He quit smoking and stopped drinking completely, and started exercising regularly. In addition, he worked consistently and "found" the energy to write new songs. (Interestingly these songs were about how people talk about everyday things, and his attempt was to slow down the pace of language and the way in which things are communicated, so that more meaning could be discovered in even the most familiar subjects.) Then, he was thrilled to receive his first substantial payment for his work, which would enable him to pay for his essential expenses for the following year. The work he was doing was creating quite a buzz in the music world, and his reputation was steadily growing.

These were signs of progress which suggested to me that the work was going well. As we continued, the work evolved and our sessions took on a new tone and focus; that is, we made good use of the here-and-now in our relationship, and how it reflected some of his ongoing issues. We looked at our interactions, exploring the way in which we were replaying his issues in our relationship. In addition, there were many instances in which we had the opportunity to access different self-states. Although this caused some affective instability, it also made it possible to integrate the conflicting states, leading to eventual groundedness.

A later phase session excerpt

MICHAEL: I'm too preoccupied with the people in my life that I depend on. My wife, the guys in the band. And other things should be more important. We should all have the freedom to think about things creatively, and explore. Instead I'm filled with anxiety, and then I blame others for it. But I make myself anxious.

[Silence for a minute; then he continues]

I'm tired – from the concert last night and talking and thinking about myself. I don't want to rehash everything. I don't want to talk about all of this. I want to take a break. But I can't here.

OLGA: Do you think I would be upset or disappointed in you?

MICHAEL: In what way? You made it clear that I can talk about anything. But I'm sure if I didn't want to come here you'd be disappointed.

[At first Michael is dubious, but then he hints at the possibility of renegotiating our relationship]

OLGA: Well, maybe you do want to leave here. Or are you accommodating to me like you have talked about doing with other people?

[I entertain the idea of a renegotiation, and whether we can be more personal and authentic. I suggest that he doesn't have to be a "good boy," as he often feels he must be]

MICHAEL: I'm past the point of impressing you. I don't need to accommodate to you. But people can often disappoint, and then they put themselves in a position to be called an asshole. If I say everything I think, I can be more disappointing.

[Michael is circling around the issue of whether he can be truly honest with me, or whether he will pay a high price for that honesty]

OLGA: Here, too, the more you say the more I could judge you like an asshole.

MICHAEL: Yes, but I would hope you wouldn't judge. Here, this is more of a partnership.

[Reminding me that I should not be aggressive with him, and not judge him, and that he is not claiming dominance in this relationship]

OLGA: Yes.

MICHAEL: Plenty of people tell me I'm an asshole. Now I have a tough skin. I prefer to run away from my problems rather than digging deep. I don't know what the point is. I don't like this psychoanalytic talk. It makes me feel worse. I'm depressed, tired. Tired of all the work. Tired of working on myself. I dreaded coming here. I don't want to be a positive person. It's a constant effort to work on myself and part of me wants to take a break. I don't want to think about myself intensively.

[Michael continues to be ambivalent about whether he can be authentic in this relationship, or whether the effort will deplete him]

OLGA: Do you think I have expectations for you to be positive, to make changes?

[I try to tease out what part of his ambivalence has to do with my effect on him. Are my comments leading him to think that I want something more from him? Realistically, of course I do, but I am willing to take a look at this]

MICHAEL: I would hope so. No, it's the world's expectations. I just want to take a break. This is when people start drinking. Like in my family. The effort to be good is just too much. You want to take a pill. I don't have breaks, like things that people do for themselves, like watching TV. I have to be in a good mood, but I want to get into the deepest depression. I think there's so much wrong with me.

But I want to be myself. But I feel like I have to hide coming here three times a week. Nobody I know does psychoanalysis. I'm always needing something to perk me up, I'm looking for something like St. John's wort, or a tea. I'm depressed even though there's lots of work I can do. But all I want to do is be in front of the TV, dirty, with the cat on my chest, for four days. I want to be taken wherever it wants to go.

[These last few exchanges reflect feelings of shame, issues around having to hide his true self, and how hard he has to work to accommodate to other people, and of course to me. He also comments on his wish to fall into passivity, and complains about how hard it is to be active; how hard it is to find his own vitality]

OLGA: You don't have to be good here. You don't have to live up to a standard.

[I try to move the feelings into the here and now of our relationship, and to assert that the "false-self" condition is something to take a look at]

MICHAEL: But I'm upset here because there's something wrong with me. And this whole week I have to work hard every night till midnight, keep the band members going, working on our stuff. [Pause] I'll try hard to stay positive. [Pause]

I want to know if I can leave here early today. Maybe I'm lazy, but that way I'll have time for lunch.

[He feels destabilized and doesn't like the conflicted feelings of the different self-states of trying to have full agency, yet trying to please others, and seeing himself as lazy, not good enough]

OLGA: This is your time, you can do whatever you like.

MICHAEL: I don't know what's wrong. It's so much effort to be good. Will I ever reprogram myself? I wish you could put a screwdriver in my head so you could fine tune me. I want to give up. While everyone is indulging in their decrepitude, everyone's living a lie. And I'm a lone soldier working overtime to get better. I'm the only lunatic who needs help. Why isn't everyone working as hard as me?

In my family I can imagine my father would go through this kind of thing and then decide to drink for a couple of weeks. It would be an excuse because he would say the doctor wouldn't give him meds. I think he was taking antidepressants or anti-anxiety meds. He justified drinking every day. So if I could take heroin and transport myself, then I could go back to dealing with everything. I don't get a break.

OLGA: Sounds like you're angry.

[I'm trying to listen to which self-state is dominant. Although this exchange started with statements about feeling depleted by having to please others, at this point there's a shift to experiencing the anger about this]

MICHAEL: [Silence] At whom?

OLGA: I don't know.

MICHAEL: Yes, probably you're right. Because of all the energy I have to put into being alive and being good. I'm angry with Dan [his manager], and in general. I confronted the band about not working hard enough. I'm angry, I'm not doing the weak stuff anymore. I used to give into their whining and demands. I don't know why people get angry when they don't get their way. Tomorrow we have a meeting to discuss future gigs, and the band and Dan will expect me to make everything easy and okay. But I'm ready to self-destruct, tell everyone to get lost, I'm not doing this anymore.

OLGA: You're feeling pushed and you're pushing back.

MICHAEL: By what? Everything's so insignificant. I feel there's been an injustice done because we did the concert and now they don't want to pay for our rehearsals. I want to assert my rights.

OLGA: What about our relationship? Do you want to complain about me?

[At this point I feel that the experience of anger is becoming intellectualized, and that it will be helpful to bring it back to the moment]

MICHAEL: Why does it have to be about you and me?

OLGA: I wonder if you feel I'm pushing you?

MICHAEL: No, I'm asking for help. There's no limit to talking about relationships, but I don't want to have to talk about you and me all the time, and now I wonder if it's at all helpful to talk to you and have you just listen.

[His response is defensive and confrontational. He tells me both that he wants to be alone, and that I don't participate fully]

OLGA: You mean you have to do all the work?

MICHAEL: No, I mean I should focus on me. I'm eating a lot. My mother is obese. Food is my substitute for meds. I'm never just okay. I don't need to be ecstatically happy. I don't want to eat because I feel sad or angry. Why do you think I'm angry? Maybe you misinterpreted my voice. I'm sometimes accused of being angry when I'm not. I'll say angrily, "I'm not angry."

[We both laugh, and then he continues]

Obviously something's up in the last week. I ate Chinese food last night, but I wasn't hungry. This week it's not helping me to think about all this.

[He is concerned that I will see him as angry. But he has insight about how he deflects anger, and returns to talking about how psychoanalysis depletes him]

OLGA: Maybe there's too much expected of you, to be mature, in a good mood.

[This addresses how depleted he feels, and how he feels he must maintain the "good boy" approach]

MICHAEL: So what do I do? I don't want to be in a bad mood. I'll see it more clearly next week. Who am I angry at?

OLGA: Somebody who's pushing you too much?

[I am suggesting that he can talk to me about what's happening between us]

MICHAEL: Where do you see the anger in me? I feel I'm in rehab being in analysis. I take it seriously, though, because my family ruined everything, and I don't want to do the same.

OLGA: So are you worried because you're becoming increasingly successful and you feel you'll be like your father and ruin everything? When you find yourself in a bad mood you feel that it's the beginning of the end for you?

[I try to help him integrate self-states of guilt about his success and transcendence of his family, versus the fear that success will be thwarted by his depression and emptiness]

MICHAEL: Maybe.

After working for about three years, it became clear that we would have to suspend our sessions in about six months. Because of the continued success of his career, Michael would be touring regularly for the foreseeable future. He and his band were offered the opportunity to do shows in different countries around the world over a period of two years, and each booking would last for several weeks. So he would be in New York for only a few days every few months. All his shows in New York City were sold out, and reviews were very favorable.

It was at this time that we agreed that it made sense for us to set a termination date. He was apologetic about the fact that he was leaving, both about the fact that he couldn't be in New York to maintain our sessions, but also apologetic that he wanted to be free to leave. At the same time he felt optimistic and relieved about his ability to now make enough money to live comfortably. He also increasingly believed that his foundation in this very difficult career was firmly established, and although careers in the arts are never guaranteed, he was quite hopeful that he would always be able to work.

As we went through this phase of the work, Michael focused on the difficulties of negotiating both within relationships and at the end of relationships. He talked quite a lot about the people in his band, and how he felt he had to be a good "parent," even when "the kids" were complaining a lot, highlighting his acceptance of the role of the adult. He also told me, "People shouldn't depend on their kids to make them happy." We talked about how perhaps the underlying message to me was that I shouldn't depend on our work together to make me happy, and that he hoped I wouldn't see him as a spoiled child who didn't appreciate my efforts.

At another point he talked about how he had to ask one of the musicians, who was unreliable and uncooperative, to leave the band. He said, "I've never broken up with anybody before." I clearly saw the reference to the fact that he had "broken up" with me. He talked a lot about the problems of dealing with certain people who are rigid and who repeat the same mistakes in life. These were references both to the people currently in his life, but also to his family of origin. He acknowledged how in some cases there are good relationships in families, but when that's not the case you have to look elsewhere. He said, "You can't start over with a family, but you can substitute with friends."

Interestingly, there were times during this termination phase when more details from his childhood emerged. He talked about his father and how anguished Michael was about their relationship. He gave some more details about what life was like in his childhood. One particularly poignant statement was made when he talked about a recurring dream he had as a child. This is the dream:

> My father had one of his violent drunken episodes, left the house, but then telephoned to ask me for forgiveness, and asked to be allowed to come back home. I said, "I'll never forgive you, even if you crawl back home and beg forgiveness on your knees." My father broke down sobbing, and disappeared, and I never saw him again.

Michael cried during this session and said he felt very guilty about abandoning his father. Still, he reiterated what he had said many times before: that he was furious with his father for "destroying himself, and the greatness he could have achieved." His father had sabotaged both himself, and to some extent the entire family. But even so, Michael said he wanted to continue a reasonable relationship with his father. He did not want to carry the same anger and resentment that had burdened him for so long. It seemed that he was finally resolving this issue.

Frequently throughout the course of our work together, it seemed as though Michael was saying that he was resigned to the fact that he had to take care of himself, and that there would never be the kind of enveloping, supportive parental love that he had always longed for. However, the emphasis shifted in the final stage of our work. At this time he took more pride in being the mature one who focuses on what needs to be done to achieve success in the world. I thought that this also reflected the way in which he was in the process of resolving his mixed feelings about the analysis ending. Together with his sadness about the relationship ending, and his gratitude toward me, were statements about the ongoing experience of connection and meaningfulness that would stay with him.

So this was the termination phase. It turned out to be a productive time, when issues around separation and loss were explored. I felt that this was the best time of our work together, perhaps because never in his life before had Michael had the opportunity to do a leave-taking in a way that was meaningful and healthy. We continued with efforts to deal with his depression effectively so that he could maintain a sense of robustness in his life, work, and relationships. He spoke about how to nurture a spirit of playfulness, which would lead to creativity, and how to avoid giving into the need to cater to people's desires to win their approval, something that would surely destroy his originality. The sense of neediness and dependency and depression became suffused with a feeling of potency that he would be able to manage the conflicting affects and self-states. The integration of agency and healthy relationships overrode his feeling of weakness, and was supplanted by a move toward creativity. However, there was an admixture of topics that I thought were unconscious and conscious allusions to the analytic work ending, and assaults on feelings of security that resulted. For one, the subjects of risk and danger came up several times. For example, he talked about how he was often careless when crossing the street, and found himself imagining that "the big trucks can't hit me." He realized that that was ridiculous, and that he was experimenting with the contrasting ideas of risk and safety, and how he needed to be aware of maintaining a balance. He repeated his concerns about "longevity" in his career, and that the way to achieve it was to not care so much about what other people think, and to be able to access his unconscious fears so that he could assume responsibility for himself without relying on me to take charge. We discussed how these thoughts pertained to the analysis ending.

The following excerpt demonstrates some of the above points.

Termination phase excerpt

MICHAEL: We're leaving on tour soon and we'll be gone the better part of the next year and a half. I started to think about a new project. I want to work with some new musicians. [More about the plans for the coming shows] I got some extra money for someone to do all the work for planning the traveling and hotels. What a break.

And I have to take a break here. I believe, though, that I can come back. It's been a journey. Yesterday was a big day [most of the money had finally come in] and the conclusion of a long chapter in my life. And now I have to start a new chapter. Even if I travel, though, I could see you. You are part of my life, so even if I don't see you, you are there. But the function of Olga is for me to be working on these issues of mine. So if I don't see you, does that mean I'm fixed, cured? Is it better to be done because it will make me stronger? In you I have a support, a crutch. Is it better to lose the crutch, and walk by myself? Or is it a crutch? Do I need to graduate? I don't remember everything my teachers told me. But does that make me a more creative person in my work, because I don't have assumptions?

OLGA: What do you think?

MICHAEL: I know I'm not a cured, stable person. I hope you don't feel bad about me ending. It would be easier for me to try to keep coming than to upset you. And yet, I have to move on.

OLGA: What would be so bad about upsetting me?

MICHAEL: That would upset me. I empathize and don't want you to be hurt or disappointed. I don't care if it's somebody I don't really like, but with you I feel that you've been there for me, and you're so much a part of me. I can't disappoint you. I'm okay with people not liking my choices, but I don't want to be an asshole. But I don't think you'll think I'm an asshole for leaving. You'd say, "If something is right you should be able to do it," and especially when it comes to my work. This leaving feels right.

Next year is scary, though. I don't want to be stuck in my old self, repeat the old patterns. But I don't want to feel bad about leaving, either. It feels like I'm abandoning my family. But I want to be strong enough to see what's behind the doors. I think I can do it. But maybe I'll be homesick.

OLGA: With every opportunity there's a loss.

MICHAEL: I've been focusing on the loss. This is how I see it. Part of my life has to be that I leave things. It requires that I not worry if you're upset, or other people in my life are upset. I have to steel myself.

OLGA: You're not running away from something or somebody here, you're going toward something.

MICHAEL: Yes, and I can see that part of me wants you to make the choice, tell me to leave, so you're responsible. Like the sound engineer we wanted to fire, and couldn't bring ourselves to do it. He finally resigned.

OLGA: So in a way I'm resigning.

MICHAEL: No, you're not. But I don't want to take the responsibility that I'm the one who's deciding to leave. I want you to take the risk of being the good or bad decider. But I know that I have decided, and that it's a good decision. It's good for me, and you will be okay with it. And I'll be traveling so much. I don't want to be sad, I want to be cheerful, and see all the potential. But I'm anxious about being with the guys [musicians] today, I don't know why, but they expect so much from me.

OLGA: Does it bring up a feeling of neediness because of their neediness?

MICHAEL: Yes. But I feel I can take care of myself. I'm not as needy as I used to be. It will be good for me, too, to be in all these new situations where everything is expected of me. Hard, but good.

Understanding of dynamics

In working with Michael, I thought it was helpful to consider what theoretical constructs might lead to an understanding of Michael's underlying dynamics. In so doing, I organized my thinking around the following description of issues: failures in development of the self; fear of impulses; and separation/individuation issues. Although these groupings provide a structure for describing the dynamics, there is considerable overlap among the categories. In some ways they are so intertwined that it is impossible to talk about one without referring back to the other issues. However, I'll discuss these topics separately, and how these issues were revealed in the sessions.

Issues in the development of the self

The first major theme revolving around the development of the self had to do with the above-mentioned conflict between feelings of despair, shame, and struggle, and opposite feelings of grandiosity, power, and entitlement.

Depression and despair permeated much of what Michael talked about in our sessions. He spoke of how he felt that he was "doomed" in some ways, mostly having to do with his heredity, and his propensity to be what he called "self-indulgent." (These issues will be discussed later.) Certainly his whole family's history, throughout many generations, was fraught with dysfunction. And yet, there was a concomitant attitude of superiority in his parents' families, leading to feelings of potential and greatness. This may have been primarily because there were several people on both sides of the family who had exceptional abilities. There were many communications from the father that he would turn his sons into superior beings, and that they would have wonderful careers that would allow them lives of luxury and prestige. This was part of the reason why Michael experienced an underlying feeling of grandiosity. In addition, Michael had some precocious abilities as a child that enabled him to understand people and how to manipulate them. This led to the feeling that he was stronger than the adults around him, and that he had special powers. In fact, he was a "parentified child," which, while it gave him the feeling that he was superior to most adults, also added a concurrent feeling of vulnerability.

In addition, although he rarely spoke about the feeling of shame, it was clear that Michael felt ashamed of the weaknesses in his background. Michael was embarrassed by the failures and dysfunction of his family members, and "where he came from." He was haunted by the cycle of accomplishment and devastation that he witnessed on his father's side of the family. Yet there was great potency and force in the vision that the father had of making his two sons into extraordinarily successful people. In fact, as time went on, Michael's brother became a musician with international prominence. Michael was a strong contender for national prominence, but he struggled to be at the top level in his field because he was overcome by doubt and anxiety. Part of him believed that he had unusual musical gifts and abilities, however, and he made up his mind that he would find a way out of the despair of his surroundings.

As mentioned earlier, while he was in his early adulthood, Michael endured much depression. However, his feeling of being outstanding stayed with him. His talents and his belief in his own greatness drew people toward him, and he was able to benefit from this. Earlier on in his life this had resulted in receiving a scholarship to a prestigious school, and finding sponsors for his artistic work, and eventually resulted in his becoming a recognized performer. He continued to enjoy major success in his field, and this reinforced his feelings of superiority. The conflict between despair and grandiosity remained a major theme throughout our work together.

The second major aspect of the issues around development of the self had to do with the sense of impoverishment and lack of agency and power that Michael felt in his life. There were many factors contributing to this feeling, of course, and some of them had to do with the absence of stable and nurturing people and events in his life. He attributed much of his feeling of lack of control/power to the fact that his family background showed a number of areas of dysfunction. Things "just seemed to happen" rather than good choices being made, and there was quite a lot of substance abuse and criminal activity. He had an overly developed sense of responsibility to make things better (psychologically) for his family, to relieve the suffering and struggles of the unhappy people with whom he was surrounded, and these efforts were often thwarted.

There were many ways in which the theme of lack of agency was talked about in our sessions. One example is how Michael talked of "always being an observer in life, not a participant," and that he was "always waiting for his life to begin." Another example of his conflict about agency was his concern about how much he needed to give in to other people, versus how much he could assert himself. Did he have to be obsequious and deferential, or could/should he advance himself, and openly utilize his power? And then, how and when does a person get what they need? He continued to be anxious about being perceived as "an asshole," meaning that people would see him as demanding too much, seeing him as "lording over them." He was afraid that people would judge him and that they would be so jealous of his success that they would malign him. He said things like: "When you're in a position of power and you take authority, you'll make people feel like you're an asshole." And "My friends, when they hear how well I'm doing, get jealous." And, "I know there are risks involved in taking charge and being an authority figure."

He felt vulnerable because he concluded that his impoverished past meant that he was not equipped to deal with life effectively. He also believed that it was dangerous to disobey authority and that he had little sense of power or agency in situations in which he had to make demands. He said that he had accomplished some of his goals in life by going along with what people wanted him to do. However, this was only one side of a conflict that he spoke about in many of the sessions. As much as he felt he needed to be obsequious, we were also able to define ways in which he was very much in tune with a feeling of needing to be his own person (healthy individuation). He wanted to be creative and innovative, and therefore had to do things in his own way. He also talked about how he resented the fact that some people in his field demanded certain considerations in order to produce a concert. He saw this as manipulation, and at one point decided to tell the person involved that he would not give in. He was sure that this would be a bad blow to his career. However, he stuck to his decision, and as it turned out it did not hurt his career.

Issues of separation/individuation

Issues of anxiety about separation and dependency and individuation persisted throughout our work together. One way this was represented was through the repeated concern Michael had about how genetics and heredity were powerful forces that threatened his sense of stability and strength. He often referred to the overwhelming issues that were present in his family. He saw that his father and his uncles started out life with potential, but that they threw away their success by being drunkards and criminals. Our discussions focused on whether he could cast off the damaging imprints of his family and the past. In effect, could he achieve a healthy separation that felt comfortable for him, and in which he took responsibility for himself?

Michael also felt that what further doomed him was the fact that he had never received the proper guidance and nurturing from his family. So he saw himself as deficient in some of the resources that people normally have and that he needed people to "excite and invigorate me." I saw this, too, as anxiety about separation and individuation, and as an insistence that ties to his family were permanent. He did not have a sense of his own vibrancy. Furthermore, his sense of emptiness led to a feeling that he always had to produce, and felt that people depended on him too much. In what seemed to be a reaction formation, the feeling of being bereft of solid ties led him to feel that he was completely independent. Moreover, he could not tolerate the neediness and dependency of others.

Thus, he felt burdened by the idea that he was entirely responsible for what was happening in his work with his band. He often talked about the feeling that "all the ideas had to come from him," or that the musicians took no actions to protect their health by giving up their bad habits of drinking, smoking, or simply having no focus on improving their work. They were "dependent" on him to make all the traveling arrangements for their tours, even to the point of waiting for him to remind them about necessary passports and visas. He had an overall feeling of having to do everything, and that people were not appreciative of his efforts. Again, this reflected his belief that he was the only mature, truly independent person in his circle (the exception was his wife, whom he experienced as being a true partner). He glorified these attributes and talked about how furious he felt about the weaknesses in his family of origin. He said that he never wanted to see certain family members, and that, if he heard that certain people in his family had died, he would not go home for the funeral. He said at one point in talking about this, "You have to destroy everything from the past and start over again and create your own world." These examples of Michael's conflict about separation and individuation were paramount at the beginning of the analysis. By the end, however, rather than feeling angry and burdened, he felt proud of the way he was able to manage so effectively in life.

Issues around fear of impulses

Another frequent topic of discussion had to do with the issue of having to "be good." By this Michael meant that he could not give in to impulses, but that he had to control himself in many ways. Of course this reflected his concerns about his family's history of alcoholism, substance abuse, and criminal behavior; his shame about the defects and deficits in his past. It also extended to other "vices" he felt he had, such as smoking, eating too much, not getting enough sleep, or having sexual liaisons outside his marriage. Within the marriage he was sometimes inactive sexually. He explained this by saying he felt depressed and depleted by his work, and that he didn't have enough energy at times to engage in sex. It seems, however, that a greater interest in sex may have felt risky to Michael, as though the boundary between psychologically healthy and unhealthy behavior would be crossed. Remember, too, that at the start of therapy, Michael was having an affair outside his marriage. He was conflicted about it at the time, although for the most part he felt that he needed the stimulation and excitement of this situation. He also liked being seen as a special person, an "artiste," who had intense passions. At the beginning of our work, Michael needed sources of external excitement and gratification. As the work progressed, he was able to use his internal resources of vitality and creativity to stimulate himself.

Another way in which Michael felt he had to "control" himself, and not give in to his impulses, was in terms of his depression and sense of discouragement. He felt very strongly that he always had to be productive, and that he couldn't show any negativity, no matter what his underlying feelings were. He described how other musicians could complain about things, whether about their lodgings, tight rehearsal schedules, or not liking a venue. But he, on the other hand, always had to present things in a positive way, and to "energize" his band members. As a result, Michael was almost always on "good behavior," and this extended to his relationship with me. It was difficult in the first year of analysis to find ways to penetrate this armor, but as time went on Michael expressed himself more fully in the sessions, and allowed himself to be whiney, irritable, or resentful, and even angry at times (for example, when he was tired and felt that he was coming to therapy for my sake, not his).

Understanding parental relationships

The history of the most formative relationships is typically helpful in understanding someone's struggles. Therefore, I will reiterate some of the major points about the parental relationships that surfaced in our work together.

The father

Michael's relationship with his father was a core issue in the analytic work that infused many aspects of Michael's personality, his thoughts, and his actions and reactions. After knowing Michael for some time it became clear that, in a way, Michael was living his life in conjunction with, and in reaction to, his father. It was almost as though Michael's belief was that his father was a superhuman figure who could make Michael great, or destroy him. As time went on in the analytic work, Michael resolved most of the issues surrounding this psychological representation, and he achieved a sense of separateness and insight about this.

In Michael's childhood his father seemed to have great power and, even more importantly, it seems that he must have been quite grandiose. Michael became quite attached to this figure of grandiosity, wanting to be as great as his father, but also to have his father's love. As a young child he believed that his father ruled the family, and that his security depended on being obedient to his father, but also on keeping him away from alcoholism. It may have also been that Michael turned to his father as a source of strength and greatness, because he felt that his mother was a weak and fragile figure. His father, in the early days, was extremely successful, and he insisted that he would make his two sons great (this was described in detail earlier in this chapter). The three men in the family were all "supermen," sharing a bond and a commitment, and a vision of future glory.

However, Michael realized as he grew older that his father was self-destructive. Not only would he drink excessively and be physically aggressive with Michael's mother, but he lost one well-paying client after another due to his alcoholism. Michael was on guard whenever his father was around, to stop his smoking (which always preceded his drinking) and then his drinking. There was much inner conflict between the view of his father as a person who would help

Michael rise to great heights, and as a destructive and abandoning figure in Michael's life. As an adult, prior to analysis, the conscious view to which he subscribed was that of bitter disappointment about his father. He told me the following: "Even if I saw my father dying I would yell at him, 'You ruined my life'." As we worked analytically, Michael changed his view of his father. He said that although he was angry about the way his father had treated everyone in his family, he also saw how sad and pathetic his father was. He knew, however, that he had to maintain an appropriate distance from his father in order to protect himself. Even after years of some estrangement, and having little opportunity to see each other, his father would call up out of the blue, asking for money. Michael knew that the money would be spent on alcohol, so he would refuse politely, and then try to engage his father in a short but meaningful conversation.

The mother

Michael knew that he had a conflictual relationship with his mother, especially when he was growing up. He said that he was very disappointed in her lack of ambition, and that she did not take care of herself. As an adult she was obese and diabetic, and complained about how bad her life was. He remembered with bitterness the neglectful aspects of her mothering. Yet, he realized when he himself became an adult how abusive his father had been toward her. As a teenager he had encouraged his mother to get a divorce, but both parents agreed that they did not want to divorce while there were still children living at home. When both children had left the parental home, they did finally get a divorce.

As Michael worked through this in the analysis he became more empathic toward his mother. He saw how constricted her life was, how she had few resources, and how she had been somewhat victimized by her circumstances. Now he was able to further integrate his mixed feelings about her, and although he almost never saw his mother since they live so far apart, he would speak to her by phone. Toward the end of the time that we worked together Michael had this to say about his mother when she called:

> She wants to see me when I travel next year. She's a good woman, and although she wasn't there for me when I was growing up, I don't hate her. I tell her I love her, and I feel bad that she had a miserable life.

In relation to what he experienced consciously, Michael presented his father as being the more salient person in his life, the one for whom he had his strongest feelings. Interestingly, Michael's relationships with women in general had been relatively good throughout his life. He had a committed and devoted relationship with his wife, and they got along very well. As a teenager he had a girlfriend who functioned almost like a "chum," whom he remembered fondly. Nevertheless, it was puzzling to me at times that Michael did not have more ambivalence about his relationships with women. As I thought about it I speculated that in his earliest days, in his highly formative years, he had a close and warm relationship with his mother. It seems reasonable to think that she turned to her son for closeness and connection when there was nobody else around. Michael pointed out that although he felt his mother neglected him at times (like the example given earlier about how she left him in his stroller outside a store so that she could go shopping), he never felt that she was abusive like his father was. He also talked about how he appreciated the fact that his mother tried to sustain the marriage, seeing this as evidence not only of her neediness but also of some strength of conviction in her personality, even though in retrospect it may have been better for her to end the union.

Defenses and resistance

Michael's defensive style was permeated by dissociation. At the start of our work, he was not able to confront the anger, dependency, and lack of agency he felt in his life that had been perpetuated by a traumatic and deprived background. He functioned under a layer of depression that had stymied his earlier efforts to achieve his goals. The utilization of dissociation made it possible for him to retain feelings of grandiosity and power, although the underlying depression needed to be worked through in order for him to integrate the various aspects of his personality, and to feel fully alive.

In addition to dissociation, Michael's defensive style was typified by intellectualization, reaction formation, and denial and avoidance. The intellectualization was most evident during the earlier sessions. He talked about subjects in a somewhat superficial way, and often quoted writers or poets whose work he had studied. In addition, he focused on what steps he needed to take to manage the concrete aspects of his life: financial worries, concerns about how to deal with his band, and how to work harder without resorting to addictive or passive behaviors. Reaction formation became evident when it was clear that Michael had so much difficulty talking about aggression, or dependency, or despair. Instead he often denied these aspects of his personality, and changed the expression of these feelings into something more positive.

Avoidance and denial were also prevalent defenses. Michael often resisted addressing sensitive subjects during the analysis. He would change the subject, or deny negative feelings. He talked at times about the burden of being in analysis, and how he needed a break. He feared that analysis would lead to uncontained aggression by giving voice to his underlying anger. Therefore, he denied his anger. He asked me how did I see anger in him, and changed the subject to one of feeling burdened and pushed. And lastly, when I brought up the idea that he had been betrayed by so many people in his life, he denied and avoided the feeling by resorting to the idea that he didn't want to complain and be seen as an "asshole."

In addition, he resisted becoming more intimately engaged with me. "Why does it have to be about you and me?" he would say. He also talked about not wanting to work so hard, not wanting to dig deeper. He avoided confrontation with me, as, for example, when I asked him if he felt I pressured him to be an adult. He denied that, and then asked for more help instead. Another example was when I asked him to be honest with me, and to give me feedback about my behavior toward him. He responded that the analysis is "more of an exercise," and that he didn't want to make me feel bad. I knew that working on our relationship was the key to working through important issues, so I had to be alert to occasions where Michael side-stepped this topic. I felt it was important to engage him at the times when he resisted deepening our intimacy. Therefore, I tried to reach him in various ways. Sometimes I allowed my annoyance or anger to come through, feeling that this encouraged genuineness, understanding, and the ability to reach inner liveliness.

Transference, countertransference, and enactment

Fundamental to analytic work, the transference, countertransference, and enactments illuminate the personalities of the patient and analyst. The relationship between the analytic participants both perpetuates and elucidates relationships from the past: old patterns, ties, and belief systems. Observations and reflections regarding the intricacies of the analytic relationship provide insights about reflexive actions and interactions, and these insights lead to pathways to new understandings and shifts in behaviors. Typically, there is a continuous shuffling around of these elements; the analyst–patient relationship builds on itself and evolves into deeper and richer insights with time. It was part of Michael's general presentation at the beginning that he kept a certain distance in our relationship. In general, I felt he treated me like so many other people in his life who turned out to be helpers: from the professional man who directed him to go to college and then gave him financial help, to his wife Jane and her parents who often gave them money when they needed it, to the people in the music field who saw something unique in him and gave him special considerations and accommodations. I was one in a series of "helpers," and I extended myself for him as the others had: I worked with him in analysis for a reduced fee. It is interesting to note, also, that we all "let go" of him when it was clear that he wanted to move on.

As time went on, in addition to the fact that he found me helpful, he also wanted more from me. I think he felt that I was withholding some important information about how to live without depression, how to be inspired, or how to maintain a vital, vigorous, and healthy state of being. However, he was afraid to push me too much. He would ask me for more, or hint at how I had not been so helpful, but then back off when I urged him to continue his thoughts. Michael's conflict about feeling dependent and wanting to be independent was acted out in many ways. For the most part he denied feeling dependent on me, although at times he was afraid he would annoy me and that then he would lose the relationship. Women in Michael's life were in a more neutral position than men. Women could be useful, companionable, and supportive, as several of the women in his life were (e.g., his early girlfriends, his wife). Men were much more ambivalent figures, since he depended on them unconsciously to provide strength and guidance in marking the way toward greatness, but they were more dangerous figures in that they could be critical or even abusive. Men (like his father and other male relatives) could be great; women (like his mother) had very little power or impact in the world.

When we started treatment I think I was in the "women" category. As time went on I became a more integrated figure, and Michael experienced me as having something powerful to offer him to make him great. However, at the times when he felt that I was withholding, he expressed more distress about how I was not helping him, and how I was controlling in the sessions. A negative transference emerged during these times. This sometimes resulted in ruptures in our relationship, points when we both felt bogged down. But we were able to process what had gone on between us, and to work out a way to reach a level of "concordance" (see Greenberg, 1995), which eased the tension. He then gained a feeling of his power and agency, even though at times it meant that there had to be a compromise between his desires and the work of the analysis.

My countertransference was marked at the beginning by a desire to be obliging and supportive, and to be able to engage the creative aspects of his personality. I soon thought of Michael as a talented person with unusual abilities (this was emphasized by the fact that he was becoming increasingly successful in the music world, and I was quite enamored of his artistic and creative excellence). Because of this halo of "greatness" and "unusual talent" I think I was not attending to Michael's intellectualization and remoteness. However, in our earlier sessions I also got carried along with Michael's depression, at times feeling that I had done everything I could think of to help him out of his despair. This led to a feeling of being "stuck" at times. He seemed so needy, and I deeply sympathized about the very real lack of nurturance in his early life. I also identified with the pressures of having to be independent and a leader early in life, having gone through some of the same situations in my own early life. I knew what it was like to experience what he told me was his experience: the sense of being pushed too hard, too early on, with no one to serve as a role model or a guide. The feeling of depression and a concomitant feeling of despair of ever having an "answer" about where energy, motivation, or inspiration comes from, were easy issues for me to understand. I also knew about and commiserated with the stresses of lonely struggling, almost as if in a void, and how it could feel as if life events were predetermined.

As time went on, we worked through this by augmenting these feelings with other self-states of vitality and agency, sometimes through humor, sometimes through anger. The ability to be curious, to feel engaged, and to be motivated to work toward a better level of functioning were all present in the work. Annoyance, anger, and disagreement produced anxiety, which then pushed us toward resolving issues. Despite his occasional resistance, he and I were both willing to delve into our relationship, and into the deeper meanings of the work we were doing. In the initial stages of the work, however, there was the unconsciously motivated enactment that we co-constructed. As I understand it now, my part in it was that I inadvertently helped him maintain the dissociation of states he did not or could not confront. As I look back, I can see how I accepted the role of helping him achieve greatness. This role continued in our work for quite a while, because I consciously derived satisfaction from the ensuing success that Michael was enjoying. Therefore, I recognize that I persisted in efforts – sometimes through indirect communication – that he be more, and better.

As the work with Michael progressed, I began to be aware of these pitfalls for me, and became conscious of the enactment. I realized that this was the same kind of "pushing" he had experienced from his father. I see in retrospect that I colluded with him to work toward superiority, investing in the grandiose fantasies without regard for the need for further examination of the despair and emptiness he felt. Thus, in a sense, I abdicated my responsibility to carry this burden of dealing with these difficult emotions, expecting him to do it, and when I contemplated my role in our work, I could see how part of me wanted to focus on moving Michael toward success. (In this way I could also experience the gratification that came from feeling that I had been a significant influence in making his life better.) I was psychologically "fed" by him. Michael's part in the enactment was the following. He could be psychologically "fed" by me, in that he had the illusion that he could achieve greatness without having to take full ownership of his aggressive strivings, or having to deal with his sense of futility. In this way, he attempted to achieve security and to dissociate the competitiveness, jealousy, or emptiness and despair that would lead to intolerable anxiety.

Thus, looking back at the course of treatment, I can see that at times in the earlier sessions I inadvertently pushed him to focus on accomplishment, to the detriment of paying attention to other issues that were more regressed. It was difficult for us to confront the hopelessness and lack of aliveness that Michael felt. However, as time went on, we were able to break through this, as both Michael and I achieved greater intimacy and authenticity in our relationship. Because we attended more carefully to the interplay of our relationship, we were able to gain an understanding of our enactment. We were able to discuss the desperation that was predicated on his belief that he had not been nurtured and therefore was doomed. We also discussed the fact that he was entitled to some kind of help from outside sources, and that he didn't have to assume complete ownership and responsibility for the resolution of these problems.

Therapeutic action: what is effective

Michael believed that the work we did together was extremely helpful. He felt less depressed and more hopeful in a realistic rather than a grandiose way. I believed that the work with Michael was rewarding for both of us. But how to conceptualize what was therapeutic, what led to the attainment of goals that resulted in a sense of well-being and creative potential? My formulations about what is effective in analysis are the following. I believe that therapeutic action results from the combination of the process of deconstruction of the rigidified, stifled aspects of the personality, together with the stabilizing aspects of the intense relational intimacy of the analytic space. The deconstruction and the relational aspects have a synergistic effect on each other, interacting and reacting in a way that leads to a continual evolution of the process. The deconstructive aspects, such as the detailed inquiry (Sullivan, 1970), making the unformulated formulated (Stern, 1997), addressing changes in self-states and affects (Bromberg, 2011), have a destabilizing effect, leading to psychic disorder that demands easement and remedy. The result is that these disturbances become part of the therapeutic relationship, affecting both patient and analyst. The disquieting features of the work are an impetus to attend to deeper aspects and meanings in past relationships, as well as the therapeutic relationship, that need to be understood and worked through, and these can be a source of motivation and aliveness. This can lead to the uncovering of enactments through the continued exploration of the relationship. That is, the repetition of previously learned beliefs and interpersonal interactions and responses can be uncovered through the analyst's ability from time to time to step outside the interaction and ask: "What is going on around here?" (Levenson, 1994). This leads to enhanced understanding of the entrenched patterns in the patient's interpersonal relationships, as well as in the conscious and unconscious fixed belief system of the patient and the analyst. In addition, the patient learns about this from understanding the mind of the other. Aron (1991) writes, "This opens up the possibility of accessing certain dormant or unformed parts of the personality, such as a sense of agency or vitality."

The therapeutic relationship is especially important in reordering the disorientation that occurs from exploring and changing old ideas and patterns. The relationship provides support, which aids in self-regulation (the regulation of competing self-states). At the same time the relationship offers challenges that lead to the possibility of negotiating new ways of being in a relationship, or what may be termed "other-regulation." There is also the opportunity to access dissociated states in the here-and-now in the secure setting of a familiar and trusted relationship, in which the analyst can "hold" some of the resulting anxiety. In addition, due to the nature of the analytic situation (the intimacy, the freedom to say whatever comes to mind, the aim of understanding the patient, and the opportunity to address one another in an authentic and personal way), the patient can gain access to the underlying unconscious issues that need to be worked out To summarize, the effects of deconstruction and the important relational aspects of the therapeutic relationship lead to both new ways of thinking and new affective experiences. This then leads to an expanded version of the self, which in turn leads to the capability of being able to think and act differently. The person has more strategies to utilize to move from one self-state to another (e.g., to move from dysregulation to regulation), or from one thought/belief pattern to another. The person has more flexibility and more resilience, and a continued ability to engage in self-reflectiveness.

To return to the work with Michael: we started our work with Michael's indelibly imprinted ideas of how his background and personality influenced or interfered with his ability to function at a higher level; in essence, his feeling that he was "doomed." At the beginning, Michael focused on presenting me with how needy and hard-working and deserving he was. My reactions to him were supportive, and I attempted to be attuned to his experience of himself. I functioned as a safe place for him to express negative, angry, or uncomfortable feelings. It became clear in retrospect that the enactment which occurred between us replicated the ongoing relationship he had had with his father. That is, the father maintained that he was needy and deserving of special attention, and Michael tried to be supportive, containing, and attuned to his father. In this case I was playing the role that Michael had played toward his father in his childhood, and Michael was responding by playing the role that his father had played with him.

As time went on, the deconstructive and unsettling aspects of the inquiry about past relationships and discussion of our current relationship led to anxiety that then had to be negotiated in the relationship. As an example, in one session I asked Michael, "What about our relationship, do you want to complain about me?" He answered, "Why does it have to be about you and me?" I said, "You can talk about whatever seems important," but then I also added, "But I wonder if I'm pushing you?" In this way there was an opportunity for change to occur; because Michael was given the chance to address annoyance and to ask for changes in the relationship with me. He was met with a response that implied mutuality, enabling him to experiment with different ways of having agency in a relationship. In addition, when there were tense moments of disequilibrium, for example, if he and I were in a power struggle or disagreed about whose needs would be met, he confronted different parts of his personality, and could therefore expand his personality. The destabilization was tempered by the interactive nature of our relationship. Michael had power in our relationship, he could move away or challenge me, and he could expect that I would be available to hold, manage, and work through the dissociated feelings that surfaced. The enactment of the conflicts between powerful and not-powerful figures (who was in charge and whose needs came first) became the playing field for working through these issues.

Another example of how changes occurred is the following. Michael remembered a dream in which his father asked for forgiveness, and Michael felt terribly guilty that he did not forgive him, and in that way abandoned him. I asked Michael to go back into those feelings of his childhood, to describe to me what it was like to be faced with such conflicting feelings. At this point Michael was able to access the confusing admixture of the longing and anger he experienced with his father, and to hold both states in his mind simultaneously. This bridging of self-states was also enacted and understood in the termination phase. Michael expressed his longing to continue the analytic relationship. At the same time he realized that he felt guilty toward me, for what he considered "abandonment" of me. But he also felt angry with me; he felt that he needed to move on and not be held back by his commitment to work analytically with me. He understood that he was re-experiencing the feelings from the past, but also working on resolving these issues with me in the present. He also understood that I would be able to tolerate his movement away from me while still "holding him in my mind" (Fonagy, 2001).

Conclusion

I called this chapter "Defying destiny" because I felt that Michael was intensely driven to prove that he could become extraordinary by overcoming the obstacles of his heredity and upbringing. Thus, he could succeed in resolving the challenge posed by the intense relationship he had with his father; to prove to his father that he was truly exceptional, that he was deserving of his father's love and attention, and yet at the same time that he could transcend his father. The motivation was multi-determined, so that while he was angry that he had to accomplish greatness without the help of his father, he also wanted to give his father the gift of his success. In the course of our work together Michael achieved insight into the reasons for his despair: that he would never get the nurturance and help on the road to greatness that he thought had been promised to him by his father – and that to some extent he felt entitled to. He felt that he should not have to accept the responsibility for himself. In many ways he now accepted that this was an old issue, and that he had to move on and create his own destiny.

The analytic relationship re-enacted these issues. In the unconscious contract that we had with each other, I promised him something special if he would work with me, some kind of resolution that would lead to an unencumbered ability to achieve a phenomenal level of greatness. He, in turn, had to promise to "stay with me," to do the work of analysis, and then I, too, would feel important. Our enactment involved us focusing on his motivation to succeed, and in so doing we avoided his feelings of emptiness and despair. In addition, there was insight and acceptance for Michael of the realization that the source of his vitality and creativeness had to emerge from himself.

There was much progress that Michael made in the course of our work. He could experience a full range of emotions, and experienced himself as a more integrated and balanced person. He also relinquished much of his sense of victimization caused by the difficult circumstances of his background. Although still harboring some resentment toward his parents, he had forgiven much of what he saw as their withholding and narcissistic behavior. He understood them better and experienced feelings of love and concern for them, and mourned the fact that they could not have had better lives, and became attuned to his own feelings of guilt about not having been a better son.

Relationships, in general, improved for Michael. He had an easier time accepting the limitations of others, and afforded himself the opportunity to experience and enjoy what was good in those relationships. His primary relationship with his wife continued to be a source of support and engagement, and he looked forward to sharing the travel and work experiences that were coming up for the two of them.

The termination of our work took place at a time which was determined by practical issues. However, in many ways I thought that this was a good time to end, and that it afforded Michael the opportunity to deal with feelings that would otherwise have been difficult to access. I felt that our work could have continued because both Michael and I enjoyed pursuing the intricacies and depth of the exploration of issues and of our relationship. Yet there were many ways in which Michael had moved to a point where he may have needed the strain of termination to deal further with his issues. For instance, the main themes of conflicts between agency and relatedness, between grandiosity and acceptance, and between a compliant good self and a truly alive self had been dealt with during the course of our work. But their resolution became deepened and solidified by the end stage issues of psychoanalysis: that of dealing with loss, separation, the boundary of finality, and the recognition that true autonomy and agency sometimes means leaving a relationship, even if it's a good one.

I believe that Michael achieved some level of realistic appraisal of who I am as a person, as well as knowing me as his analyst. He talked about how he felt my voice, and our work, would continue in his head, and how he appreciated the work and the relationship we had. The intimacy in our relationship had deepened over time, and we were able to be authentic and to confront each other in the here-and-now. I believe that Michael terminated the analytic work with feelings of healthy empowerment and resourcefulness, and that we both gained insight and understanding from the experience we shared. I know that we both felt the loss of what had become a vital and enriching experience.

References

Aron, L. (1991). The patient's experience of the analyst's subjectivity. *Psychoanalytic Dialogues*, *1*(1), 29–51.

Bromberg, P. M. (2011). *Awakening the Dreamer: Clinical Journeys*. New York: Routledge.

Fonagy, P. (2001). *Attachment Theory and Psychoanalysis*. New York: Other Press.

Greenberg, J. (1995). Psychoanalytic technique and the interactive matrix. *Psychoanalytic Quarterly*, *64*, 1–22.

Levenson, E. A. (1994). The uses of disorder – Chaos theory and psychoanalysis. *Contemporary Psychoanalysis*, *30*, 5–24.

Stern, D. B. (1997). *Unformulated Experience: From Dissociation to Imagination in Psychoanalysis*. Hillsdale, NJ: Analytic Press.

Sullivan, H. S. (1970). *The Psychiatric Interview*. New York: W. W. Norton.

Commentary on Cheselka's case

Daniel Gensler

Dr. Cheselka has offered the reader of this book a case that balances relational and intrapsychic factors which explain the patient, the therapy, and its successful conclusion. Her patient was a gifted singer, song writer, and musician who was afraid that he would not be able to fulfill his potential because of his family background ("negative genes," negative early parenting, substance abuse, and dysfunction). He was also concerned about his tendency to manipulate and cheat people. His mother was sexually promiscuous, lonely, jealous, resentful, complaining, and accusing. His father was an off-and-on alcoholic, a problem that compromised his career substantially. The parents fought a lot. When his parents cut off the patient's financial support at age 19, he was drinking and depressed and dropped out of school. He started to get back on his feet with the financial help of a friend. He married a musician, became less depressed, but stayed poor.

An early transference theme centered on a need to impress the therapist with how needy yet hard-working and deserving he was. Her early countertransferential reaction was to be supportive and encouraging, admiring his endurance and persistence in overcoming his problems. An early formulation of his personality dynamics was that it was difficult for him to find inner vigor in his personality because he was so conflicted about separateness, aggression, and dependency, and because he was so immersed in narcissistic defenses of turning the feeling of being doomed into feeling special and entitled.

As the work continued, patient and therapist started to examine here-and-now matters in their own relationship, and how these matters reflected some of the patient's ongoing issues. In the course of this examination, the patient accessed different states of self that had always been there but that he was now first able to articulate safely with another person. "Although this caused some affective instability, it also made it possible to integrate the conflicting states, leading to eventual groundedness." These self-states included feelings of depletion, passivity, and anger, and the need to be regarded well and to be seen as a good person. Using the therapy relationship, Dr. Cheselka brought out the patient's preference to avoid or not to recognize these feelings and self-states. When she felt annoyed with him for side-stepping these matters, she sometimes let it be seen, believing that this encouraged genuineness, understanding, and the ability to reach more of his inner liveliness. As she turned the discussion repeatedly back to their relationship, she made the patient feel controlled and influenced, provoking reactions that were useful both to enliven the therapeutic interaction and to bring out similar, relevant relationships and feelings in the patient's past. For example, they both came to realize that her turning their attention back to their own relationship felt for the patient like the same kind of "pushing" he had experienced from his father.

The therapist also came to see that she had been colluding with the patient in the acceptance of his superiority, investing in the grandiose fantasies he cherished for his future but ignoring the further need to examine the emptiness he felt. This realization helped her open up to his underlying despair.

Toward the end of therapy, the patient started to resign himself to the fact that he had to take care of himself, and that there would never be the kind of enveloping, supportive parental love that he had always longed for. He also started to take more pride, rather than to be resentful, over becoming the mature one who focuses on what needs to be done in order to achieve success. In this way, his long-standing sense of neediness, dependency, and depression became suffused with a feeling of potency that he would be able to manage conflicting affects and self-states in the service of his own goals.

By the end of the chapter, Dr. Cheselka had succeeded in balancing analysis of her patient's personality and analysis of their interaction. She also stated her belief that therapeutic action comes out of that balance. She wrote:

> The effects of deconstruction and the important relational aspects of the therapeutic relationship lead to both new ways of thinking and new affective experiences. This then leads to an expanded version of the self, which in turn leads to the capability of being able to think and act differently.

Elsewhere she elaborated on the relational contribution to the positive therapeutic effect of her work with her patient. For example, she noted that when she and her patient were in a power struggle or disagreed about whose needs would be met regarding controlling the topic of therapy sessions, he confronted different parts of his personality, and thereby could expand his personality. She gave him the chance to work out for the first time in a safe way his experience of feeling alternately powerful and not powerful with the person with whom he was in conflict. This experience extended back to his childhood regarding who was in charge and whose needs would come first, and allowed him to work through these issues in the transference and in the current therapy relationship.

In her chapter, Dr. Cheselka presents much of the case first, including a detailed section in the middle of the presentation of her advance with the patient into here-and-now work. This first portion of her chapter (largely case presentation) is followed by an extensive discussion of the patient's personality issues, including self-development, separation–individuation, defenses, and resistance. This discussion also covers the therapy relationship with its transference, countertransference, and enactments in helpful detail. This detail includes her effort to address the therapy relationship and its issues, her patient's resistance to this, the relation of his resistance to his avoidance of some of his own central conflicts (such as ambivalence and conflict over independence and dependence), and close attention to the enactments and countertransferences that were occurring. There is new clinical material in this discussion, and I wish she had included more of this material earlier over the course of the case presentation.

A dangling thread was the place of sexuality in Michael's life. At the start of the case presentation, there was a reference to his living with two women, having sex parties, an affair along the way, and his good relationship with his wife by the end. Cheselka wrote:

> [A]t the start of therapy, Michael was having an affair outside his marriage. He was conflicted about it at the time, although for the most part he felt that he needed the stimulation and excitement of this situation. He also liked being seen as a special person, an "artiste," who had intense passions. At the beginning of our work, Michael needed sources of external excitement and gratification. As the work progressed, he was able to use his internal resources of vitality and creativity to stimulate himself.

Yet she also wrote: "It was puzzling to me at times that Michael did not have more ambivalence about his relationships with women." The affairs offered external sources of liveliness to compensate for feeling despairing and empty, but did they not also signify some ambivalence about women?

Dr. Cheselka writes well and the case comes alive. The work was a success, and so is a good advertisement for psychoanalysis and psychoanalytic therapy. I am proud to be in the same profession as the author of this chapter.

Chapter 5

The dance of dissociation in healing trauma

Heather MacIntosh

A recent surge in writing about dissociation within the relational psychoanalytic literature has provided the clinical reader with poignant and prosaic examples of the travails and potentially transformative experience of analytic work with highly dissociative patients (MacIntosh, 2015). Key writers in this field provide detailed case descriptions along with thoughtful theoretical commentary to guide clinicians in their approach to this challenging work (Bromberg, 2011; Davies, 2001; Stern, 2010). An emphasis on working within the dissociative enactments and in attempting to bridge the dissociative gap between the symbolized and that which is outside of the patient's current capacity to be symbolized is suggested as a key mechanism in the process of change (Bromberg, 2012; Stern, 2011). Bromberg argues that while dissociation is protective, it robs the traumatized patient of the capacity for self-reflection, intersubjectivity, intrapsychic conflict, and self-regulation (Bromberg, 2011). These key writers would argue that working at the level of the dissociative enactment is not only necessary but, in fact, inevitable and ubiquitous (Bromberg, 2006, 2011; Davies, 1999; Stern, 1997, 2003, 2010).

In an enactment, past experiences are relived in all of their lost affectivity and behavioral stuckness. Through this dissociative portal, the patient's world comes alive in the analytic relationship, whereas intersubjectivity dissolves under the pull of each partner's dissociation and reliving (Bromberg, 2006). The analytic sphere becomes the seat of repetition and the relationship another inevitable and painful failure. The trouble is that as the enactment pulls both members of the dyad into its steady and powerful power, the analyst, too, is swirling in the morass, potentially only finding their way to dry land through that most famous of escapes: blaming the patient. The analyst may simply only know that something isn't quite right, that they aren't being the analyst they wish they could be; that they are stuck in something unknowable and unseeable. It is only when they can begin to wrestle their way out from under this oppressive fog of dissociation that something new, different and surprising bursts open: a new co-constructed experience (Bromberg, 2001, 2003; Davies, 2006; Stern, 2004).

It is necessary that the analyst resolve their own dissociation for successful resolution of the enactment to be possible. The enactment can only dissolve into something new when explicit awareness of what is trying to poke through the implicit communications of the underbelly of the patient's traumatic dissociation that is ensnaring the dyad can be attained. Analysts are encouraged to tune into shifting self-states in their patients and reciprocal shifts in themselves to sense burgeoning enactments (Bromberg, 2011; Stern, 2003). This is especially challenging, since one of the key characteristics of dissociative enactments is a difficulty figuring out what is going on and putting words to what is happening in the analysis.

Helping patients build their self-regulatory capacities to allow for a broadening of tolerance for affect and painful resurgences of traumatic material is believed to hasten the growing symbolization of traumatic material held outside of awareness through dissociation. This process is seen as an important step in creating the context for that which is expressed through dissociative enactment in the relational space of patient and analyst to become symbolized and available for exploration and resolution. In fact, Bromberg (2011) suggests that without this process, for trauma survivors, the unsymbolized affects and memories of traumatized patients remain outside of relational and intrapsychic space such that there is no room or capacity for conflict within the patient's mind that would allow for the working through and resolution of these states and experiences. These dissociative enactments represent "memories that cannot be remembered or forgotten" (Krystal, 2002) which become triggered within a relational field but cannot be felt or known and so must be behaviorally acted out (Stern, 2013).

These writers have brought the concept of dissociation back into the analytic fold and provide an important vehicle for the ongoing exploration of the impact of dissociation upon the analytic relationship and mechanisms of change in psychoanalysis with those who have experienced developmental trauma that is severe enough to induce high levels of dissociation (MacIntosh, 2015). However, within the walls of these words there is embedded an assumption of a benign enough developmental history in the analyst or, at least, a benevolent unconscious against which the analyst need not be afraid. The analyst approaches the dissociative enactment with curiosity, clouded awareness, and, at times, frustration, but within the writings of these relational contributors one does not have a sense that they are afraid of what may be dancing in the dissociative spaces within themselves, the analyst, as they engage in this wordless experiencing with their patient, the highly traumatized, deeply suffering soul.

So, what might this look like in the case of an analyst who has anything but a benign developmental history and a patient whose early life was something out of the deepest darkest places imaginable? Discussions of the impact of the personal trauma histories of psychoanalysts are only beginning to emerge in the literature. While some notable figures in our field, including Henry Krystal who wrote about his childhood experiences in forced labor camps in the Holocaust (Krystal, 2002) and Wilfred Bion who wrote of his combat experiences in the First World War (Bion and Bion, 1997), analysts who have written about their personal experiences of trauma are few and far between (Kuchuck, 2013). More recently, authors, including Stolorow (2007), Orange (2014), and Davies (1999), among others, have made references to the impact of personal experiences of trauma upon their lives and work as analysts. Notably, the majority of writers within the field who have shared personal stories of trauma have written about extra-familial traumas such as those related to combat and the Holocaust, adult traumas, and losses. Recently, Tiemann (2012, 2016) explored the impact of her personal history of early developmental trauma upon her own experience of psychoanalysis and in her work with a patient. She argued that her own trauma both informs her capacity for empathy and understanding as well as imbuing her with certain struggles and anxieties such as fearing that her patients may intuit things about her own "deficits" (Tiemann, 2016, p. 77) and that, at times, her own experience of being triggered "obstructs self-reflection and creates doubt in my capacity and right to do this work" (p. 77). The importance of the traumatized analyst's personal analysis and working through of their own traumas is emphasized by all writers who tiptoe into the topic of the personal trauma history of analysts.

There is a scarcity of writing about personal experiences of intra-familial trauma and how these impact the psychoanalytic work. In a recent research study I had the opportunity to interview 45 psychoanalytically oriented clinicians about their personal experiences of trauma and how these impacted their lives and work. The majority of these clinicians reported histories of interpersonal and intra-familial traumas. They indicated that one of their primary motivations to participate in the study was that they felt there to be a professional prohibition against the exploration of the analyst's own traumas and that an aggregated analysis of personal narratives might bring these stories to light in a way that would not impinge upon their professional "safety." And so, where are we, the working walking wounded, to turn for wisdom when our own deep, dark places are awoken in the work?

In my own life, the impact of traumas experienced throughout childhood has played a major role in my development, life course, and decisions about vocation. In particular a promising career as a classical singer was obfuscated by the sequelae of physical injuries related to untreated preverbal trauma: I found my way to psychoanalysis through trauma and my desire to make meaning and engage in healing relationships. These are the traumas that hunt and haunt because these are the traumas that can only be lived in the body and spoken through ghost-like impressions of memories. These are the traumas that come to visit in the enacted domain with other deeply traumatized patients whose traumas also inhabit the non-verbal, dissociated realm of experience.

And so I found myself with "William," a man who had experienced unknown horrors in his early development, things unspoken and unsymbolized not just because of their horrors but also because of his preverbal developmental stage at the time of their occurrence. William and I found ourselves dancing in the deep, dark dissociation together as I attempted to help him find more of his life in the light and less in the dark corners of himself as enacted in isolated parks and retraumatizing scenarios of reliving trauma. Our shared preverbal trauma came alive between us, giving me insight and empathy and threatening to drown me in my own dissociative cloak as it became alive in the silent spaces between us.

William

William referred himself to me after reading a paper I had written on developmental trauma and dissociation. William had a long history of alcoholism, anxiety, phobias, interpersonal difficulties, and what he called a sex addiction. He wryly told me that, given these struggles, perhaps looking a little deeper into his history might be a good idea. Up until the point when I met him, William had never managed to tolerate staying in any psychotherapeutic relationship, bailing in terror after a few sessions and sticking with self-help group 12-step programs where anonymity gave him a small sense of safety.

In initial sessions William was open and talkative, ready to engage and eager to come to understand more about the process of therapy. William felt that he had done enough reading to know that he needed therapy and he felt prepared for what he imagined would be a very traumatic experience. William was respectful, gentle, curious, and open, but, underneath that external presentation there ran a deep current of something else; something darker, something that I felt immediately upon meeting him, the best word for which was "creepy." I felt the feeling that I imagine ghost hunters feel in the presence of something they describe as paranormal: air chills and feels thick as treacle and you feel as if you are in the presence of something sinister. This is not how I would hope to feel upon first meeting a new patient, but this creepy, sinister feeling was present and at the forefront of my mind from our first meeting. William was clearly in great distress and appeared to be highly dissociative, yet he continued to function in his work as a mid-level research assistant. William had limited financial resources and limited insurance coverage, and he had calculated that we had 18 months of twice-weekly sessions to solve his problems.

Presenting problems

At the time that William began therapy he was reportedly dealing with significant trauma symptoms, including frequent nightmares, occasional flashbacks, severe hypervigilance and hyperarousal, exaggerated startle reflex, interpersonal mistrust, affective dysregulation, and the aforementioned dissociative symptoms. William described experiencing a long history of dissociative episodes and shifting of states of affect and consciousness such that his experience of being himself was vastly different when he was at work, at home alone, or with his friends from self-help groups. Similarly, William reported that he had discrete periods in his history where dissociation dominated his life. In particular, he described a period around the time when he began having flashbacks of sexual abuse by his father where he would reportedly "lose" vast amounts of time and find himself coming out of a dissociative state wandering in parks late at night. Consuming alcohol preceded these episodes. Eventually, he became aware that during these dissociative episodes he was trolling parks and bath houses in order to meet up with men he had been communicating with on the Internet who would sodomize him without the use of a condom, assuming the role of the dominant but gentle older man, teaching the younger man about sexuality. While in this state, he called himself Geoffrey and behaved as though he were a much younger man. William became aware of this activity when he "came to" in the middle of being sodomized by a man in a park. William became hysterical, crying, screaming in pain, and curling into a fetal position, soiling himself and yelling at the man to leave him alone. Following this event, William entered a rehabilitation program for alcohol abuse and had himself tested for HIV and other sexually transmitted infections. Since that time, William struggled with holding onto himself in times of stress and would still, at times, wake up in the morning to find replies in his email folder from people who wrote to "Geoffrey"; meaning that he had posted another ad in the night looking, once again, for men. William thought of himself as heterosexual and denied any homoerotic fantasies or desires, but "Geoffrey" clearly had other feelings and desires.

During his 30-day stay in a rehabilitation facility, night staff told William that he would walk the halls in the night, find a corner, and curl up into a ball whimpering like a small child. When night staff would find him and try to take him back to bed, he would just say, over and over again, "Daddy says I'm a bad boy" and "I'm sorry, I pooed my pants, I'm sorry, I'm sorry, I'm sorry." William was not able to recall these events when prompted the following day.

In addition to severe dissociative symptoms, William came into therapy hoping to find a greater sense of self and safety in relationships. He indicated that he could not trust others, did not feel safe with women, and had many "odd" interpersonal responses such as feeling compelled to reach out and touch women's breasts. William was very forthright about his inability to trust women but that women were the only safe people because men were "bad." This unmanageable bind had been making relationships very difficult for William throughout his whole life. In addition, William was seeking to understand his sense of himself as "bad" in relation to his experiences with his mother and his inability to find women attractive and desirable unless they had some bisexual or lesbian leanings. William quickly figured out that I am a lesbian and told me, in telling me that I am a lesbian, that that was a good thing and made me a safe person in his life. I suppose William must have a good "gaydar" because this was certainly not something that I proffered him in response to his statement that only queer women were safe women.

Background

William had just ended a long-term relationship with his girlfriend who, he stated, was the sanest girlfriend he had ever had. He was socially isolated and did not have any close friends or connections with family. William did not have any children and, interestingly, had a vasectomy at the age of 21, against doctor's orders, to ensure that this would never happen. He felt extremely certain that he could never be a parent and did not want to continue a family line of trauma and dysfunction.

William is the second in a sibling of four boys. As the smallest of the brothers in stature, his brothers frequently physically assaulted him in this dog-eat-dog family. William described his father as benign but absent. His father drank to excess, frequently cheated on his wife, and had a huge collection of pornography scattered throughout the house. William's descriptions of his father are bifurcated. On the one hand, he was the parent who was safer in that he didn't beat or berate him. On the other hand, he was the parent about whom William has flashbacks of sexual abuse. These two fathers appeared to be separate in his mind.

William called his mother "mommy dearest" with a snide, twisted smile. He described his mother as physically and emotionally violent in one moment and then, hidden in bed, leaving William attending to her and the other children in the next moment. William's descriptions of his mother's tirades were vivid and affectively frozen in time. As he described her screaming and yelling at the children and telling them that they were horrible, just as bad as their bastard father, they were horrible because of sex, they were horrible because they are men and men only want sex and on and on, I could virtually see the scenes flashing in front of his eyes. He described the model scene of dinner every day; his mother having made something hideous that required no effort, exploding over something unpredictable and running off to her room from whence she would scream expletives and throw things down the stairs at her husband, the louse for whatever ill he had caused her, while the boys sat in silence, attempting to eat the repugnant meal laid out before them. William reported that his mother was frequently hospitalized for migraines but that he was told in later years that she was hospitalized for depression and administered ECT. William believed that the sexual abuse by his father occurred during these periods of hospitalization as well as during his infancy and early childhood under the guise of intimate care.

William had two failed marriages. His first marriage was to a childhood sweetheart who had also been sexually abused in her childhood, and who committed suicide when they were both 19. William's second marriage was to a woman who treated him with contempt and disdain, leaving him when she started tracing gay porn on his computer. It was during this marriage that William began to experience escalating alcohol use, sexually addictive and compulsive behavior, severe dissociative symptoms, and the onset of the flashbacks that were associated with his fugue-like episodes with men.

My experiences with William

At the beginning of this therapy William was open and engaged, sharing what he knew of his history and being relatively honest about his significant memory gaps and challenges with linearity of thought. In spite of William's openness I felt the treacle in the air between us [...] something dissociated, unsymbolized, and filled with the darkness of abuse. During sessions William would move from topic to topic tangentially and it was very hard to follow, track, and attune to him. While he was very attuned to shifts in my affective state, his interpretations of what he was picking up from me were always filtered through a lens of danger and rejection. Any comment or question about how I might be more able to understand his experience was interpreted through the expectations of: I did something wrong and she's trying to get rid of me. At the same time, William had a great sense of humor and was able to laugh at how hard therapy could be. He often said, "I feel horrible so this must be working." These small moments of meeting made the yuckiness somehow bearable. As much as I feared being pulled into the sludge, I liked William, I felt compassionately toward him, and I wished and hoped that all that was in the realm of the "real" between us could banish the darkness of all that was unsymbolized and being enacted silently in the dissociative spaces between us. I wanted to help him, and yet I feared I would be pulled into the mire of his darkness, as it aroused an awakening of my own.

Themes in the therapy included: there is nowhere and no one that is safe, all men are evil and I am a man so I must be evil; I cannot have a healthy relationship; I am too messed up; and: if I know everything I will die. Exploring any of these themes was virtually impossible, as any attempts at empathic conjecture and exploration of his experience of himself led to dissociative state shifts and affective disavowal. Of course, I was also very aware of the ever-present risk that stress might potentiate a relapse, leading William back down the dark hole of Internet porn, alcohol, and dangerous sexual liaisons, and so I too tended to pull back and put on the therapeutic brakes as intense affects arose in him.

William struggled to stay present and to follow any linear path of mental exploration in sessions. He frequently forgot what had been said in sessions and what he was thinking about and feeling outside of sessions. Occasionally, he wrote something to bring in to the session, but if I asked him about it he could not remember what he had written. In an attempt to work on this, I started writing session summary notes with him at the end of sessions but he would end up losing them; we abandoned that idea. As weeks rolled into months I found myself slipping into a dissociation that felt shared – I too was having trouble remembering what was happening in sessions; I too was finding it difficult to track and follow our process; I too was feeling anxious and fearful about the process.

Eventually, William agreed to allow me to tape the sessions to help us understand the triggers and exacerbating factors to dissociation in sessions, especially since, in the intense dissociation in sessions, I often could not remember the moment before we went off on a tangential leap away from where we had been exploring either. The tape recording was for both of us; I found myself needing to review tapes of sessions between sessions to track my own process of being sucked into the deep, dark dissociative hole and losing my own mind. I began to feel that the deep, dark places of my own early traumas were dancing in the dissociative enactment with his deep, dark places. There we were, engaged in a verbal exchange while somewhere in the silence between us was playing an unconscious story of our wounded preverbal selves. As frightened as I was that my unsymbolized traumas might, in some way, come to life with his in a way that could be painful and difficult for me, I was more concerned about how what was dissociated in me might, in some way, harm him. He had been so deeply harmed by so many. I turned to colleagues and supervision to keep one foot on dry ground. As much as what is dissociated is powerful in its pull, at least, I thought, I was aware that there was something happening in the spaces between us.

The following is an excerpt from one of the first sessions that I taped. In it one can feel both of us slipping in and out of connection with one another and ourselves.

HEATHER: As you talk, I am reminded of the conversation we were having the other day and we were getting close to something and you were having a pain that was coming and going and lots of feelings were coming up for you [...] do you remember that?

WILLIAM: Yes, vaguely, the pain has been coming on and off since then [...] especially whenever I think of being here. [Said with sarcasm and laughter]

HEATHER: Ahhhh [...] that's great. [...] [Also said with sarcasm, both laugh [...] coming in and out of affect]

WILLIAM: Here it is again, I even tried to go into the pain, I did what I did with my shingles [...] becoming one with the pain [...] so I could have some control of it [...] not that I'd need control. [...] [More sarcasm]

HEATHER: No [...]

WILLIAM: And it just made it worse, the trick didn't work.

HEATHER: I just remembered what you said [...] one of the things you said was [...] it was so bad [...] someone is going to die [...] do you remember saying something like that?

WILLIAM: Vaguely.

HEATHER: I'm just connecting the dots a bit with the idea that there is something inside you that you have talked about that says, if I feel and know and enter that space in my mind that is not available to me, that I am on the edges of it, someone will die and I notice that you have used the same phrase with respect to James [friend in rehab who comes in and out of psychosis] [...] that he has to stay insane to stay alive and I wonder about the horrible conflict you must be feeling inside as you move forward in this process [...] there is some very strong message inside that knowing is very, very dangerous.

WILLIAM: I'm terrified of this but, I want this [...]

HEATHER: This is such a strong message inside you that knowing, knowing the truth of what happened to you and your family will destroy you.

WILLIAM: Yes […] [very quiet] […] it will kill me, too.
HEATHER: If you let yourself get close to these feelings, memories […] they can hurt you […]
WILLIAM: Never, never, ever be safe.
HEATHER: It's an intractable bind […] that you talk about with such poignancy the thing that you long for, longing for closeness, longing for right relationships, longing for safety, is the very thing that is the most dangerous in the world for you.
WILLIAM: [Long silence.] Yeah, can't […] can't let anyone close […] never be safe […]
HEATHER: Mmmm.
WILLIAM: [Long silence]
HEATHER: You look sad […] what's going on? […] What are you feeling in there?
WILLIAM: Not sure. [He is drifting away, staring into space, slow, monotone speech]
HEATHER: Not sure? How much of you is with me?
WILLIAM: Some of me […] I'm falling into the fog again.
HEATHER: The fog is pulling you away?
WILLIAM: I'm not trying to get away.
HEATHER: Okay […] it's coming though […] I can feel you slipping away […] if you were to stay with me […] to feel and talk about what you are feeling […] can you imagine what that might be?
WILLIAM: I'm slipping down the hole.
HEATHER: Which hole?
WILLIAM: A black hole.
HEATHER: Hmmmm […] what's in there?
WILLIAM: Death.

I could feel the pull, I was trying to stay out of the hole myself, trying to keep one foot on dry land to help him come back to the room but I was not terribly successful. What the reader cannot see/feel is that while my words were trying to pull him back into the here-and-now my own state was slipping away with him.

HEATHER: Hmmm […] [silence] stay with me […] try to stay out of the fuzzy fog […] [trying to hold him present with my voice] try to stay with me and we will talk about the feeling that you are so aware of the danger of closeness and the danger of remembering, the danger of being sane, in a way, that can pull you into a black hole and in the black hole is death […] knowing, being, feeling, remembering is so dangerous you will die.
WILLIAM: Too scary.
HEATHER: Too scary?
WILLIAM: I don't like feeling insane […] I don't like feeling […]

HEATHER: It's too much.

WILLIAM: It takes me to the worst places. [He seems to be in pain, holds his head as he does when feelings and memories threaten to emerge, again [...] changes the subject]

WILLIAM: I went to a meeting [...] [Seems completely disconnected and tangential]

HEATHER: Which meeting?

WILLIAM: Saturday morning AA [...] there were all these women there my age who are single and they were all coming up to me [...]

HEATHER: Sorry, I didn't catch the connection [...] I didn't hear something there [...] we were talking about how dangerous it is to feel things and then you mentioned the meeting.

WILLIAM: Oh, it's just that my head keeps going over to there.

HEATHER: To the meeting? Do you know what the connection is for you between those two things?

WILLIAM: They are all at 20 years of sobriety, every time I think about the women emailing me [...] very attractive, very successful, all of them are blonde [...] [laughs] [...] hurts! [Holds his head again, looks like he's being attacked]

HEATHER: Hurts?

WILLIAM: My head hurts again.

HEATHER: I'm just really aware that we were talking about some really intense stuff and then we took a jump off to an AA meeting with a bunch of women and there seems to be a real connection for you but I am having a hard time finding my way into it and, you still have the pain in your head so we're still there in some way [...]

WILLIAM: The ones at the meeting anyhow, any one of them might be a viable, intimate, healthy relationship, and I wouldn't feel like it was based on my having to puke my soul onto the floor first.

HEATHER: Oh, okay, I'm getting there.

WILLIAM: The goal is finding the safety somewhere.

HEATHER: You want the safety, safety is dangerous [...] maybe one of them [...]

WILLIAM: Got it [...]

HEATHER: Okay, I'm with you [...]

WILLIAM: It's hard for me sometimes too!

HEATHER: We're in this together [...] [Both laugh]

WILLIAM: It's a surprisingly useful skill [...]

HEATHER: Tangentiality?

WILLIAM: Yeah, I go wildly off [...] it's predictable.

HEATHER: Yes, the unpredictable predictable?

WILLIAM: [...] Something about too much or too fast.

HEATHER: Linearity of thought is too [...] hard?

WILLIAM: Yeah.

HEATHER: And for you?

WILLIAM: Yeah […] always, you wouldn't want people to know what you think and feel […] you've got to control that.

HEATHER: So when we get too close, we've got to move.

WILLIAM: We don't know where we are […] we just think […]

HEATHER: So we are talking about how safety is dangerous, knowing is dangerous and feelings will take you to a place of inevitable death and, there is something about that that takes you to the desire for relationship, that takes you to the memory of the AA meeting and the women who seemed to notice you and with whom you would not need to vomit onto the floor with your horribleness, and then, as we look at the links between those two events […] you tell me that nothing is linear because you are trying to be someone you're not, you don't know who you are? [Questioning […] looking to understand?]

WILLIAM: Every one of us whoever you talk to […] addiction is a disease of avoidance and hiding.

And so, round the mulberry bush once again. We were lost, we regained our footing, we got lost again, and finally we came back together. For William, being found meant feeling, knowing, remembering, tolerating, imagining a future in relationships. For William, being found was terrifying, and yet, being lost was unbearable.

Sessions like this one continued for many months. Many times I imagined that I should pull out of the therapy with William. I feared that I was not helping him, at best, and hurting him, at worst. On the one hand, I imagined that I had a capacity for empathy that others might not as I focused my energies on trying to stay tapped into what was happening in the dissociative mire between us. Having experienced preverbal traumas, I did feel that I could understand, in a way that others might not, the struggle to understand, tolerate, and regulate physiological states of traumatic reliving that have no words, images, or ways of being understood. And yet, on the other hand, perhaps this understanding was no understanding at all. Perhaps it was a fallacy; alleged twinship in the guise of intersubjective conjunctions that were actually the deepest, most debased aspects of our shared trauma history confusing and misleading me away from the path of healing and toward an eruption of destructive dissociation. Perhaps it was not the enacted realm providing tendrils of the unsymbolized up to the light but, rather, simply a retraumatizing spiral of something sinister embedded in our shared dissociation that would prevent William from finding the solace and relief he so desired. I "brought" William to supervision. I discussed William in my own analysis. I shared my fears that I might hurt him. I explored my feelings of lurking darkness, creepiness, and swirling, unspoken traumas. I dove deep into my own unsymbolized void as it was triggered in the work with William. I worked diligently to do all that I could, with my own helpers, to help William.

Over the course of our 18-month, twice-a-week intensive psychotherapy process, William was able to climb his way out of the dissociative hole.

He became more steady in his innards, less dissociative, gained more control over his addictive urges, began engaging in some physical activity, started to make a couple of friends at 12-step groups, and began moving up toward positions of greater responsibility in his work. With a clearer mind he was better able to use his emotions and instincts about others as useful information rather than things of which to be wary. I will be honest when I say that I don't quite know how this happened – well, other than the usual ways in which these things happen – perseverance, patience, caring and deep empathic focus. I too became less dissociative when I was with William. We two became less dissociative together. There were no moments, like those described in the works of Bromberg, Davies, and Stern, where something emerged, erupted, escaped into symbolic forms of conscious leading to a new experience of understanding and awareness. No "ah-ha" moments. Perhaps, then, for a dyad where the symbols are not available to be understood due to their preverbal forms, what is mutative is not the emergence into consciousness of something new but, rather, the sticking with it, the perseverance of two souls on a journey together, as the vapors of early trauma, the embodied memories – smells, feelings, tastes, imprints on flesh – these vapors and their accompanying terrors, grief, and arousal must simply have a space in which to be slowly dissolved into the air so that they can dissipate into the shared dissociative space, to slowly set the tortured patient free from the cloak of darkness in which they had been wrapped. When William left treatment, he smiled, he laughed, he had space in himself for something more; thoughts and feelings about a life for himself that might be different than the one he imagined was his destiny. I imagine that William is not done in his work but I do believe he is much further along on his journey to healing and, perhaps, through the work with William, I am a little less afraid of what lurks in my deep, dark underbelly and how these unsymbolized, unknowable traumas of my own may, someday, inadvertently hurt a patient about whom I care deeply.

References

Bion, W. R. and Bion, F. (1997). *War Memoirs, 1917–1919*. London: Karnac.

Bromberg, P. (2001). The gorilla did it: Some thoughts on dissociation, the real, and the really real. *Psychoanalytic Dialogues, 11*(3), 385–404. doi:10.1080/10481881109348619.

Bromberg, P. (2003). One need not be a house to be haunted: On enactment, dissociation, and the dread of "not-me" – A case study. *Psychoanalytic Dialogues, 13*(5), 689–709. doi:10.1080/10481881309348764.

Bromberg, P. (2006). *Awakening the Dreamer: Clinical Journeys*. Mahwah, NJ: Analytic Press.

Bromberg, P. (2011). *The Shadow of the Tsunami and the Growth of the Relational Mind*. New York: Routledge/Taylor & Francis Group.

Bromberg, P. (2012). Stumbling along and hanging in: If this be technique, make the most of it! *Psychoanalytic Inquiry, 32*(1), 3–17. doi:10.1080/07351690.2011.553161.

Davies, J. M. (1999). Getting cold feet, defining "safe enough" borders: Dissociation, multiplicity, and integration in the analyst's experience. *Psychoanalytic Quarterly, 68*, 184–208.
Davies, J. M. (2001). Back to the future in psychoanalysis: Trauma, dissociation, and the nature of unconscious processes. In M. Dimen & A. Harris (Eds.), *Storms in Her Head: Freud and the Construction of Hysteria* (pp. 245–264). New York: Other Press.
Davies, J. M. (2006). *On the Nature of the Self: Multiplicity, Unconscious Conflict and Fantasy in Relational Psychoanalysis*. Paper presented at the International Association for Psychoanalytic Self Psychology, Chicago, IL.
Krystal, H. (2002). What cannot be remembered or forgotten. In J. Kaufmann (Ed.), *Loss of the Assumptive World: A Theory of Traumatic Loss* (pp. 213–219). New York: Brunner-Routledge.
Kuchuck, S. (2013). *Clinical Implications of the Psychoanalyst's Life Experience: When the Personal Becomes Professional*. New York: Routledge.
MacIntosh, H. B. (2015). Titration of technique: Clinical exploration of the integration of trauma model and relational psychoanalytic approaches to the treatment of dissociative identity disorder. *Psychoanalytic Psychology, 32*(3), 517–538. doi:10.1037/a0035533.
Orange, D. M. (2014). Out of time: Siblings as trauma transmitters, protectors, sources of courage: Meeting Ron Bodansky's protest. *Psychoanalytic Inquiry, 34*(3), 251–261. doi:10.1080/07351690.2014.889482.
Stern, D. B. (1997). *Unformulated Experience: From Dissociation to Imagination in Psychoanalysis*. Mahwah, NJ: Analytic Press.
Stern, D. B. (2003). The fusion of horizons: Dissociation, enactment, and understanding. *Psychoanalytic Dialogues, 13*(6), 843–873. doi:10.1080/10481881309348770.
Stern, D. B. (2004). The eye sees itself: Dissociation, enactment, and the achievement of conflict. *Contemporary Psychoanalysis, 40*(2), 197–237.
Stern, D. B. (2010). *Partners in Thought: Working with Unformulated Experience, Dissociation, and Enactment*. New York: Routledge/Taylor & Francis Group.
Stern, D. B. (2011). The hard-to-engage patient: A treatment failure. *Psychoanalytic Dialogues, 21*(5), 596–606.
Stern, D. B. (2013). Philip, me, and not me: A personal and professional introduction to the special issue celebrating the work of Philip Bromberg. *Contemporary Psychoanalysis, 49*(3), 311–322.
Stolorow, R. D. (2007). *Trauma and Human Existence: Autobiographical, Psychoanalytic, and Philosophical Reflections*. London and New York: Routledge.
Tiemann, J. (2012). The survivor-analyst as analysand: An autobiographical account of an analytic treatment of complex trauma. *International Journal of Psychoanalytic Self Psychology, 7*(4), 533–558. doi:10.1080/15551024.2012.686164.
Tiemann, J. (2016). "Call me Johanna": The challenge of building intimacy between two complex trauma survivors within an analytic dyad. *International Journal of Psychoanalytic Self Psychology, 11*(1), 75–88. doi:10.1080/15551024.2016.1107421.

Commentary on MacIntosh's case

Creepiness

Susan Kolod

Dr. MacIntosh describes a successful psychoanalytic psychotherapy in which the dissociated traumas of both therapist and patient contribute to ongoing enactments. She emphasizes that therapists must analyze their own dissociation in order to resolve transference/countertransference enactments, and notes correctly that "Discussions of the impact of the personal trauma histories of psychoanalysts are only beginning to emerge in the literature." Dr. MacIntosh tells of how her own dissociated traumas were triggered by her patient: "I dove deep into my own unsymbolized void as it was triggered in the work with William."

What struck me immediately in this presentation was Dr. MacIntosh's sense, right from their first meeting, that there was something "creepy" about her patient. She writes, "William was respectful, gentle, curious and open but, underneath that external presentation there ran a deep current of something else; something darker, something that I felt immediately upon meeting him […] the best word for which was 'creepy'." Although Dr. MacIntosh attributes the creepiness to dissociation, there must be more to it than that. "Creepiness" is not a word that usually comes to mind when working with deeply dissociated patients.

There are many great creepy characters in literature and film: the child murderer played by Peter Lorre in Fritz Lang's classic film *M*, the charitable but depraved Svidrigailov from Dostoyevsky's *Crime and Punishment*, the falsely humble Uriah Heep from Dickens' *David Copperfield*, and the many psychopathic characters from the fiction of Patricia Highsmith. Although one could argue that dissociation is an element of creepiness, a more straightforward view is that people seem creepy when they project hidden ulterior motives, usually of a manipulative or predatory nature, concealed under a surface presentation of vulnerability, softness, and affability.

Certainly, in William's history, there is enough to qualify him as creepy. In particular, Dr. MacIntosh describes him "trolling parks and bath houses to meet up with men […] who would sodomize him without the use of a condom." These men assumed the role of the dominant but gentle older man, teaching the younger man about sexuality. William had a different name, Geoffrey, when he engaged in this trolling activity. But he would suddenly "come to" in the middle of being sodomized and run away, crying and screaming hysterically. William, who was sexually molested by his father "under the guise of intimate infant care," was clearly re-creating this scenario.

The story reported above, which at first looks like the sad repetition of abuse and victimization of a child by an adult who is supposed to be caring, also has elements of something much more aggressive. William, after all, sought out these contacts. The older men respond to Geoffrey, doing what he asks, but are then suddenly treated as abusers and tormentors by William. Although he describes soliciting and engaging in this behavior in a dissociative state, one wonders whether the "coming to" and the screaming and crying isn't part of the dynamic; switching from abused to abuser and doing, rather than being "done to." It seems likely that this paradigm was played out in the therapy relationship as well. I wonder whether Dr. MacIntosh sensed that she might be asked to perform certain acts, only to be treated as an abuser and tormentor when she agreed to them.

But you don't need to be a therapist, let alone a therapist with a trauma history, to recognize creepiness when you see it. What was Dr. MacIntosh perceiving about William that forced her to confront her own history in order to help him? Perhaps the presenting symptoms and course of treatment can provide some clues.

William sought treatment, he says, because he suffered from nightmares, flashbacks of sexual abuse from his father, hypervigilance, hyperarousal, exaggerated startle reflex, interpersonal mistrust, dysregulation, and dissociative episodes. As the therapy progressed, dominant themes included a sense that nowhere and no one is safe, that as all men are evil he must be evil, that he could not have a healthy relationship, and if he knew everything he would die.

William and Dr. MacIntosh reached a very unusual arrangement. William stated that he could afford twice-weekly psychotherapy for only 18 months. He required Dr. MacIntosh to solve his problems within this time frame. By "his problems" I assume he meant those described above. I wonder how Dr. MacIntosh felt about this arrangement. Did she think it was possible that they would be able to tackle and conquer such severe symptomatology in such a short time?

However, she did agree. By the time the 18 months had elapsed she noted that "He became more steady in his innards, less dissociative, had more control over his addictive urges, began engaging in some physical activity, started to make a couple of friends and began moving up toward positions of greater responsibility at work."

Dr. MacIntosh cured him of some symptoms – clearly he was helped by her – but the symptoms she cured were not the ones with which he came into treatment and expected to be rid of in 18 months. Was he less "creepy" at the end of treatment?

The main thesis of Dr. MacIntosh's chapter is that she needed to confront and understand the ways in which her own traumatic history intertwined with William's and contributed to a tendency to dissociate along with her patient. This is an important and original idea. However, Dr. MacIntosh does not reveal the nature of her trauma. Understanding that this is something she may not want to make public, it is nevertheless important to know the specifics if we are to understand how her history interacted with his.

My hypothesis, based only on the written presentation, is that in perceiving William as creepy, Dr. MacIntosh was tapping into what she alludes to as her dissociated trauma. Thus, for example, if it was sexual trauma, she may have perceived unconsciously that William, under the identity of Geoffrey, was a type of sexual predator. If she had been manipulated and lied to, she might be perceiving that William had sociopathic tendencies. But we never get a sense from the presentation if and how these things played out in their relationship. Did they ever talk about their interaction? How did William feel about the therapist? What kind of transference did he develop toward her? She talks about her countertransference but it is never explained or seemingly understood, except for her assertion that William tapped into her own dissociated trauma. I would like to know more about how that happened. It is truly impressive how devoted and involved she became with William, discussing the feelings he evoked in her both in supervision and in her own analysis. I wish she had revealed what she found out. What was he tapping into and how did she come to understand it so that she was able to be useful to him?

To go back to the unusual frame: I wonder whether, in addition to financial constraints, William wanted to prevent the therapist from getting too close to the sinister, predatory part of his personality. After all, he does refer to himself as "evil." I would take that seriously. Perhaps he was protecting her from Geoffrey.

There is no arguing with success, and this is a successful treatment judging from the outcome after only 18 months. However, there are so many questions – so many issues left unexplored. And, in particular, the issue of William's creepiness is never really explained.

Chapter 6

Surviving sexual abuse

A chameleon looks in the mirror

Alyson Feit

This case presentation is about transformation, regrowth, possibility, and yes, metamorphosis. It is the story of a man who has been badly treated by life, and whose memories of abuse have been difficult for both of us to bear. Peter's initial presentation was not dissimilar to that of Kafka's Gregor Artsa, who awakens one morning in shock and horror to find himself transformed into a giant insect. Peter has always felt that the story of his early life transformed him into something grotesque and has assumed that anyone who really gets to know him will react with shock and repulsion – reactions familiar to him from his early family experiences. Yet, throughout the course of treatment, Peter and I have used the language of shared experience, be it popular culture, politics, music, or NPR, to find a way in which he could feel less repellent, more like others, more human, sometimes using a joke to make the work more bearable, or sometimes just bearable for one additional moment at a time. His second transformation, the one achieved in interpersonal psychoanalysis, has been of a very different kind.

At our first meeting, I found Peter in the waiting room in a charcoal-gray sweatshirt. He was sitting hunched over with the hood up, tightly drawn, almost obscuring his face. During the meeting he could not make eye contact. He seemed not even to be able to figure out how to sit in the chair. Sometimes he sat in a fetal position, eyes downcast. Then, seemingly out of nowhere, he would sit up in alarm with his eyes darting everywhere, his body practically arching toward the door. He had trouble answering questions. He appeared to be trying hard to describe the chronology of his life but would trail off, confused at many junctures. For just a moment I felt that I was a therapist in an inpatient ward.

I did not comment on his body postures, on his strange manner of dress, on his difficulty maintaining a consistent, running dialogue. Yet I remember thinking how fragile he was, or perhaps he was delusional – I wasn't sure. But I felt full of dread that so fragile a man was in my care. I asked whether he felt comfortable with me or preferred a referral to a different therapist. At this point he sat up straight and looked me in the eye. In a very focused, direct manner he explained that he had spent years being bounced around from one therapist to another and did not want a referral. We met a few times and shortly thereafter began regular psychoanalysis. Within a week after the psychoanalysis began, his presentation changed markedly. He began to make eye contact. It became easier to follow his conversation. Two weeks into the analysis he made his first joke. I laughed. We had begun.

Peter was born in the Midwest. He has a sister who is three years his senior. At the time of his birth his parents were together, but they had divorced by the time he was 6 years old. His mom and dad were high school sweethearts who got married and gave birth to Peter's sister a year later. His father worked in a factory; his mother held down a number of odd jobs. Following the divorce, from the ages of 6 through 14 Peter moved ten times, living mostly with his mom but also with a series of relatives, including an aunt, his grandparents, and eventually his mom and stepdad. The early moves appear to be largely a reflection of his mom looking to start a new life following her divorce. She spent a great deal of time reliving her adolescence, partying with various men, and drinking a lot. She had little good to say about Peter, telling him he was strange, peculiar. He felt like a burden to a woman who was obviously not up for the task. She also found his obvious intelligence to be an oddity.

From the beginning, Peter was quite candid about a childhood that was characterized by sexual and physical abuse. He was sexually molested by his father from the age of 4 through the age of 6. His parents had had a violent marriage. He noted that his father had been incarcerated at one point after breaking his mother's arm. On another occasion, after raping her, his father locked his mother in the bathroom for several days. He gave her food through a small space under the door. When his mother left his father his own sexual abuse by his father stopped, but he was immediately approached by his sister to have sexual intercourse with her.

He remembers this first occasion well. He was sitting in front of the television watching cartoons when his sister came home. She was agitated about something and asked him to go into a corner of the room and masturbate until he had an erection. He cried and refused. She threatened him that unless he tried to penetrate her she would tell the children at his school that he didn't know how to have sex. He was unable to penetrate her at such a young age, but did his best. They continued to have sexual contact, eventually including intercourse, throughout their childhood until he was 14 or so. Although he was coerced into having sex with her as a young boy, as he grew older he began to seek her out, and as they became teenagers she used to withhold sex from him and tease him maliciously in a variety of ways. Often this would involve having sex with her boyfriends and leaving the door open for him to watch. He still remembers the complicated feelings of rage and lust, coupled with shame and humiliation.

Peter has endured numerous other sexually inappropriate overtures. One particular incident involved a babysitter who sat him on her lap and asked him to suck her breast. He remembers being surprised that milk didn't come out. Memories of physical abuse are sporadic. He remembers his mother hitting him so hard that she broke a spoon on his head. His father terrorized him continually.

On one occasion he teased Peter mercilessly about his affection for his puppy, took out a rifle, and shot the dog while Peter, helpless, sat on the floor crying. On other occasions he would lift Peter's shirt and lick his lips while commenting on Peter's soft skin.

The culture of violence had a traumatizing effect on young Peter, who was always anxious at school and had a hard time fitting in. He found solace in television and the movies. When he watched television as a child he often half-convinced himself that he *was* the protagonist in the show. This imaginative world took him away from the reality of everyday life and gave him a space where he felt unburdened by the pressures of his real-world existence. This imaginative capacity saved him. He created whole fantasy worlds that often seemed more real than his everyday existence. By the time Peter was 12 or so his mother's habit of moving herself and her two children from place to place worked well for him, as he had difficulty fitting in. His interest in pop culture often had him half-convinced that he was a pop celebrity, and he dressed flamboyantly in purple leather pants and an orange-tasseled button-down shirt. This did not work well in the rural environment where he grew up and he was harassed quite frequently by the local farm boys. Yet he refused to change. Despite his many relocations he occasionally made friends, who would defend him when bullies called him "queer." His friends would retort, "He is *not* queer." This often left him feeling confused, as these interactions made him feel that being queer was something so bad that his friends had to deny it was true of him. His sister also routinely called him "queer" when she pushed him away after they had finished sexual intercourse, so the term left him confused, as it seemed to bear little relationship to the sex or gender of one's sexual partner.

Although this harassment early in his life clearly had sequelae that have followed him into adulthood, there is, and always was, something about Peter that was quite resilient. According to his memory, he made little effort to blend into the rural community in which he lived and he paints a somewhat humorous picture of himself in high school. "The local boys dressed in cowboy boots and flannel shirts while I continued to dress in tight leather and pink tank tops." After graduating from high school, Peter left his rural community. Prior to moving to New York City, he traveled a great deal. Everywhere he went, rather than rebelling against the prevailing subculture as he had during his teenage years, he learned to mimic it perfectly in order to fit in. He soon learned how to use his incredible verbal intelligence to chat, flirt, and flatter. He was Proteus incarnate and could fit in anywhere and everywhere. He had an assortment of wardrobes and could chat about everything from baby strollers to Byron to Belarus. He became a sought-after hipster in the city, a popular guest among artists at the very chic gallery openings. He moved often, attended a few college classes, and took up an assortment of odd jobs. He had a number of relationships with women throughout his twenties, but shortly before treatment began he had become involved with a man he met at a party. They have now been together for three years.

Before discussing the course of treatment, I think it is important to note that from our first meeting, Peter made it very clear that any therapeutic intervention must be predicated on a feeling of sexual safety. I described that at our first meeting Peter dressed in a sweatshirt whose hood almost totally obscured his face. During that session I paid scant attention to whether or not he was attractive, as my attention was more attuned to his interpersonal behaviors, which were skittish and peculiar. Yet, I did pay close attention to the fact that in our second consultation session Peter was careful to mention that one of his most pressing difficulties was around women who flirted constantly with him and pressed him for a sexual relationship. At the time my internal response to that was surprise; I had not really noticed how handsome he was [...] perhaps because the hood obscured much of his face. He went on to talk about how his mother and grandmother discussed his body in ways that made him uncomfortable, admiring his legs, buttocks, and face. I noted to myself that he was clearly hypervigilant about his appearance and I was careful to refrain from commenting on his physical appearance. During the first few months of treatment he tested out my neutral stance by talking at great length about his tattoos, flexing his muscles, and playing with his zipper. Throughout our work together I have refrained from commenting on his physical person, which I thought would reinforce his feelings of safety in the room. Objectification and sexualization by his parents have deeply intruded on Peter's image of his body and his identity as related to his body. Throughout the treatment I have been concerned about his extraordinary self-consciousness and have only occasionally remarked on his physical presence.

And now: a few words about the course of therapy itself. As you will read below, over the years we have worked together, Peter's life has changed a great deal with regard to his intimate life, his professional success, and his artistic expression. Within this short period of time he has established his first long-term, committed relationship and has begun to advance professionally. His work is now valued by his employers and rewarded with extra pay and promotions. He has also begun a second career as an artist where he has achieved a real measure of success. I believe that his achievements are linked to a feeling of emotional security, a security based primarily in the reliable connection of two new relationships: one with his partner and the other with his analyst.

Peter's treatment has been a complicated one. In the initial stages, which overlapped with the first year of analysis, much of our work together focused on his experience of fragmentation and his inability to voice dissociated memories and feelings. A second stage of the work, which coincided with the second year of treatment, focused on the consolidation of these experiences. This enabled him to be able to understand better the world and his place in it. By this I mean that by describing and bringing fragmented experiences together under the same rubric, Peter was able to begin to recognize and identify significant aspects of who he was and what had shaped him. The identity elements that began to be fleshed out included Peter as a gay male, a trauma survivor, and as a person who grew up poor. This led to an exploration of his sense of identification with oppressed minorities and disadvantaged others. During this stage of the treatment, Peter began to see himself less as a passive victim who was forced to revisit many iterations of past trauma. He was able to link up life experiences in the formation of a more coherent sense of self. In the third stage, Peter internalized the playful aspects of our analytic work and was therefore no longer preoccupied with the task of unifying all of his thoughts and experiences into a coherent whole. This experience replicated the psychoanalysis itself, where continuity and the logical progression of ideas were not always necessary, and experimentation and free association were encouraged. Thus, in this final stage of work, Peter began to experiment with thinking of himself as comprising a fusion of many different identities, often overlapping and changing, even if they appeared to contradict one another. His art has served as a vehicle for his imaginative expression and creativity as he has continued to struggle with the pain and pleasure of introspection.

During the initial stage of treatment, Peter struggled with feelings of fragmentation, with little sense of the "me-ness" normally achieved through internalized self–other patterns of interaction. His very first words at our initial consultation were "I don't know who I am." He described overwhelming anxiety when I left the room to obtain the HIPPA form and said: "Don't do that again. When I am left with my own thoughts I have no idea who I am [...] I think my main problem, the reason I am here at all, is that I have no identity." It was hard to get him to describe this incredible feeling of lost-ness, alone-ness, barrenness. I found myself thinking of the existential philosophers who had a similar sense of disorientation in a world that felt meaningless, confusing, even absurd. His sense of himself appeared to be a series of disjointed experiences that he associated with himself, but which lacked any integrative framework. Much of the work during this period of time focused on fragmented memories of sexual abuse and neglect. He was enraged – both at his father for the sexual abuse of early childhood, and at his sister, whom he repeatedly referred to as his rapist. He felt angry, and battered by the world at large, and destroyed by his mother's emotional neglect as a child. Most difficult of all was the realization that he still wanted her attention as an adult, although she continued to have only a passing interest in him. This was what was most intolerable for him – to be so unimportant to her – and he was conflicted about whether to cut off contact with her entirely.

He explicitly discussed his fantasy of me as his mother, one who heard what he said and whose responses revealed a careful consideration of his thoughts and feelings. But he felt acutely and painfully the limitations of the analytic situation. In thinking of him, I recalled the words of the poet Herman de Coninck who wrote about his wife: "if only he could, just like that, leave her for another country, another I, another wife – but if he did, he'd only leave himself behind." Thus, throughout this period, Peter learned to mourn and to tolerate the pain and the absence of his biological mother, who would likely disappoint while he struggled with the fact that she was his blood, his history. At the same time, Peter's gut-level feeling about how much I cared about him and genuinely enjoyed his company enabled him to find value in himself and in a relationship with another, and thereby to imagine himself as one who is valued and cherished. This was sometimes achieved by simple questions which let him know that I was listening and attending to the salient details of his life. For example, during our second session he stated that he did not know how to figure out how to pay off high credit card bills that he had accrued due to college debt. I asked if he had attempted to bargain his rate down with the credit card companies. He had never heard of that. Shortly thereafter he referred to the fact that he felt his limitations were as much about his parents' disinterest in teaching him "the rules of how the world works" as much as they were a reflection of more overt abuse and emotional abandonment. Numerous times since the credit card conversation he has referred to it as the moment when he knew that "you would do the things for me that my mother never would."

Early in the treatment I observed that Peter fought every attempt I made to question the exclusively positive light in which he saw me. Once he alluded to his love affair with old movies and told me point blank that he was not going to find any "seams in my stockings" because he was not ready. I began to accept the fact that Peter himself understood a great deal about his own developmental needs. He appeared to have a keen sense of the positive maternal transference as necessary for the equilibrium of his self-state. The connection was perhaps too precious and too fragile to call into question. The risk of falling back into a fragmented state of self-confusion was too great. At times I wondered whether I should risk the positive connection by being more confrontational. Was it useful to reinforce the natural inherent resources Peter possessed and to help him engage these resources in his current adaptation? Or was it better to challenge and question the compensatory narcissistic behaviors that he evidenced in his sense of superiority, boastfulness, and snide mocking of others? During this first stage I followed Peter's own lead with the belief that the secure attachment he was developing with me was essential for him to learn to explore, play, imagine, and interact socially with others with less anxiety, more freedom, and, hence, more potential for growth.

My decision to err on the side of empathy for a while was in large measure informed by the intense nightmares and flashbacks that interfered with his ability to function in the world. His feelings of fragmentation were often coupled with violent sexual imagery. Explorations of these horrific dreams took up a great deal of our time together. The dream I mentioned at the beginning of this presentation is fairly representative of this first stage of therapy. In this dream, as in many others, Peter imagined that his body itself was assembled in pieces that felt stuck together in bizarre and grotesque ways. He depicted his head as grossly misshapen as a result of his early experiences. Nothing resided where his genitals should be, while his eyes looked like breasts. The mutual gaze that would have connected him with his mother in a positive way had not taken place for him, and had been replaced by her general distaste for him. Instead, his needs for comfort and affirmation were channeled into auto-erotic sexuality and his incestuous interactions with his sister.

I tried to follow his lead about how much sexual trauma was appropriate to try to assimilate at any given moment while other sessions focused on simple facts of his life that he wanted to understand and change. For example, Peter had never had a stable job and had bounced around in non-profit agencies, as well as in literary ventures. He was stymied by how to manage conflicts in his current position in a social service agency. During one session I commented that he seemed like "a man of action," trying to gently point out his propensity to get into confrontations at work without considering the possibility of negotiation and the mutual resolution of conflict. He eagerly took up these words and used them often to reflect on his own behavioral choices that tended to be quite flamboyant and reactive in style. During this period of time his behavior at work underwent a marked change. Nine months into treatment he was given a significant promotion. Three months later he was offered a new job at twice his salary.

This may seem like a great deal of change in a very short time, but I think that it is in large measure because I have only briefly alluded to Peter's incredible intelligence, particularly his verbal aptitude Although he only attended a few college courses, he is a self-taught renaissance man who is comfortable talking about many topics, including politics, music, history, and technology, among others. He also appears to have a significant artistic bent. These talents have afforded a number of interesting opportunities, and as the analysis reached its one-year mark he was offered two book deals. After some reflection he turned both offers down because he could not find the necessary motivation to take on this kind of major task.

Attempts at understanding his inability to choose a course of action and follow through with either book deal, or with one of several jobs he was offered, had me confused. I soon learned that these were the first of many opportunities he would turn down for lack of initiative and agency. Peter's incredible ability to adapt to his surroundings and make others feel good afforded him many such opportunities. But his skill and charm were a mixed blessing, and during the first stage of the analysis Peter did remind me very much of a chameleon. Like Woody Allen's Zelig, he appeared to successfully adopt the roles and behaviors of his social surroundings. As in Helena Deutsch's description of the "As If" personality, he had an incredible ability to become whatever person was suggested by the emotional forces and pressures of the moment. Yet, as time went on, this slowly evolved into something that looked slightly different. I mark the second stage of our work together by Peter's developing ability to evaluate more carefully each circumstance to figure out which had value for him. Unlike the "As If" Peter, who was compelled to respond to social pressures of the moment and to become the person he imagined the other wanted him to be, this Peter made a more reflective choice. In other words, he was able to begin to think about and then choose those roles which were of specific value to him. Over this period of time those choices were refined and enhanced, and resulted in a new sense of agency and confidence in his ability to choose situations that would continue to support his development.

During this second period of the analysis, when a certain amount of internal consolidation occurred, Peter began to feel more comfortable expressing his anger. He often used it sarcastically, to mock the president, or various pop culture stars and fashion icons, as well as the local dry-cleaner and most work colleagues. He was an indignant social critic. He felt superior to most people in politics and business – smarter, cooler, funnier. He had a tremendously humorous and sarcastic wit. He was also a brilliant mimic. At the time, I understood these feelings and behaviors as a way for Peter to compensate for and avoid looking internally at his own feelings of inadequacy. He needed to express the angers of his past toward contemporary politicians, style-makers, and food gurus, as it gave him a means of pushing outward rather than inward at a time when he simply could not bear to look too closely at himself. It was easy to understand this need, as the grotesque images of his dream material revealed that his grim, unconscious beliefs were those of someone who felt disgusting, defective, and deserving to be abandoned by anyone to whom he felt close. During this second stage of treatment the dreams were horrific, and frequently referenced the confusion of being wanted and then rejected by his sister, or the experience of being unwanted by his mother who had repeatedly stated that he was a boy and that boys grew up to be aggressive and violent, as his father had been. Some of the more disturbing nightmares appeared to reference his terror of his father who was often depicted as an internalized animal who could not be expelled. At other times his father was depicted as a bat that was circling and lunging. Sometimes he was a red man who comes and knocks calmly on his door with a large pink, shiny penis. These memories made him dimly aware that his sexual abuse by his father may well have included painful anal penetration. Other dreams were more vague. Sometimes there was religious imagery and Peter was Jesus on the cross, with a perverse, sexualized creature having his way with him. The nights he had those dreams he awakened with dry screams and could not fall asleep again. He felt trapped in his own mind, his own body, and destined to mentally torture himself without end with the monstrous creatures of his own creation.

Although themes of sex and humiliation were common in Peter's nightmares, his sexual desires changed over the course of treatment. For the first two years of treatment, Peter was very committed to a gay identity. He stated that throughout his teens and twenties he had a series of sexual relationships with both men and women, but that he had realized he was gay when he met his partner. This changed two years into treatment and in the past year Peter has not really identified with a particular sexual orientation. His complicated sexual past includes numerous traumatic sexual experiences with strangers. He describes himself as distraught and out of control sexually prior to treatment. The most significant event was a one-time visit to an adult movie theater where four or five men performed oral sex on him. Peter described how immediately thereafter he pulled out much of his hair from its roots and scrubbed himself raw in the shower. In his current relationship he was careful to delay sex for a number of months, as he sensed early on that he wanted this relationship to be "different." His current monogamous relationship is very satisfying to him, although he continues to feel sexual desire for both men and women.

The third stage of treatment commenced when Peter was able to be a great deal more open about his confusion as to his sexual orientation, as well as some gender confusion. This final stage of treatment involved using a great deal of dream material in our sessions. The content of these dreams was often difficult for us both to bear. His sexual response to the nightmares was also confusing and made the final stage of our work particularly challenging (e.g., in one dream, Peter was forced to witness a brutal rape scene and awoke in panic, screaming, with an erect penis. In a second dream, he himself was the rapist who could not contain his own need to annihilate the other).[1] Peter's ability to write down his dreams under these circumstances allowed us to use some of his most horrific fears of himself as victim becoming a perpetrator and characterized some of the most difficult clinical moments of our work together. I often marveled at his dedication to the work even during the most horrific circumstances. He also forced himself to wake up his partner and share his panic, which was a marked change from his earlier behavior of quietly exiting their bedroom when panic struck.

Hearing these dreams can be difficult, and I often think that analysis with a woman reminds him of his relationship with his sister who was his first sexual interest. After hearing these dreams I was always careful not to force an interpretation. As Peter has had such complicated sexual relationships with all the members of his nuclear family, I do not presume to know whom the protagonists in his dream life represent. After some time Peter discusses his thoughts, namely that in the first dream he is looking at his sister while she is having sex with someone else – a sadistic and seductive manipulation familiar in their history. This sadistic fantasy makes him want to kill her. On the other hand, he may be the abused woman who is in pain in the dream and is full of rage toward his sister who is the male inflicting the pain. He goes on to discuss his complicated feelings about sexual attraction – the fact that he can be attracted to women, but currently prefers sex with men and wants to stay with his current male partner. He goes on to talk about his second dream, where he is disconnected from his desire – his penis is big and engorged but he's not interested. At this point in treatment I reflect to myself that Peter's anxiety and anger at times may prevent him from connecting with his sexual interest – that while he continues to struggle over his attraction to women he is terrified by his desire; his seduction by his sister was followed by sadistic toying. This remains a source of anger toward women and he is reluctant to expose himself to that combination of frustrated desire and humiliation. Perhaps he awakens his partner to confirm their relationship in the face of his desire for an attractive woman. I find it important also to remember that Peter may identify with the man in the second dream who is afraid of his own penis, since heterosexual desire from an early age has been defined by his mother as violent and aggressive.

As time has evolved, Peter has become less invested in his identity as a man who is strictly interested in other men. Our work has expanded to explore sexual identity, which in turn led to Peter's interest in making art. In this final stage of treatment, Peter had spent a number of months fantasizing about me as his new mother, who would demand that he actually write a novel or begin to produce some art. At one point I asked him what it would be like for him if I did actually ask him to produce something and followed up on it. He said it would allow him to work hard and to stick to something for the first time in his life because someone gave a damn. In particular he wanted to be accountable to produce art rather than to just talk about it. I suggested he simply do it and I would ask about it on a regular basis. He grabbed hold of the idea quickly. Within a week he bought art supplies. He obtained cheap canvases, mirrors, and "found objects" that were appropriate for his craft. He took up his art in earnest. His first pieces appeared in group shows, and within a couple of years he had begun his career as a solo artist.

Many of his works integrate pieces of mirror, and the artistic process itself often includes Peter gazing into the mirror as he paints and draws around it. This freedom, namely to experiment and to create, to rotate and to fit together shards and pieces of glass, is a physical manifestation of his internal experience. Through analysis and through his art he continues to imagine and re-imagine. This shaping and reshaping have opened up potential avenues for his desires and wishes for himself, despite the potential to make himself vulnerable to shame and rejection. Themes of trans-generational transmission of trauma often arise, but in his work he transforms the mirror and uses his traumatic past as a means for self-transformation through active expression in the world. In this way, Peter is a man who contradicts expectations, who uses both material in the world and his very own body in the spirit of Ovid who famously stated *materiam superabat opus* – the workmanship has surpassed the raw materials. I feel grateful to have played a role in this continuing transformation.

Note

1 To ensure Peter's confidentiality I will not write up the explicit content of these dreams, but hope that I present enough information for the sake of clarity.

Commentary on Feit's case

Elizabeth Hegeman

The most pressing question posed by this case description is: How is it possible that a man who has been so brutally tortured, degraded, and sexually invaded by his family members, so isolated at crucial times during his childhood and adolescence, has been able to make such splendid use of an analysis without working through any rage or sadism in the transference? As Dr. Feit points out, it seems like "a great deal of change in a very short time." She attributes Peter'a vocational, interpersonal, and creative triumphs to an incredible intelligence, but any sound developmental understanding would require much more to explain the presence of such apparent ego strength. We will have to examine the nature of the analytic relationship for the possible explanation. It may also be that there were mitigating factors in Peter's development that others who write about trauma have found hard to describe without sacrificing protection of confidentiality, or relationships, hobbies, transient contacts, or friendships, the memories of which will only emerge later in the treatment.

From the beginning, Dr. Feit sounds as though she acted with considerable courage in agreeing to work with Peter, and at every stage of the treatment. I wonder if her early question as to whether he wanted a referral may have been an indication of her own ambivalence. Even if she suspected that his initial presentation was a test for her, Dr. Feit took a leap in choosing analysis, rather than beginning with supportive work, or "installing resources" as one does in EMDR. Plunging into analysis went against conventional wisdom, and ran the risk of uncovering even more serious pathology or regression, given his history. But I think that the key to the success of this treatment was her recognition that Peter needed parenting as well as analysis, and she must have provided that. To succeed in juggling those sometimes conflicting roles, sometimes structuring, nurturing, or advising him, sometimes holding back to allow for his own self-discovery, must have required considerable attunement. The key to this must have been the mutual recognition of shared humor. Dr. Feit comments that when Peter made his fist joke, "we had begun." The "we" is the crucial element in Peter's repair.

An example of the kind of courage needed to work with Peter took place when Dr. Feit dared to challenge him to produce art – even though he may have clearly been asking for her to be the someone who gave a damn, and even though she considered him to be in the third stage of treatment (signaled by his open exploration of gender identity and object choice), Dr. Feit must have sensed that she was risking a lot by allowing what he might perceive as a demand for performance to enter the relationship. A demanding woman, even one who had showed herself to be on his side, could present a provocation for Peter if he was as damaged as might be expected from his history.

The metaphor of the mirror, a reflection to be feared, and shattered, whose pieces can be rearranged so as to transform the self, is a potent reference to the analytic gaze and its power as well as a reference to Peter's shattered self. It is significant that in his artwork Peter feels able to play with the pieces of the broken mirror, as he feels able to play within his analysis. The use of a mirror itself in his art is transgressive, breaking the convention of the flat surface upon which depth and images are imposed, and reflecting – or deflecting – a shattered self and a shattered world. The mirrors in his work and in his mind could also represent the observer-analyst who is watching him become more whole, and/or the self-observer who is putting himself together.

It is still possible that there is more to be worked through in this analysis which appears to have excluded anger and criticism of the analyst; perhaps some mutual idealization is still in play at this stage of the treatment. But if the patient's relatedness and creativity have progressed so remarkably, this treatment has already met the criteria for "Love and Work." It is also possible that as Dr. Feit hints, some people who have been very hurt and hated do manage to gather enough strength (perhaps through self-observation as a defense) so that when a more nurturing relationship and environment do appear, they can readily take advantage of it. This case presentation stretches the upper limits of this theory that great resilience can sometimes emerge from great pain. Another, related point is that some severely traumatized patients can develop deeply internalizing defenses that result in unusual creativity. Peter's inner self-image, a pastiche of grotesque self-elements, is a work of art in a sense – it enables him to contain a range of feelings coming from being attacked, and not attacking back. In this way a character structure develops, as in some dissociative identity disordered patients, which allows them to discontinuously inhabit a world made up of such horrors and contradictory realities that it is unbearable, and yet somehow allows him to survive psychically without inflicting it upon others.

We have much to learn about the sources of this strength, the moments of creative leap that take place in the creation of self, perhaps a different self, as a form of resistance to systematic oppression. Much study has been devoted to the role of trauma in the development of the antisocial personality (e.g., Chefetz, 2015; Gartner, in press) and its relation to destructive developmental history; but we have yet to formulate fully the dynamics of those horribly abused children who do *not* go on to express their rage externally. Richard Gartner has estimated that four out of five male children who are sexually abused do *not* go on to become abusers (2002). Every one of such patients I have worked with has been unusually intelligent and/or creative in some way that elaborated and helped each of them process their own history, usually in some way that helped or protected others as well as concretizing their own unformulated experience. Becoming a lawyer helps consolidate and express the rage, teaching creative writing passes on to others the satisfaction of putting pain into words, volunteering with Samaritans or another suicide hotline helps a victim become someone who soothes a suffering other, rather than a soul condemned to repeat the horrors in the active role.

References

Chefetz, R. (2015). *Intensive Psychotherapy for Persistent Dissociative Processes: The Fear of Feeling Real.* New York: Norton.

Gartner, R. (2002). Personal communication, December.

Gartner, R. (in press). *Understanding the Sexual Betrayal of Boys and Men: The Trauma of Sexual Abuse.* New York and Abingdon: Routledge.

Chapter 7

Failure to thrive

An eye for the I, and an ear for the here

Sigalit Levy

This is a case presentation of a continuing psychoanalysis of a 30-year-old gay man who entered treatment owing to increasing anxiety and depression. Underlying many of his difficulties was his dissociated rage that was enacted inside and outside the treatment. Efforts to resolve this led to an impasse that turned out to be related to his idiosyncratic way of thinking and seeing the world. The patient would use his senses to orient and express himself instead of formulating his thoughts and feelings into words. As the analysis progressed, he became more adept at using words to communicate feelings and thoughts. Also discussed are theoretical themes of the perception of change in psychoanalysis, and the difference between curiosity and interest and its effect on the therapeutic process.

> The eye – it cannot choose but see;
> We cannot bid the ear be still;
> Our bodies feel, where'er they be,
> Against or with our will.
> (William Wordsworth, 1798)

The application which Dylan submitted for treatment more than three years ago gave the impression of having been written by a man overwhelmed by multiple stressors, to which he reluctantly decided to seek help. The help he sought, namely therapy, was a last resort, coming at the end of a series of failed efforts to manage a patched-up life.

As I scanned the waiting room trying to identify my patient, I noticed a man who looked at me with an effortful appearance of patience, a look, I would find out, intended to conceal intense anticipation. I greeted a young man who seemed physically ill. Thin, of average height, and frail-looking, he wore a look of false ease meant to conceal what he would later call the "bundle of anxiety" he carried inside. His walk was self-conscious, and when he entered the room he crashed into a chair as if he found rescue in sitting down. He was pale and apparently conscious of his receding hairline, which he camouflaged with a razor shave and a wool hat. He was dressed in multiple, oversized layers of clothing that seemed excessive for the season and formed the impression of someone younger than his stated age of 28. As the treatment unfolded, I learned that the clothes were meant to conceal what he believed to be an awkward figure of which he was painfully self-conscious. These clothes were a visual metaphor as well, presenting a portrait of a fragile self buried under layers of defenses, conflicts, and idiosyncrasies, which would take years into treatment to shed.

Dylan seemed haunted. He had a sharp look in his eyes as he struggled to seize my gaze and escape it at the same time. In this first session his speech drifted from rambling to hesitant, and at times he required probing to engage in conversation. In the first year of treatment difficulties in almost all areas of his life surfaced. He had trouble in the domains of work, finances, social life, and relationships. He struggled with his attachment to his overbearing mother, and he had few words to say about his father, present in his absence. I came to learn that Dylan's presentation – thin, pale, and sickly – reflected an internal sense of feeling ill or deformed. It was as though he had an adult version of the developmental disorder, "Failure to Thrive."

Dylan is a gay man of Hispanic descent, who, despite his clearly stated identity as gay, had tremendous difficulty accepting this about himself. Put simply, he did not approve. Rather, he was self-conscious, self-deprecating, and often felt that his perception of his compromised masculinity, along with certain feminine traits he bore, made him, to use his own words, a "freak of nature."

As he spoke about his difficulties in the first session, Dylan quickly became overwhelmed. He cried and shivered in a mixture of distress and anxiety. Acutely aware of his failure to maintain his composure, Dylan was ashamed. As the session progressed, I, too, was flooded with feelings of emptiness and futility.

Dylan's overtly humble and unassuming presentation masked a sharp critical streak and an underlying rage. As he was talking, it seemed as though a repressed anger was fighting to claim itself. When I asked him how he manages his anger he replied, "I rarely get angry." I said, "Interesting you should say this, since, as you were talking, I had a sense that anger is fighting to push its way through, as if it were to knock this door down." "Oh, this," he said apathetically. "Sometimes it explodes. In the classroom, I may get so angry with students that I will impulsively throw books or chalk and scream at the top of my lungs. But they understand."

Dylan is an English teacher and an assistant principal. At the time, he was single and struggling to recover from a destructive relationship with a man who was addicted to drugs and alcohol and had a volatile temper. Dylan broke off this four-year relationship seven months before beginning treatment, but feelings of guilt, dread, and longing for this man remained. Dylan, who had used a variety of drugs since high school to try to modulate overwhelming affect, shared with his boyfriend an affinity for drugs. Following the break-up, Dylan gradually tapered off his drug use. Without drugs, a debilitating anxiety – periodically escalating into panic attacks – surfaced. Dylan's inability to manage his anxiety even with the help of anti-anxiety medication (Lexapro, 20 ml) was what eventually motivated him to seek treatment.

Later in the session, when he was calm, he proceeded to talk about his mother. Although he openly (but superficially) described her as critical and overbearing, what emerged was his love and attachment to her. "If anyone in the world loves me, it must be her," he said. When I asked him about how he experienced talking to me, he said, "You remind me of my mother – your hair, and she would like your handbag." So, with mom's dubious blessing, we embarked upon this journey.

As acute as Dylan's depression was at our first meeting, his mood in the following sessions bore little resemblance to his mood in the initial session. He seemed to find solace and relief in the structure of therapy. In subsequent sessions I learned that Dylan is a "good son" to his mother. Having two aggressive and masculine brothers, Dylan had been, to use his own words, "the daughter that my mother never had." Despite his vagueness, I learned that Dylan still lived with his mother and was bound to her by complicated ties. Since he was young, she had been in the habit of confiding in him. She would also ask that he help her with errands and household chores. In return, she would protect him – at times – from physical and emotional attacks by his brothers, who appeared to have targeted him because of his homosexuality.

Just as she protected him from his brothers in childhood and adolescence, in adulthood Dylan's mother gave him shelter from a world that overwhelmed him. He had lived with her since college, and she overlooked his frequent lapses to give her modest monthly payments. Parenthetically, Dylan was a "good patient" in a superficial way, not unlike the way he was a "good son" to his mother. In treatment he was motivated, and transitioned readily and smoothly to coming twice a week, and, six months later, to three times a week for psychoanalysis. He came reliably and punctually for sessions, and he engaged in the work. In exchange for this, I, too, provided him with a kind of refuge. I protected him from external stressors by helping him regulate his feelings, and our sessions provided him with order and structure. Periodically, when I remembered our initial meeting, I could scarcely believe the extent of the pain and distress I saw in Dylan. It would be almost a year into treatment before these feelings would unexpectedly resurface.

Dylan was easy to be with. He was a "patient patient," agreeable and attentive. At times one could almost forget he was there. Eventually I would understand the roots of Dylan's ability to make people feel so at ease around him. One day he told me,

> I always felt like a burden. No matter what, I had no business asking for anything – further burdening. Never even contemplated how you would respond to it. So I have to go above and beyond to get accepted. I was gay – a big problem in my family's life – and it kept surfacing and resurfacing. With my father I thought, "If I can appease him, it will be by avoiding him." I realized I could be hidden and invisible among anyone.

But Dylan longed to get closer to his family. As he put it, "I used to have this incredible urge to know, so I did it through snooping." I suggested this might have been a reaction to feeling that he could not have access to his parents more directly.

Dylan emerged from this childhood a cynical man who did not miss an opportunity to relate, as comic scenarios, the painful events of his past and the sad story of his current life. These stories were entertaining. But by being comfortable and amused I was soon part of the very problem I had been designated to cure.

Doubtful of the clarity of his thinking and ridden with anxiety, Dylan became vigilant to clues that would help him orient himself. Either before or after each session, he would comment on information that he gathered through his senses. With time, I came to realize that these communications of his were ways of registering experiences that were outside of his immediate awareness and therefore not available to speak about more explicitly. For instance, at the end of one of our first analytic sessions, Dylan got up, glanced at the open window, and mumbled irritably, "It smells like spring. I am not ready for spring." I readily proposed, "You want the world to be in perfect synchrony with you." He nodded in acknowledgment and left the room. Although my comment was highly speculative at the time, our exchange led me to think about Dylan's way of being that is self-contained – a closed-off self-system. Over time, it became clear that he experienced environmental changes as an intrusion into his solipsistic self. In supervision, we thought about proposing to Dylan that his experience reflected a need for me to be in perfect synchrony with him. But it wasn't clear that Dylan could engage in such a direct interpersonal exchange during those moments. These were times when he seemed to attend to external cues as a result of interpersonal (probably maternal) failure to provide a stable and safe experience of reality. Thus, Dylan's focus on environmental impingements suggested a need for me to be in synchrony with him, not to stand outside his experience of longing for perfect unity and look at it with him.

One time upon entering the room, Dylan sniffed intensely and concluded, "It smells like mothballs in here." Sensing this odor suggested that he felt like an old man at the ripe age of 28. This in turn brought to mind his mother's frequent reference to him, when he was a child, as being "8 going on 80." Perhaps, too, the mothballs were a reference to the parts of his identity that remained "closeted."

Levenson proposes, "That which is not analyzed will be enacted" (1994). Dylan's comments on his sensory experiences often revealed the existence of unconscious experiences that were not articulated, or perhaps even formulated. One striking instance of this was when Dylan got off the couch at the end of one session, appearing distracted, and proceeded to sniff the soles of his shoes. He murmured in a perturbed manner, "Smells like dog poop, doesn't it?" I instinctively suggested, "You may not appreciate my analytic efforts in the session." Surprisingly, Dylan did not seem fazed by my interpretation. In the following session he presented a dream in which he was seated in his car, half his body covered in feces, with no desire to get out or escape. Being particular about cleanliness and acutely sensitive to smells, he could not understand the strange comfort he felt in the car. One way in which we came to understand the dream was that it reflected Dylan's growing realization that there were aspects of himself and his life that "stank." He is stuck with these parts of himself, but also comfortable with them.

During a different phase in analysis, Dylan entered the room and said it smelled of alcohol. He then said my walk seemed unsteady. Clearly he thought I had been drinking. This interesting beginning marked a shift in the way he viewed me in the transference. Initially I was a maternal figure to him, but now I had become a paternal one – unstable, unreliable, and prone to addictive behaviors. This shift brought to the forefront associated feelings of loss that followed his parent's divorce and the painful break-up with his boyfriend. Dylan communicated the breadth of his sufferings after his parents' divorce with the words, "It was always difficult at home, but after my father left, all hell broke loose." Dylan referred to his father as a "borderline alcoholic." To his mother, however, her ex-husband was simply a "drunk."

As I gradually got to know Dylan, I came to understand the degree to which he operated as a solipsistic, self-enclosed system. He would orient himself in space and time with the use of his senses and fantasies, checking back and forth between this world and external reality. This served as an alternative to a fuller engagement with life. He had immense difficulties trusting that which was outside of himself, and was resistant to developing an interest in reflecting upon his own processes and looking at himself and the outside world in a new way. When I made interpretations or other analytic interventions, Dylan would often pause and seem to contemplate, but eventually reply only with "Perhaps." It did not take long to see that this was Dylan's way of appearing to comply with my efforts while at the same time deflecting them. Much work had to be done before Dylan became more open to learning about his inner life, engage in self-reflection, and to join me in the process of analytic inquiry. This work marked the next challenging phase of the analysis.

Dylan was uncomfortable with his sexuality. With the exception of his father, he was open about it with his immediate family and close friends, but otherwise he walked a fine line that involved trying to conceal his sexuality from those who he thought would rather not know. Dylan suspected that his father knew he was gay, but he felt he could not be open with him. He felt this created a great deal of distance and discomfort between them. Initially Dylan believed that his discretion was designed to protect others from their discomfort with his homosexuality. Eventually, he recognized that he was projecting his own discomfort onto others, and that his secrecy with his father was born of a fear of a more intimate relationship with him. Later in treatment, I suggested that his silence may have been a result of a yearning to be seen, even superficially, as a heterosexual, and thus as a more masculine man, in his father's eyes. Dylan agreed.

Speaking of his father, he said, "This is the last mirror that I can look at and see reflected back to me an image of a heterosexual man."

This brief vignette sheds some light on Dylan's way of engaging with the world. Uncomfortable in social settings and highly distrustful of others, Dylan would retreat into a world of fantasy. In treatment, Dylan started to call this his "parallel universe." He disclosed to me that he often pictured an imaginary friend in the passenger seat of his car while he was driving, keeping him company and sharing intimate moments. Besides revealing the obvious theme of loneliness, I saw this fantasy as adaptive. It afforded Dylan a feeling of mastery and control over a world whose social demands were complicated and difficult to negotiate. But as Dylan became increasingly dependent on this fantasy, he allowed less and less input from the outside. He came to experience himself as master of his own fate, managing his feelings, desires, and needs with little contact from the world. Whenever he was confronted with a bit of reality that did not correspond to his fantasies or idiosyncratic ideas, he would grow anxious. In analysis, he would challenge these impinging bits of reality in ways that, at times, were almost irrational. Outside of the analytic setting, he reacted to such intrusions with rage. The latter was most poignantly evident in his driving. He liked to drive; it gave him a sense of mastery and agency, and compensated for feelings of stagnation and futility. His car became the vehicle for his aggressive drives. Yet, if he was empowered by the car's speed, its enclosing body protected him and offered him anonymity. The combination of power and anonymity left him prone to aggressive and impulsive moves on the road. At times this led to dangerous encounters, and made him anxious and afraid about the possible consequences of his actions. Dylan was most sensitive to being cut off, experiencing it as a violent intrusion of his basic sense of self. He would retaliate by swerving in front of the offending driver, as if only "an eye for an eye" were just. These moves would compromise his own safety as well as that of others.

Dylan's parents divorced when he was 7 years old. The divorce followed the unveiling of an affair that his mother was having with a neighbor whom she eventually married. When his father left the house, Dylan became the target of sadistic physical and emotional attacks by his brothers. At times his parents protected him from these attacks, but it came with a price. The unspoken deal was that in exchange for this protection Dylan had to fulfill certain chores; duties that he felt were humiliatingly feminine in nature.

Dylan was scarred by a number of experiences growing up. The pain of childhood humiliations surfaced in treatment when he revealed the details of his home life. The boundaries at home were loose, privacy was compromised, and he was prematurely exposed to graphic sexual material such as in the following sadistic "game."

Adolescence game: "penis on a platter"

Dylan's brothers began to taunt him with this game when he was 11 years old, the age when they began to suspect he was homosexual. "They used to contemplate it together," Dylan recalled:

> One of them will hold a plate, place a slightly erect penis on it, cover it from both sides with a bun, garnish it, and add potato chips on the side. First time I was presented with it was when I was watching TV. At first I was like, "oh," then it turned to "ewe." It was a lot like that in the house, "oh" turning to "ewe."

In analysis we made frequent reference to this sadistic game. Told initially as a comical anecdote, Dylan came to refer to the hurtful game as "tragic." "Don't get me wrong," he said at one point. "I appreciated the creativity. But it forced me to remember that I am not like all of them, that I am different."

Feeling different from his siblings he thought about ways to keep attention away from himself. He found escape in politics and the news. He read newspapers compulsively, became fascinated with the Census, and memorized demographic information about various countries and states. Dylan found order and certainty in these clear-cut data. Holding the data in mind kept underlying anxiety about his uncertain identity at bay. It was at this time that Dylan started to develop a rich fantasy life in which he pretended to be a "different child with a different life." He immersed himself in this fantasy, and began to create imaginary friends with whom he engaged in activities and conversation. Although this rich fantasy world helped Dylan survive the unfortunate events of his childhood, he carried these fantasies far into adulthood. Dylan was stuck in time.

Childhood memory

"It was a beautiful summer day. The lawn was freshly mowed and I was running and jumping joyfully letting out a happy scream while my hands were lifted upwards." These moments of spontaneous expression of joy were brutally interrupted when his father screamed, "Stop acting like a girl." Dylan remembered intense feelings of shame imposed upon him for being feminine, inappropriate, and awkward in his open display of emotions. Moreover, the horror on his father's face haunted him. It registered, in his mind, as the condescension he would find from the world if he were to express his feelings openly or appear feminine. In listening to Dylan I could picture his joyful leap, frozen in time, in an awkward space, a spontaneous display of joy at once replaced with the shame of having done something inappropriate. Dylan traced his contempt for expressions of feelings back to this scene. "I don't do that," he would say dismissively when he reported observing other people express feelings of any kind.

To minimize his self-consciousness and acute sensitivity to other people's impressions of him, Dylan withdrew into a life of rigid structures and idiosyncrasies. He worked, socialized little, and escaped into an endless world of daydreams. The dreams as presented had a quality of a still life: devoid of desire or feelings. Dylan's frozen sense of self was also captured in his night-time dreams. During this point in treatment, Dylan's dreams were short and repetitive. They were cycles of futile, frustrating acts, such as putting up signs that were taken down, searching aimlessly for his car keys, and driving futilely in circles, never reaching a destination.

Dylan felt that his body was awkward, and he was uncomfortable in it. He thought he was too skinny. He felt that the thinness of his torso was in juxtaposition to his relatively large extremities. I thought that Dylan's experience of his body was disproportionate to his feelings about his self. The first took up much of Dylan's mental space; the second, oddly little. It seemed that Dylan experienced his body as if it were a suit that was too big, a set of clothes that strangely continued to grow while the person inside remained a perpetual child. Further, Dylan felt that his physical awkwardness compromised his masculinity and made him look and feel odd. The following dream sheds some light on Dylan's way of feeling, and how he positioned himself in space and time. He reported this dream at the beginning of analysis while lying on the couch.

A dream

> I am driving in my car and from the rear view mirror I could see an explosion. A plane exploded, disintegrated by losing its tail and is left awkwardly floating in the air. Never crashing into the ground. Just hanging up there as some freak of nature.

This dream, as we understood it, captured Dylan's sense of self. He felt that he was emasculated by his mother who nurtured his feminine traits. He was also angry at his father who failed to rescue him from his overbearing mother. Looked at another way, the dream could be a representation of his early memory of jumping joyously and then being left hanging after being chastised by his father. It also suggests vigilance and anticipation of the fatal crash that may occur if Dylan were to leave his world of fantasy and live in the larger world. Entering that world, with his feet placed on the ground, would expose him to the pain of his early injuries. Put simply, the dream seemed to capture Dylan's fear that the worst was yet to come. The dream also suggested self-destructiveness that is not yet experienced consciously.

As a transference dream, it intimated anxiety about his inability to see me while lying on the couch, thus being forced to develop new ways of relating in order to feel grounded in the context of analysis.

Themes of loss and abandonment intensified when I took a summer vacation. When I returned, Dylan reported that "all hell broke loose" in my absence.

Within a two-week period, both his 16-year-old dog and his best friend died. Dylan had trouble regulating the intense feelings with which he was flooded. The initial shock he felt was quickly replaced with rage at his friend for refusing to "die gracefully." While others would see this friend's tenacious efforts to hold onto life as being courageous, Dylan felt only contempt. He felt that his friend was causing him and important others in his life unnecessary pain. He was exasperated with his dying friend. "Why could he not accept his death gracefully, in the very same way that I would, or the way they show it in the movies?" he asked. Dylan's disapproval of his friend's struggle was not only a result of his difficulty regulating his feelings of loss and sadness, but also a way of distancing himself from his own affect. His intense contempt suggested that he felt contempt for himself because of the vulnerability and fear he felt inside.

My vacation stimulated a variety of feelings in Dylan that ranged from longing to anxiety. But it mobilized anger most intensely. That anger was directed toward women, including me and his mother. The way in which Dylan was trying to make sense of the complexity of his feelings at the time introduced a fascinating phase into our work. He was faced with a growing feeling that women were anxiety-provoking, petty, unreliable, burdening, confusing, and clingy, but he was also struggling to fit me into that prototype. Interestingly, this work took place at a time when Dylan was relatively open with me, and his manner indicated a growing trust and comfort. He looked for clues that would give him evidence that I fit the image he projected onto me, even though any such clues challenged his growing sense of me as caring and trustworthy. He resorted to efforts to collect information about me through his senses. He would sniff the room on his way in, try to catch a glimpse of the contents of my bag, and comment on my clothing. He found my dresses too fashionable for work, concluded I showed poor judgment, and noted that if I wore the same pants twice in a week would mean, according to his mother's rules, that I was "dirty." He was confused because he did not know how to incorporate these observations and their meaning into his growing trust of me. Because of my own sensitivity to privacy, Dylan's intrusiveness at that time felt suffocating. If felt as if he had become the intrusive mother, and I the suffocated child. I felt how stifling and enraging it is to be constantly under scrutiny for behavior that is benign. Perhaps it was not coincidental that Dylan became more open with his criticism and devaluation of me at a time when I was becoming more attentive to ideas about the privacy of the self in the context of analysis. This was also a time in which I was making an effort to adopt a more nuanced and less confrontational approach toward treatment. Thus, Dylan's criticism of me was particularly challenging. Despite this, I felt that it was important to not impose boundaries upon his behavior. I wanted him to feel free to behave badly. I was hoping that with this freedom he would no longer feel pressure to accommodate himself to my interpretations and observations, but rather let me know what he really felt.

It turned out that giving him this freedom was fruitful. Dylan was finally able to express his feelings of hatred and resentment toward women, and his mother in particular, with whom he began to say he had a "love–hate" relationship. He continued to struggle to fit me into his projected image of a hateful mother. Concrete, factual information meant a lot to Dylan, who tended to judge people based on their gender, sociocultural background, and demographics. The lack of information about the facts of my life made Dylan anxious and confused. He doubted the knowledge of me he had gathered from his experience of me, and felt that he could not fully trust that understanding of me unless it were grounded in biographical data.

I refer specifically to Dylan's intense desire to know about me as curiosity rather than as interest. I think of curiosity as an experience *in relation* to the other, yet not a *relational or related* experience. Although the *Oxford English Dictionary* offers similar definitions of curiosity and interest, the definitions do diverge somewhat. Curiosity is defined as a "strong desire to know *something*," while interest is defined as a "state of wanting to know about *someone*." Curiosity is synonymous with inquisitiveness, nosiness, prying, and snooping, while interest is synonymous with attention, notice, awareness, and relevance. In German, the word curiosity, *neu gier*, stems from the Latin and can be literally translated as "greed for news," while the word interest, *inter esse*, is translated as "between and to be," which means "to be into it." Thus, I felt that curiosity better captured Dylan's feelings about me. In his interactions with me, I experienced Dylan as nosy and prying, rather than as genuinely interested. Dylan's prying is not surprising given that he was treated as an object in childhood, not as someone worthy of genuine concern or regard. He was not interested in actively engaging with me in a process of collaborative inquiry, but rather in sating his "greed for news" or information about me. When we discussed Dylan's curiosity, he rattled off a number of questions he had about me. At one point he said, "If I only knew your age and marital status there would be a whole lot of judgments I will be able to make solely based on this information." It was intriguing for me that Dylan kept relying so heavily on rather superficial, factual data to validate his internal experiences of other people.

My focus on the differences between curiosity and interest emerged out of attention to their expressions in the transference and countertransference. Over time, Dylan shifted from curiosity to more genuine interest in me. I believe that the more he was able to experience my genuine interest in him, the more he could afford to be interested in who I was. When he was curious, his interpersonal style was relatively distant and rigid; when he was interested, he was more open, related, and engaged. In the latter state, both of us could get to know ourselves and the other through dialectic inquiry. This shift is in some ways like a "mobius strip," in which the change is constant and yet imperceptible.

At this point in treatment I, too, found myself preoccupied with an intense curiosity to understand why Dylan does what he does, why he is a relentless detective collecting information with his senses. Why would he not ask directly any questions to which he wanted answers? Why would he resort to secretive methods of collecting data? For that matter, why had I not asked him why?

Why did it not occur to me that I could? I enlisted all my supervisors' expertise to help me solve this riddle. The result was much speculation but little clarity. Enactment, as I understand it, is an uncanny force that catches its participants in a whirlpool of actions and leaves them feeling as if they have little control and no meaningful voice. Retroactive reflection on the *particular feelings* that dominate the enactments helps to gain clarity and make analytic sense of it. Thus, it was only later that I gained some clarity into the nature of this phase in which Dylan and I were both engaged in passionate acts of spying on each other. We were circling and sniffing around for information or clues that would tell us something about the other. Dylan's reliance on the senses may follow from an inability to trust his own thoughts. Rather than rely on his mind, he would turn to a more primitive medium to organize himself.

During the following months, when Dylan would be making some speculations about those around him – partner, mother, or myself – I would suggest that when he wanted to know something about somebody he could ask. Dylan was intrigued enough by this to wonder why he had not been asking all along. Did he really want his questions answered? Having the answers put before him, we came to understand, made it impossible for him to maintain his fantasies – fantasies that he had carefully crafted and religiously protected. Maintaining his fantasies protected him from himself, too – the critical, judgmental self that was a victim of social prejudice and had come to use that very tool against himself and others. When we looked into this further, Dylan said, "Funny, I Google everybody, but I never typed in your name. I don't know why. Weird. I Google people all the time. But not you." We thought this was some measure of Dylan's ambivalence about knowing me. "What you know can hurt you. What you don't won't," he said. And I thought that this choice not to know was a way of protecting himself, his fantasy of me, and what we had come to have between us. I encouraged Dylan nonetheless to bring into the analytic inquiry questions that intrigued him. In airing these questions, I told him that he might not only find out more about me, but about himself as well.

Dylan felt that the discrepancy between his mother's words and her actions led to his mistrust of eliciting answers to his questions. Rather than ask and get unsatisfactory answers, he would scan the environment for clues, which were more reliable than his mother's words.

Dylan arrived for one of the following sessions unusually tired. He had gone to sleep quite late after watching several hours of a show called *Serial Killers*. He was disturbed by the show's images of torture devices that the killers used to manipulate their female victims. The torture devices fascinated him the most. He was troubled by his fascination. Seeing them was disturbing, but somehow also pleasurable. With these images, Dylan felt that he was partially able to anchor and satisfy (in fantasy) his hateful feelings toward women. This was the beginning of a phase in which Dylan was able to explore his negative feelings toward women, and his mother and me in particular. Often protective of his mother and ridden with guilt about his negative feelings toward her, Dylan now painted a picture of an overbearing female who hated women and devalued men. After analyzing a dream in which a mother figure was referred to as "white trash," I asked Dylan what he made of this expression with regard to a mother. "I would hate to think about my mother this way," he said. He paused, and then proceeded matter-of-factly,

> She is not educated though. She burps. She farts. She curses. She runs around naked. She yells, she hits, she steals, she cheats. She is the least refined woman I know. It's funny; she wanted me to go to church with her this Sunday. I said, "No way." Later she said, "I went to church and I did not burst into flames."

Dylan had lived with his mother since college. He was bound to her in an enmeshed and symbiotic way. He was burdened by their interdependency and resented himself and her for not being able to leave the relationship. It was a relentless source of aggravation. In treatment, Dylan's mother began to emerge as an intrusive presence who related to her son in much the same way that he related to me. His mother snooped around his room, went through his mail, and periodically paid some of his bills. While the latter may have seemed a generous gesture on her part, Dylan felt that she was expressing her disapproval of him, and of the way he handled his finances. The gestures were neither solicited nor appreciated by Dylan and he experienced them as intrusions into his privacy. In treatment, a significant shift occurred when Dylan began to appreciate that his extended stay at home compromised his personal growth more than it protected him. Finally, Dylan was able to move out. The opportunity presented itself when his brother bought a house and offered Dylan to move in with him. This house would serve as a transitional space. Here Dylan would adapt to more independent living while continuing to separate from his mother. Although he was able to physically separate from her, it was much more difficult for him to separate psychologically, and he was plagued with guilt and anxiety.

Leaving home in the context of the stability and safety of treatment paved the way for more vulnerable feelings and needs to emerge. These were the very feelings that Dylan had been contemptuous of whenever he noticed them in himself or in others. As he became more aware of his own needs to be nurtured and comforted, he would curl up on the couch, aching to share these feelings with another person. He expressed what he felt was a painful longing to be hugged and held in the intimacy of the analytic relationship. As these feelings deepened, Dylan was able to mobilize himself and seek out a close relationship outside of the analytic dyad. He connected with a man and became strongly attached to him. This man was able to offer experiences of safety and intimacy, and Dylan was able to have sex for the first time without the influence of substances. A few months into the relationship the boyfriend moved to a different state. For two years this relationship became a long-distance one, in which the frequency of the meetings was controlled by the other man. They met once a year for a few days but they otherwise relied on frequent phone conversations. Periodically, Dylan would experience fitful rage and frustration at the lack of physical contact. Despite this, Dylan did not want to move on to a more fulfilling relationship. His frustration and longing have been frequently explored. We have come to understand that this relationship offered Dylan a transitional space in which he could exist between reality and fantasy. The relationship was real enough to stir longing for a more fulfilling one; yet it was not real enough to bring him fully out into the world, to leave his domain of fantasy. Paradoxically the physical distance allowed Dylan to fill this gap with fantasies and to imagine a relationship that was far more substantial than it really was. Periodically when he was confronted with real information about this man's behavior or character, he would burst into fits of envy and rage. There have been undercurrents of sadomasochism in this relationship, but thus far Dylan has been only marginally open in engaging in a collaborative exploration of this. Recently Dylan has begun to date men who are interested in a richer and more intimate relationship.

Following a period of adjustment to living away from home, Dylan began to thrive. He gained control over his finances. He started to work out regularly, to pay greater attention to a regime of healthy eating, and he managed to gain considerable weight. More comfortable with his appearance, Dylan began to coordinate his attire to the season. He was able, for the first time in his adult life, to wear short-sleeved shirts, flip-flops, and shorts. He began to socialize more, to spend more time outdoors, and to taper off his anti-anxiety medication.

I recall a particular time when I was walking toward the waiting room to greet Dylan and saw him halfway through the room as he walked toward me. It was one of those moments in which the scene appears like a photograph taken with an out-of-focus lens. The image of the pale and sickly-looking man whom I initially met blurred into this well-built, tanned, healthy, attractive man who carried himself with a new sense of vitality. Clearly, the change in outward appearance reflected a significant internal change: change that I recall feeling moved and pleased by. But to my surprise, Dylan was more judgmental in his remarks at the beginning of the sessions. Soon, his former pattern of casually and irresponsibly handling his analytic bills increased. He forgot to pay me at the time we agreed upon, he did not arrange to take enough cash from the ATM, he would pay me half today and half "next time," he would elaborately count the money as I was waiting, feeling slighted. He could not remember exactly how much the bill was and often short-changed me. All this was handled in a casual manner. "Oh well, I guess I owe you five bucks. Here, I have three," he would say, promising to give me "eight quarters to boot" next time. When I proposed to Dylan that we should analyze the implications of these behaviors, he grew unusually anxious. I told him that the manner in which he was handling my fees felt slighting and hostile; that it felt that he may be having a hard time acknowledging that I have something of value to offer. Dylan had great difficulty engaging in a collaborative exploration of his hostility toward me and its dynamic roots.

A yearning for independence, entitlement, a longing for the fanciful carefree days of childhood in which one's concrete needs are taken care of – these themes, too, were explored. There was a lack of regard for my own needs. Dylan admitted that in his experiences with important women in his life, he felt that everything he had to offer was contingent upon his giving something up. As a child, if he would not cater to his mother's needs, she would become punitive and sometimes banish him from the dinner table. "Wouldn't it be crazy of me to expect that you will now have to prove to me that our relationship is not contingent upon some exchange on my part?" he asked. And yet, it seemed that Dylan was acting out because he sensed he had unwittingly given me something. My gratification at his growth enraged him, since it echoed the way in which he was satisfying his narcissistically involved mother. His protest took a similar form that it had against his mother when he neglected to manage his finances responsibly.

Dylan's act of short-changing me also brought to mind the elusive process of change. Periodically, when I would make reference to the various changes that occurred in his life, he would shift restlessly on the couch and say nervously, "Shooting pains into the eye." I was fascinated not only by the extent of Dylan's visceral reaction but also by its context. Why would he have an adverse reaction to a reference to progress and change? Dylan was able to reflect on this. Shooting pains in the eye were a measure of his refusal to see that which is painful, a physical manifestation of the pain associated with increased awareness and growth. Change was also recognition of the evolutions of the "I" – the self and identity – as he knows it to be. Interpersonally, it was a measure of his impulse to attack me. Note the phrase, "shooting pains into the eye" not "my eye." "You have an eye for the I," he would remark periodically when I would share with him an observation or insight. Although Dylan appreciated my ability to see things about him and shed some light or "flag" blind spots, it was difficult for him not to be invisible anymore. In addition, acknowledging progress meant that I contributed something of value that may enhance feelings of obligation and dependency. He would then be vulnerable to being held hostage by me the way he was by his mother. Put this way, at which point would holding become withholding or holding back? Reference to progress also brought some concerns Dylan had associated with change. Yes, there has been change, but he was wondering if this change would fade or disappear once our work is over and we part ways. We understood then that Dylan was short-changing me – or paying with change – in part because he feared that his progress was contingent upon my actual presence in his life. In addition, by my giving him a bill, he seemed to experience our relationship as a repetition of his merger with his narcissistic mother. With my bills, I, too, as a self-congratulatory analyst, pained him with narcissistic shots into his I, his identity.

Looked at in another way, this may be some indication of Dylan's ambivalence about change. Paying with change may be seen as a symbolic acknowledgment of his progress, a change he may like to be able to undo should he become overwhelmed with it. Themes of compliance and "as-if" change were introduced into the analysis, which led to further thoughts about this elusive process of change.

I think of change as "magic mushrooms." I recall that as a child, on my way to school on a damp day in winter, I noticed that the front lawn was spotted with mushrooms. They grew overnight, and seemed magical and majestic with their intricate details and inviting texture. I have come to associate analytic change with these mushrooms. Therapeutic change develops in the dark, in the private space in which the mutual efforts of patient and analyst are left unattended. There the light of analytic inquiry does not interfere with the delicate formation of change. Sometimes when Dylan reacted in a way that took both of us by surprise, I was puzzled. I was concerned. Why did I not see Dylan's depression, ease, or new sense of compassion coming? Was I misattuned? I have come to realize that this is a central part of change. The process may feel deceptively stale, even futile, but it takes place underground, growing in mysterious chambers until it surfaces and becomes visible. It is stumbled upon with a feeling of surprise, and there is a sense of magic and wonder as if to ask, "How and why now?"

It is not easy to talk about patients' progress without seeming too self-congratulatory. I chose the following vignette from one of our recent sessions to illustrate Dylan's development through the course of analysis. Recently, Dylan matriculated in a graduate program at a prestigious university. It was a long-time aspiration, which he was finally able to pursue. At the end of the hour when Dylan got off the couch and began to gather his belongings, I commented on the elegant jacket he was wearing. I thought he was making a special effort to dress up for his evening classes. Dylan nodded in acknowledgment, straightened out his jacket, glanced out of the window, and said offhandedly, "It's gotten cooler out. I thought I could get away with it."

Reference

Levenson, E. A. (1994). The uses of disorder – Chaos theory and psychoanalysis. *Contemporary Psychoanalysis*, *30*, 5–24.

Commentary on Levy's case

Ira Moses

Dr. Levy provides us with a clinically rich case report highlighted by her observations of the patient's behaviors as well as her own thought processes during this very productive treatment. I will attempt to demonstrate how traditional interpersonalists, particularly through Harry Stack Sullivan's (1953a, 1953b) and later Ed Levenson's (1988) operational perspective with their use of inquiry, might view this case. It is important to note that though the terms *interpersonal* and *relational* are often used interchangeably, they have become quite distinct. Traditional interpersonal psychoanalysis contributed several theoretical and technical innovations. The most radical was the reframing of the analytic process to be a function of a two-person, "participant-observer" model. In addition, they introduced *inquiry* as a major analytic technique; included the study of interpersonal security operations; expanded the field of intrapsychic phenomena to include "unformulated experience," and further expanded the domain of analysis to include more difficult patients with an appreciation of the patient's adjustment to living in the world. Of particular importance was Sullivan's interest in the data for analysts' inference with his emphasis on operationalism. In contrast, modern relational theorists emphasize a different level of inference as it privileges reverie, implicit knowledge, intersubjectivity, mutuality, and multiple self-states. Sullivan, in contrast, was concerned about the analyst becoming lost in reverie at the expense of not hearing the patient.

For the purpose of this discussion I will simply focus on how the interpersonalists would use inquiry to further the patient's awareness of their inner world and to examine how the therapist's assumptions and observations may or may not be in alignment. It is worth mentioning that Dr. Levy's patient would present numerous challenges to any therapist as he presents problems on multiple levels: significant anxiety and depression; history of abuse from siblings; drug dependency; poor body image; inadequate affect regulation as manifested by his rage outbursts; gender identity conflicts; and individuation and separation problems living in his mother's attic.

What is inquiry?

Inquiry was developed by Sullivan (1954) and later elaborated by Levenson (1988), Moses (1992), and Cooper (1995) as an essential component of analytic technique. Sullivan (1954) was quite critical of what he felt to be the ever-increasing intellectualized, highly interpretive approach of his time. He implored us to be more curious and to actively ask questions in order to be sure that we know what is being told. He wrote:

> A patient tells me the obvious and I wonder what he means, and ask further questions. [...] [The patient] begins to see [...] that statements which seem obvious to him may be remarkably uncommunicative to the other person. [And worse than that] [...] they may permit the inexperienced [therapist] to assume that he knows something that is not the case [...] [only to later realize] *that he has been galloping off on a little path of private fantasy.*
>
> (Sullivan, 1954, p. 8)

For Sullivan, it was axiomatic that "The analyst should never forget that conclusions about the subjective experience of the patient can only result in an inference, never a fact" (1953a, p. 73).

I would like to underscore that the goal of the inquiry is not necessarily to have patients answer but rather begin to help them internalize the analyst's inquiry, i.e., our curiosity about their experience. It is to help the patient "think inward" (Antonovsky, 1978, p. 308), to introspect, in the face of avoidance and anxiety. When faced with obstacles, the analyst retreats all too quickly into their own reverie, assuming that the patient cannot associate, or think, or mentalize.

It is through this unique perspective of inquiry as a check against our reverie from which Dr. Levy's work will be discussed. The reader should note that this review will be an exercise for heuristic purposes and not an evaluation of Dr. Levy's work per se.

Dr. Levy writes:

> Dylan's comments on his sensory experiences often revealed the existence of unconscious experiences that were not articulated, or perhaps even formulated. One striking instance of this was when Dylan got off the couch at the end of one session, appearing distracted, and proceeded to sniff the soles of his shoes. He murmured in a perturbed manner, "Smells like dog poop, doesn't it?" I instinctively suggested, "You may not appreciate my analytic efforts in the session." *Surprisingly, Dylan did not seem fazed by my interpretation.*

How might an interpersonal inquiry approach this interaction differently in an effort to help the patient expand upon what is happening rather than the customary efforts of offering an interpretation? (I also wondered: by the word "instinctively," does she mean to say that she responded immediately or is there a more unconscious substrate to her choice of words?) The more obvious question, of course, is: why does he bring it up at the very end of the session when discussion would be impossible? Of additional concern, from an interpersonal perspective, is what Dr. Levy chooses to say: "you may not appreciate." Had she heard his tone as perturbed and wonders if he was actually angry and annoyed at her? Most interesting was his reaction to her interpretation as she describes "did not seem fazed," which could be indicative of a certain dismissiveness or disregard. Since for Sullivan psychiatry is the study of interpersonal relations, the patient's reaction to Dr. Levy – his not seeming "fazed" – may be just as critical a subject for inquiry as the intrapsychic material and, therefore, our inquiry into both realms may serve toward expanding the material. Her interpretation may be correct but may not be the most germane in that moment. We could play with this further by suggesting that her saying "you may not appreciate" could be a way of actually minimizing his reaction which may have been stronger, as suggested by his association that something smells like shit. Is the patient inviting her to smell it along with him? One could observe out loud and wonder why he has to actually sniff the sole of his shoe. We can think of at least three possibilities. Can't he smell it without sticking his nose into it? Does he like the smell? Does he feel Dr. Levy is trying to stick his nose into something? The point of these multiple inquiries is to argue for specificity by staying as close as possible to the patient's expression and then facilitating the patient's elaboration of his experiences. In other words, inquiry can free the therapist from trying to figure out meaning on her own and use inquiry to help the patient bring form to that which had been unformulated. Dr. Levy may be accurate when she writes: "Dylan's comments on his sensory experiences often revealed the existence of unconscious experiences that were not articulated, or perhaps even formulated." It is the very interactions through inquiry which may help the patient formulate that which had been unformulated. Interpretation and the analyst's "understanding" of the phenomena may paradoxically get in the way of the patient's formulation by imposing the analyst's conceptual understanding upon the patient's psyche. We are reminded of Freud's warning that interpretations can become appendages to the mind of the patient. (One often hears these appended interpretations during initial interview when the patient is describing what they learned from previous therapies.)

To continue our exercise in inquiry, we see that the patient's "shit" is quite central in the following dream in which I have highlighted two specific references. She writes:

> In the following session, he presented a dream in which he was seated in his car, half his body covered with feces, with *no desire to get out or escape.* Being particular about cleanliness and acutely sensitive to smells, he could not understand *the strange comfort* he felt in the car. One way in which we came to understand the dream is that it reflected Dylan's growing realization

> that there were aspects of himself and his life that "stank." He is stuck with these parts of himself, but also comfortable with them [emphasis added].

It is his lack of desire "to get out" and his comfort with his stink that presents a central difficulty for the analyst. Dylan's resistance to change is revealed by his comfort of sitting in his shit (perhaps similar to the toddler who finds comfort in a dirty diaper, protesting any effort to have it changed). As we know, if a behavior is comfortable (ego-syntonic) it is difficult to change until it is made ego-dystonic. It would then follow that the inquiry into the patient's experience of his "strange comfort" could be an essential subject for exploration. One might hypothesize that this comfort with his stink could be part of his problems in relatedness in that others would find some of his behavior off-putting if not odious (e.g., his tantrum in front of his class).

Inquiry into the transference

The patient offers considerable material about the transference, perhaps suggesting that he feels comfortable enough to expose the negative transference. Dr. Levy writes:

> During a different phase in analysis, Dylan entered the room and said it smelled of alcohol. He then said my walk seemed unsteady. *Clearly he thought I had been drinking*. This interesting beginning marked a shift in the way he viewed me in the transference. Initially, I was a maternal figure to him, but now I had become a paternal one – unstable, unreliable, and prone to addictive behaviors. This shift brought to the forefront associated feelings of loss that followed his parents' divorce and the painful break-up with his boyfriend. Dylan communicated the breadth of his suffering after his parents' divorce with the words, "It was always difficult at home, but after my father left, all hell broke loose." Dylan referred to his father as a "borderline alcoholic." To his mother, however, her ex-husband was simply a "drunk" [emphasis added].

Why, then, did he think Dr. Levy smelled of alcohol? Her walk seemed unsteady? Was he starting to see flaws in the analyst who needed to be perfect? Dr. Levy concludes, "*Clearly he thought I had been drinking.*" Rather than the analyst filling in a narrative about why he might be seeing her as his father, why not see what the patient can make of it by the use of inquiry and ask questions such as: Why now at this time in treatment did he smell alcohol? Was his transference being shaken up by a previous experience in the session and perhaps his smelling the alcohol was, paradoxically, a way to excuse his analyst's loss of steadiness in the sessions? It may have been terrifying that her unsteadiness was due to her deterioration that could not be excused by drinking. Dr. Levy keenly observes the patient's reaction to her interpretations:

> When I would make interpretations or other analytic interventions, Dylan would often pause and seem to contemplate, but eventually reply only with, "Perhaps." It did not take long to see that this was Dylan's way of appearing to comply with my efforts while at the same time deflecting them.

Dr. Levy runs into the all too common reaction as the patient responds reactively, rather than reflectively, to her observations with a certain manifest indifference and insouciance. His not being "fazed" as cited above and this most recent response of "perhaps" nicely illustrates his attitude toward Dr. Levy's efforts.

Security operations

Unlike the defense mechanisms which are mostly unconscious intrapsychic mechanisms identified by Freud, Sullivan proposed a set of interpersonal interactions and modes of relating to the other as a way to manage anxiety. Here are some quite illustrative examples as noted by Levy:

> Parenthetically, Dylan was a "good patient" in a superficial way, not unlike the way he was a "good son" to his mother. In treatment he was motivated, and transitioned readily and smoothly to coming twice a week, and six months later, to three times a week for psychoanalysis. He came reliably and punctually for sessions, and he engaged in the work. In exchange for this, I provided him with a kind of refuge. [...] *Dylan was easy to be with.* He was a "patient patient," agreeable and attentive. At times one could almost forget he was there [emphasis added].

Dr. Levy reasons:

> Despite this, I felt that it was important to not impose boundaries upon his behavior. I wanted him to feel free to behave badly. I was hoping that with this freedom he would no longer feel pressure to accommodate himself to my interpretations and observations, but rather let me know what he really felt.

Her efforts to work with his rather enduring character defense by not imposing boundaries may be equally problematic in that it appears to be counter to her countertransference rather than a systematic analysis and inquiry into his compliant behavior. It is quite common, in Dr. Levy's defense, for analysts to have major countertransference struggles with setting boundaries and thus to err on the side of being too strict or, more likely, too loose. She is to be credited for being mindful and attentive to the reactions of the patient and to allow herself to adjust her approach to interpretation.

> Eventually I would understand the roots of Dylan's ability to make people feel so at ease around him. [...] "I always felt like a burden. No matter what, I had no business asking for anything – further burdening."

At this juncture the analyst can begin to think about ways to work through the patient's need to please by examining his comments about being "a burden." Does he also worry about burdening Dr. Levy as if she was just like his mother? As Levenson and others have noted, it is often impossible not to get caught up in a reciprocal transference/countertransference interaction of earlier patterns of relatedness (which is often referred to as an "enactment"). Dr. Levy, however, is able to step back and examine her participation in the enactment and thereby can disentangle herself through an inquiry.

> Dylan emerged from this childhood a cynical man who did not miss an opportunity to tell, as comic scenarios, the painful events of his past and the sad story of his current life. These stories were entertaining. But by being comfortable and amused, I was soon part of the very problem I had been designated to cure.

Once the analyst can see how she is participating in these enactments she can begin to offer a more integrated response in lieu of a repetition.

Transference issues

As we read, the patient's transference was quickly revealed.

> "You remind me of my mother – your hair, and she would like your handbag." So, with mom's dubious blessing, we embarked upon this journey.

And later:

> He found my dresses too fashionable for work, concluded I showed poor judgment, and noted that if I wore the same pants twice in a week would mean, according to his mother's rules, that I was "dirty." [...]
>
> Because of my own sensitivity to privacy, Dylan's intrusiveness at that time felt suffocating. It felt as if he had become the intrusive mother, and I the suffocated child. I felt how stifling and enraging it is to be constantly under scrutiny for behavior that is benign. Perhaps it was not coincidental that Dylan became more open with his criticism and devaluation of me at a time when I was becoming more attentive to ideas about the privacy of the self in the context of analysis. This was also a time in which I was making an effort to adopt a more nuanced and less confrontational approach toward treatment.

This vignette nicely illustrates some of the unique challenges women analysts face when dealing with transferences from male patients in reference to their looks and dress. It appears that the patient is overstimulated as well as highly conflicted, as manifested by the confluence of sexual and punitive associations (dress was too fashionable [...] mother's rules would indicate that this is "dirty"). Dr. Levy seemed to be suppressing her annoyance with his intrusions and thus was feeling suffocated. I think that in this session inquiry may have helped by focusing the patient to look inward rather than externally toward the analyst, inviting the patient to describe more fully, to elaborate on his associations with "dirty." Helping him expand on his internalization of his mother's harsh voice may allow him to gain a new perspective on it.

Resistance

Dr. Levy observes:

> He was not interested in actively engaging with me in a process of collaborative inquiry, but rather in sating his "greed for news" or information about me: "If I only knew your age and marital status there would be a whole lot of judgments I will be able to make solely based on this information." It was intriguing for me that Dylan kept relying so heavily on rather superficial, factual data to validate his internal experiences of other people.

This exchange, for the purpose of my discussion, is a very critical one, since it deals with the most difficult aspect of working with inquiry. For Sullivan the key struggle was working with the patient's barriers to communication. The analyst should expect that inquiry, when we approach the most conflict-laden material, will be no easy task. (I would offer the quip that if it is too easy to talk about it then it's not that important.) Inquiring at these times about the patient's experience of our inquiry may also be helpful. The patient's inability to collaborate with inquiry may be seen as indicative of his lack of collaboration throughout his life. At these junctures one may begin to think out loud with the patient as to why he is having trouble, what else may be on his mind, and so on.

Conclusion

I think we would all agree that any intervention – be it interpretation, observation, or inquiry – is part of a matrix of interventions which must be embedded in analytic empathy with attention to the patient's sense of security. Thus, I would hope that my review of Dr. Levy's interactions with the patient will give the reader an idea of how the analyst may help patients inquire into their own experiences against the undertow of avoidance and anxiety in order that they develop the tools to help their emotional and introspective growth.

References

Antonovsky, A. M. (1978). The thinking cure – Some thoughts on thinking in psychoanalysis. *Contemporary Psychoanalysis, 14*, 388–403.

Cooper, A. (1995). The detailed inquiry. In M. Lionells, J. Fiscalini, C. II Mann, & D. B. Stern (Eds.), *Handbook of Interpersonal Psychoanalysis* (pp. 679–694). Hillsdale, NY: The Analytic Press.

Moses, I. (1992). The analyst's questions (panel presentation) – Resistance to asking questions. *Contemporary Psychoanalysis, 28*, 300–308.

Sullivan, H. S. (1953a). *Conceptions of Modern Psychiatry*. New York: W. W. Norton.

Sullivan, H. S. (1953b). *The Interpersonal Theory of Psychiatry*. New York: W. W. Norton.

Sullivan, H. S. (1954). *The Psychiatric Interview*. New York: W. W. Norton and Co.

Chapter 8

Faced with death

Death in the countertransference

Orsoly Hunyady

> Sally had her hands around my throat; she was choking me. Her face was contorted with rage and she was ranting about something with conviction and vehemence. I felt my throat closing up. My own strength was just enough to prevent her from coming closer and strengthening her grip. I pushed her away as much as I could. We held each other at arm's length, my holding her by her shoulders, keeping her at that steady distance, while trying to catch my breath to say something. As I felt the strength in my arm dissipate, I found suddenly that Sally and I were sitting on a dark hardwood floor. I was then holding her in my arms; wrapped her in them; and she was crying silently, eyes closed.

Then I woke up.

In this chapter I seek to address the emotional depth with which we engage with our patients, and highlight the fact that so much of the work necessarily and inevitably takes place on an unconscious level for both patient and therapist. I will describe two dreams I had about patients and will talk about how having these dreams affected the treatments with some patients. With those who function in a less concrete manner, report more dreams of their own, and generally seem to be more connected to their unconscious, my dreams would have had less importance. Perhaps in these other cases I would not have had the dreams in the first place, because by generating the dreams I was unconsciously trying to facilitate a stifled clinical process – a process that I was not able to advance from a conscious stance. With these two particular people perhaps I had to have the dreams myself for both of us.

The dream I recounted above about Sally had great emotional resonance, as it occurred the night before I was going to see her for our weekly session. Once I woke up from the dream, I instantly thought that dreaming was my way of finding the words and having the breath to say to them, i.e., getting out of the strong grip of the transference–countertransference and being finally able to comment on it. So, paradoxically, as nightmarish as the dream was, I felt relief when thinking of my work with Sally upon awaking.

At this point I had been seeing Sally for several years, and her anger was present in most sessions, although it was never openly directed at me. She had a lot to be angry about and, accordingly, we spent a great deal of time articulating the various facets of her frustrations, disappointments, and hurts; how she was victimized in various situations as well as how she herself came to be a critical, dissatisfied, distrusting, and often dismissive person. We talked about not only how she experienced her anger and where it was coming from, but also how it was expressed, and how other people reacted to it. In other words, we attended to Sally's anger in a consistent way, working actively with it, given that it had such prominence in her emotional life. Generally, when I opened up the space to talk about the ways in which she was angry with me, my inquiries tended only to confuse her, as she did not experience any anger toward me consciously. Despite my efforts and our explicit conversations about anger, however, not much seemed to have changed in Sally's internal and external world for years.

What I was not fully aware of all this time is how oppressive and suffocating our work felt to me. Sally's anger was seemingly omnipresent; in fact in some ways her identity had been organized around it; therefore it did not leave much room for other feelings and experiences in her life. Although her anger was not openly directed at me, it certainly felt constraining. Upon reflecting on the dream, I further realized that we had been locked into a power struggle from the beginning of the treatment (as it was depicted in the dream quite literally). I wanted to stabilize Sally by keeping her at a distance, while she insisted on having and expressing her rage and doing away with my efforts (and with me) – and, of course, with the distance.

So, the following day, as she ran through her story of the week and described her outrage about her boss's behavior, I thought about my dream. Even though I would have wanted to, I was not able to allow myself to share it with her. Once the session was over, I had to grapple with my disappointment in myself and tried to understand why I couldn't bring up the dream, especially given that my inability to speak was the very experience that the dream was unconsciously designed to capture and explain. As I imagined what it would have been like to tell Sally that she had been in a dream of mine, I came to understand that the depiction of intense connection between Sally and me, openly communicated by the dream through our physical contact, was implying more intimacy than what either one of us could allow in the room. Through the dream I finally became aware of how much I was affected by Sally, how intensely I felt about her anger, how impossible these feelings made it for me to express my countertransferential reactions, and also how intensely connected I felt with her, sharing in her struggles precisely through fighting to keep her at arm's length. I finally stopped pushing back against her push; I no longer needed to intellectualize and stay away from "us" and the touch that existed between us from the beginning – and through these changes we transitioned into the second part of the dream. I realized later, too, that in the dream Sally's anger – which I always experienced as a form of adolescent rage – became unconsciously associated with my younger daughter's tantrums which were frequent at the time and that often ended with us sitting on the dark hardwood floor of our apartment, with me hugging her while she cried. In that sense I brought Sally into my home, into my world; this was another expression of the shift in intimacy that the dream conveyed for me.

To provide some context, let me tell you more about where Sally is coming from and how all this relates to her own interpersonal dynamics. She was born into an immigrant household as the first child of a bicultural couple, and was followed by a younger sister. During childhood she dealt with various manifestations of discrimination, never fully feeling part of any group or community. Her relationship to each of her parents was very distinct. In Sally's experience her mother had always been volatile, unpredictable, overly critical, and intrusive. She always had to be "in the know" about Sally's whereabouts and tried to control Sally's behavior through guilt trips, threats, and promises. This was especially true when it came to providing financial support in early adulthood. In one example, Sally's mother offered to help out with her student loans, but when Sally made a life decision with which the mother disagreed, she simply stopped sending the checks, leaving her daughter in financial peril and intense anxiety. And rage. Each time this happened, Sally promised herself that she would not rely on her mother again, but when the time came and her mother again became involved, Sally could not refuse because she needed the money. In turn, her mother needed Sally to navigate the world of English for her, to translate and explain bills, talk to doctors, and read official documents. She demanded these "services" from her daughter, and her aggression was fueled by her own anxiety, sense of inadequacy, and resentment over feeling dependent on her daughter. Sally's mother considered and openly described Sally as a child who "treated her own mother disrespectfully," who lacked gratitude, who was difficult, emotionally reactive, angry, and generally disagreeable. She always contrasted this view of Sally with that of her younger sibling who was the "good one," having adapted to her mother's volatility and unpredictability in a very different manner. In turn, Sally felt mistreated and angry most of the time, while silently developing self-hatred and a conviction that she was impossible to love.

Sally's relationship to her father was quite different. For many years, Sally considered him to be an ally in weathering her mother's moods and criticisms. She saw him as the reasonable one of the two, the person to whom she could turn in case she needed something. However, once her parents divorced, her father traveled a lot for work, and so Sally's relationship with him was largely based on fantasy, rather than real, lived, and shared experiences. Sally was close to 8 years old when her sister was born, so her teenage years were spent with very little supervision, while she was also put in charge of a toddler – because both of her parents had to work to make ends meet. Sally grew very resentful of this situation and started to act out; her grades did not suffer unduly, but she grew closer to a girl who ran into trouble with the law. They experimented with drugs, alcohol, and certainly with defiance toward any and all authority. At that point Sally's father was living and working in another city, away from the family, and, following a particularly vicious fight with her mother, Sally fled to him. He was going to be her salvation: she was planning on staying with him and finishing high school there. But her father, instead of taking her in, laid out the reasons for Sally to return to her mother and sister and simply sent her home. This was a shocking, almost traumatic event for Sally, who now felt completely trapped, having had her fantasy shattered of a father to whom she thought she could turn to. The lonely and vulnerable feelings created by this event accumulated anger and bitterness. Sally embraced a tough exterior and an overt feistiness; she grew fiercely independent, while her sensitive side became hidden, lonely, and fraught with fears and sadness.

By the time we met, Sally was in her mid-thirties and had matured considerably since her teenage years. She reined in her anger enough to get along with people at work; because she was also a competent, effective, hard-working person, she became quite successful. At the same time, she resented the fact that she ended up being the one who took care of others – including her colleagues, friends, and romantic partners. This resentment dated back to her teenage years, when she had to assume a caretaking role that was burdensome to her. In her thirties she was still unable to structure and partake in relationships so that they were more mutually satisfying and her own needs were met by others.

Sally has a strong voice, talks loudly, and is always full of opinions. She doesn't ask, she demands. Even more frequently, she blames and resents others for not giving her what she wanted – that which she hadn't been able to ask for in the first place. She felt strongly that authority figures were insensitive, incompetent, immature, and unpredictable. And while she couldn't stay away from them entirely, she resented her dependence on them and felt a lot of anger over having to do their emotional work for them. With her mother, she still has frequent interactions in which her mother is extremely critical, is then rebuffed by Sally, and then she becomes offended, calls Sally names, yells at her for being mean and disrespectful, and then cuts off all communication with her. During these episodes Sally tries first to reason with her mother, and then tries not to be affected. But each of these occasions brings up the lack of her other parent, as well as the lack of an ally – someone who would "have her back."

When thinking about this now, I wonder again about my dream. I wonder whether I was choked by my own frustration over the desire to spend time with my own daughter instead of Sally or to spend time with Sally as my child; that instead of accepting Sally and spending time with her in the way she was actually able to, I wanted her to change and (perhaps even magically?) turn into someone whom I could hold close, and who could relax into my arms after a tantrum, who – at the end of the day – is and feels safe with me, someone whom I don't have to defend against. I wonder whether in this way I resembled Sally's mother, who kept Sally at a distance, treated her efforts to have her needs met as inappropriate, her anger and disappointment as accusatory and suffocating. Perhaps, like her mother, I wished that Sally were simply someone else and not herself (i.e., more like her sister). Simultaneously it may have been also true, of course, that I resembled Sally when she experienced feelings of suffocation in response to her mother's aggression.

In the first part of the dream the forces with which we put pressure on each other locked us into a mutual embrace of some kind. No movement in the treatment was feasible because it felt impossible and dangerous for each of us to loosen our grip (defensive attack and counter-defensive hold). From my end, letting Sally get closer would have meant that I had failed to protect myself from her destructiveness – as she so often felt vis-à-vis her mother. From her end, I suspect that abandoning the attack would have meant isolation and giving up on seeking a connection altogether. With the loosening of my arm, two things happened: I made myself more vulnerable to her grip on my throat, and also caused an imbalance in her. She had been depending on my counter-resistance to maintain balance. She depended on me for keeping her away, feeling offended or angry, challenging and critical. It was expected that I would not take her in when she was in need, I would not risk closeness with her, and would not express my own needs and desires. As I stopped defending myself (unwittingly and unbeknownst to me – not consciously), I created a new situation in which Sally had to regain her balance in a new way. How exactly this was conveyed I am not sure – given that I did not directly share my dream – but something in my demeanor must have shifted. I could now see an alternative to the power struggle and mutual defensiveness. The second part of the dream formulated an experience that had never been consciously felt or expressed between mother and daughter (or father and daughter, for that matter). Perhaps her fingers on my throat were grabbing for words that never came, and her hostility (at least in part) was a reaction to being kept at a distance. Sally was not aware of how she was contributing to the dynamic of power struggles and to being disappointed by her mother. Neither one of them could acknowledge, either, how strong Sally's wish was for connection, understanding, and tenderness. All of this, of course, applies to the mother herself, because her own mother had been cold, distant, critical, and unavailable, from whom Sally's mother escaped by moving to the United States. She then transferred her own need for closeness to her daughter, but I believe her dependence and desire scared her. Thus, when either one of them needed closeness or experienced the fear of separation, it was communicated through guilt-tripping, blaming, and vindictiveness (i.e., in a form of anger, as a defense against the fear raised by the desire). In this way the actual need could be denied, and instead the focus could be on who did what wrong, who failed to respect whom, and who needed to be punished and how.

It is worth considering for a moment not just who I represented for Sally, but who Sally represented for me in the dream, given that it was the product of my mind with its own transference to her. Sally probably stood in for my own anger, which I was holding at arm's length because of my own disappointments and losses. It is possible that I have never let myself feel the levels of injustice, outrage, and bitterness that were oozing from Sally, and this made it more difficult for me to connect with and embrace her. She also evoked others in my life who were aggressive and dismissive toward me, and who I have been fighting off for a long time. Maybe the dream also spoke to my own sense of loss I have felt since leaving my own country. Our power struggle was definitely a way for both of us to avoid the much more deep and solemn tears that followed from feeling unwanted and unseen – and not knowing why. In fact, the second part of my dream may be seen as an elaboration on the first part: perhaps being choked was really about choking *up*. Perhaps we were both holding on tight and struggling hard (internally as well as with each other) to keep the tears away by closing our throats; these tears probably desperately wanted to well up but could have done so only in an embracing, open environment.

Sally originally came to treatment to "move on" following a break-up that had taken place during the previous year involving her boyfriend and her. During the previous year the boyfriend had moved to New York for work, and they decided that Sally would follow him six months later, leaving behind a close circle of friends and a well-paid stable job. Once she arrived, however, he seemed to have changed. He was depressed, elusive, not himself. Sally started to catch him out in lies, and when pressed, he admitted to cheating and wanted to break off the relationship. This was completely bewildering for Sally, who then fell into a depression. She took a job she didn't care for, and tried to make friends – in vain. She came to me mainly because she could not wrap her head around what had happened to her relationship, and her ex-boyfriend was not willing to talk to her or process it together. She felt completely left to her own devices and was lacking essential information to make sense of what had gone wrong. In other words, she was mystified why a man, who had been so important to her, for whom she had sacrificed so much, would leave her just when they were about to embark on a shared journey. How reminiscent of her failed trip to be with her father.

I believe that for years, Sally felt that our treatment was useless, because I was not able to tell her what went on in her ex-boyfriend's head. After a while she no longer felt ambivalent about the break-up itself, because she no longer believed that her ex-boyfriend would have been a good life partner for her. Still, she felt furious about how she had been treated by him – especially being lied to and being deprived of information so that she could not understand and learn from what had happened, and in so doing move on. Anger from her childhood, which returned in response to this more recent betrayal and loss, in addition to frustration at yet another incompetent authority figure (me), whom she was supposed to rely on, made her feel helpless, furious, and miserable.

Nothing changed radically or immediately after I had the dream either, but I did feel different with Sally in the room. I no longer felt suffocated, controlled, helpless, or angry; I felt freer to talk about whatever came to mind, including "weak" and vulnerable feelings, anxieties, and desires that people often experience. I stopped being afraid of being put down or otherwise attacked by her; I didn't brace myself for her rage any more. It took several more months to directly address specific reactions I had to her, but every time I did bring something up, we grew a little closer. Sally, in turn, began to "own" more of the destructive self-criticism as well as her intense aggression toward others; she began to see how her aggression protected her against more vulnerable feelings, and we both felt we could cooperate in talking about various challenges, interactions in her life, and intense feelings accompanying those challenges and interactions. When she did talk about losing her boyfriend, Sally sounded different and she also cried in a different way. In the first year of the treatment, her tears seemed to come from a dissociated place. She would talk about her boyfriend largely with anger, spite, and contempt, and tears just flowed silently down her face. Following my dream I noticed that Sally's sadness became much more pronounced and "present"; it was heavy and strong; the tears formed less of a continuous flow in the background or on the side; instead the crying became more occasional. When she did cry, her tears became central and more emotionally connected. In retrospect, I think that we first needed to work through her issues with her mother so that she could trust me, mourn with me, and then deal more directly with men and the feelings that they evoked in her.

Soon afterward, Sally emerged from her depression and began dating again. She went through a series of relationships in which her partners at some point became ambivalent and undecided about her and the future of the relationship. A clearer picture began to emerge in terms of how other people – especially men – experienced Sally, because other people also started to talk to her more directly. She was perceived to be strong, feisty, and combative; as demanding, but competent; someone who knows what she wants – a straight shooter. She grappled intensely with this image. Her experience of men as being weak, "not being together," and ultimately being disappointing prevailed for a long time, but slowly the connections were made between what she conveyed to them about herself on the one hand, and their fear and ambivalence toward her, on the other. We talked about what it was like for her father when she showed up on his doorstep. He must have been both intimidated by the task of taking care of her and (therefore?) also must have thought that she was perfectly capable of taking care of herself at home. He was blind or ignorant to the depth and the nature of conflict, intimidation, and pain that she had been forced to endure with her mother. We also talked about her own ambivalence about feeling dependent, and "appearing weak" – as well as the kinds of men she picked, those who were likely to affirm and validate her negative prior expectations. As the mystification subsided as to why her relationships turned out the way they did, it became a difficult challenge not to berate or despise herself for the role she played in these dynamics. Interestingly, she did not project this critical attitude onto me, but she dismissed whatever I tried to say about it, as when I advocated for greater self-acceptance. At that point we were able to joke about her dismissiveness.

These days I look forward to our sessions. I can argue more comfortably with Sally, and so I feel the need to argue less. We both trust each other more, and have more tolerance of our differences in experience. In the end I feel more like the mother and caretaker of Sally.

In the first part of my dream – and early on in the treatment – the power struggle and the mutuality of our defensive hold on (of) one another represented a kind of symmetry and lack of differentiation, which eventually gave way to an asymmetry in our positions and our roles, so that I could provide safety and she could relax more and focus on herself and her experiences. I do believe, however, that it was very important to first survive her grip by using all of my own strength, before I could open myself up to being vulnerable, which eventually shifted our dynamic. Sally's life has changed. Her most recent relationship, though, went through a long period of instability and ambivalence, and has lasted thus far. Sally is now married with a child on the way, and she plans on moving away from the beloved hated New York City, with all of its complicated memories: struggles, disappointments, and reclamations. She says she is now ready for a slower pace and more stability.

As I mentioned above, Sally did not have many dreams that she shared with me, and so I have decided to present our work together in relation to one of my own. I made this choice in part because I wanted to address more directly the role of countertransference in psychoanalytically informed treatments. These days I don't think it is too controversial to say that – following the interpersonal and relational traditions – we can conceptualize transference and resistance as mutually (and unconsciously) co-constructed phenomena. This means that as therapists we have access to the clinical process both from the inside through our own experiences and countertransferences, *and* from the outside by listening to the patient's experiences. Through this example of my work with Sally, I wanted to illuminate what it means in practice (at least for me) to work from the "inside out," in the sense of using my own (conscious and unconscious) subjectivity to serve the therapeutic process. The next example demonstrates even more clearly how my own reactions to the patient had to be formulated, recognized, and reflected upon to bring about psychic movement, and also how my own countertransference highlighted key aspects of other people's experiences in the patient's life.

The second case which I want to describe may be thought of as a short-term treatment or alternatively as an unusually extended consultation, in that the patient and I never committed explicitly to a set frame – even though our weekly meetings certainly functioned like regular sessions.

One day I received a phone call from an aging European woman who was worried about her husband, and felt that he would benefit from talking to a professional. She quickly described his symptoms, and in a worried tone asked what my thoughts were. I asked her whether *he* was interested in talking, and whether he was able to come to the phone. She answered that he did not want to talk on the phone, but that he also thought something was wrong with him and would like to meet. So I scheduled a meeting and clarified that if he is the patient he will have to speak for himself. She was deferential and agreeable.

When Mr. Z came in, I realized that he needed a lot of physical help. He appeared to be about 90 years old (he was actually 79); he had a very difficult time with simple movements, which he executed at an extremely slow pace. His wife helped him to take his coat off and led him to the couch in my office, then she kind of stood around looking a little lost. She appeared to be slightly younger than him, certainly in better shape, and I understood why she managed their shared life almost single-handedly. He did not seem capable of or interested in taking charge.

Once I was left alone with Mr. Z, something shifted slightly. He looked at me directly, and I felt that he was measuring me up. When I asked him why he was seeking help he described his symptoms very much as his wife had summarized them on the phone: his physical decline was recent and very fast. He had always been a very active person, and he was not able to function by himself anymore. He listed all the medical ailments with which he had been diagnosed and for which he took medication. None of these conditions were life-threatening; they added up to a general age-related deterioration. Some symptoms were still under investigation; the doctors could not give him a conclusive diagnosis and did not know how to cure them. All of this made him feel helpless and depressed. He said he was in a bad mood most of the time, did not feel like doing anything, did not feel like eating, and barely slept at all. He rarely left the house; he had little contact with people. He felt isolated, disconnected, and empty. These feelings had begun about two years earlier, when he retired – and his life had shrunk radically. Formerly, he had owned his own business, always making deals, supervising the work of his employees, always "on the go," seeking out the latest technology and new opportunities. He had been used to being the boss who looked after his employees and, of course, his own family. Two years earlier he had been forced to close up shop because he could no longer afford the rent, and he had to sell the business. He also sold his exquisite playing card collection, which he had built up for over 40 years. Two of his best friends died that same year, and others had moved away since. In a matter of months, his entire life (and lifestyle) – which used to feel fulfilling, involved, connected – changed. Then he fell ill and became virtually incapacitated very rapidly. After describing all this, he began talking about his wife with a lot of appreciation. Despite his chronic grumpiness and tendency to control everything, he said, she always stood by him, supported him, and now he could not even exist without her help. She accepted this, he said, with grace and understanding. He was grateful for her; she was the only thing he had left in the world, he said. He added a little later that he was also grateful for their son, who was doing well. He was head of a research institute in California, and had remarried – finally – to a nice, likable woman. A good woman, he said again, with a son of her own. But Mr. Z and his wife did not want to worry him with how bad things had become. I heard a whisper of shame in how he said it; it was their own problem.

As he talked, slowly, I felt more and more clueless about how I might be of help. I asked only a few questions, punctuating his story, to bring into focus the tremendous losses he had experienced in such a short period of time, and how he had been so used to operating like a very different person. The flat tone of his answers communicated that he had been through this kind of conversation with several other doctors, who had been worried about his emotional state and suggested that he see a psychotherapist. Mr. Z himself did not seem especially worried, and gave the impression that he was just doing his job by relating the facts. I did not hear volatility in him or any form of suicidality, but rather a complete lack of interest, a total helplessness, hopelessness, and disengagement, and an ongoing low-grade agitation over the frustration of how difficult everyday activities had become and, yes, how clueless the doctors seemed, and who, by the way, were the only people he talked to other than his wife. We set another appointment, and because it was so difficult for them to get around and because they had to travel for over two hours to get into Manhattan, I agreed to talk in the morning before each session to confirm or cancel, depending on weather conditions and his current physical state.

That night I had a striking dream:

> I was sitting in my office, and across from me sat a person, wrapped in a dark cloak, head bent down. I was leaning forward to see his face, and as I got closer, he lifted his face; the hood of the cloak shifted backwards, and suddenly the face of Death was revealed. It was a decomposing, skeletal face with glaring eyes looking straight at me. I gasped, pulled back, completely terrified – and was instantly jolted out of sleep.

There was no question in my mind that the dream was about my session with Mr. Z. First, I took it as a clear, visual symbolization of feelings I had experienced earlier in the day: that Mr. Z was dying; he had given up, let go because he did not see any reason to live. Facing his complete physical deterioration and imminent death had made me terrified and depressed while sitting in my office with him. The image of the decomposing skeletal face stayed with me for days. I was not sure that I could handle this new challenge; I was not ready to deal with all of my own feelings around death and loss – as I would have to if I were to continue working with him. I would have had to come up with something in the face of Death. For a while the terror and withdrawal dominated my response to him and my thoughts about working with him. Repeatedly, I imagined him being found dead at home by his wife; falling on the street; or sitting at home doing nothing, wanting to do nothing, being interested in nothing. All of it felt heavy and I could not feel my way through the helplessness; I could not think of anything to relieve Mr. Z's depression. I contemplated his defeat and the present pointlessness of those things that had been important to him in the past, the things that had constituted his previous life. Now there was nothing left for him, and his memories constituted loss rather than life. Implicitly I assumed that his physical deterioration was brought on by his psychological (and actual) losses; perhaps they were the physical manifestations of his emotional deterioration.

As I was brewing in these feelings, it occurred to me that Mr. Z was extremely lucky that his wife was not pulling away from him the way that I was.

She seemed involved, frightened but persistent, taking charge and providing all the help needed [...] keeping him around. But why would they, then, seek out therapy? It occurred to me just then that probably his wife felt (unconsciously?) precisely as I did. She probably experienced the same fears and sense of helplessness. I started to wonder whether I should talk to her as well, or include her in the sessions and treat them as a couple, because Mr. Z's depression might be very closely related to his wife "owning" all the dread and the fears and the feelings of being lost, as well as the energy and the subjective compulsion to act. And while I decided against the option of directly involving her in our sessions, I did start to contemplate Mr. Z in his interpersonal context.

When I had the dream about Mr. Z, we had already begun our individual therapy together. In the dream I had leaned closer to him, and I wanted to see his face. I did not let him simply hide under the dark cloak, which means that at some level I must have been ready to see what was underneath and experience the terror of the situation in order to work with it. Two other things came to me in relation to understanding the dream at this early point. One was that Mr. Z's face in the dream looked nothing like his real face: it was completely depersonalized and generic – and although I did not know much about him yet as a person, I began to wonder whether this was a reflection of some process that had been developing in him as well as between him and his wife. Because the face in the dream lacked flesh, it lacked idiosyncrasy as well. The features that make a face concrete and familiar were absent; it had become non-specific and unrecognizable. The *only* thing I could see was deterioration itself. This, I thought, probably speaks to his current experience of life, in that his life became almost unrecognizable, dominated by loss and lack. I imagined that his interactions with various doctors had exacerbated this feeling, because they looked at his body and commented endlessly on his physical decline, seeing him as one of the many people they examine every day.

The other thing I could not shake off about the dream was the pair of glaring eyes; these were in complete contrast to how Mr. Z spoke in session and the deteriorating, dying face in the dream. However, the glare was oddly reminiscent of the first time Mr. Z and I made eye contact in session. The eyes (Is) were far from being extinguished, empty, or disengaged. I had no good sense what feeling they were conveying, but they looked directly at me with some expectation. Perhaps this expectation was also terrifying to me. How can I measure up? What can I offer? One thing was certain: I would not be able to see more of him without also being looked at.

During the following sessions, each of which was scheduled individually at the end of the previous meeting, I was active and exploratory; I asked question after question – wanting to fill out the picture and transform Mr. Z from a symbol of death and dread into an actual person, for myself as well as for himself. In addition, I felt the need to "do" something – anything.

And so he told me about his present circumstances and his experiences of them in detail: his doctors' appointments and the frustrations that came with them, his worries about his house, his annoyance with the man who bought his card collection, his son's job of which he felt proud. We also talked about how and when he started to collect cards, what kind of a father he had been and would have wanted to be, how he met his wife, when and why he immigrated, and the ups and downs of his business over several decades. After a while I saw glimpses of the vital man he once was. He had been hard-headed and difficult to deal with, to be sure – very old school, but respectable. Mr. Z worked hard his entire life; he took obligations and responsibilities seriously, and he had accomplished a lot. He showed self-reflection and even humor from time to time. He did need a lot of nudging along the way as he told his story, running out of breath often – both literally and metaphorically speaking, but the pictured filled out slowly. Mr. Z was no longer hiding – and no longer a skeleton, either.

As he became more of a whole person to me, Mr. Z also became visibly more alive in sessions. I imagine this was because he connected to the lost parts of himself and because he was experiencing something new. By the pure fact of having to describe himself to a stranger (a young professional woman at that), not only did he become able to recount his life story, he also showed some motivation to depict his life accurately, and he even wanted to impress me. He was curious about what I was going to do with everything he told me. Whereas at home all his memories had been transformed into painful losses, things – like his card collection – that he no longer had, in my office these memories could come alive again and the mere act of describing them to me created a new connection between himself and another person. In turn, I witnessed not only what he had become, what life had turned into for him near the end, but also what it had been like in the past. We both realized in the telling that while he had had the chance, he used his personal resources well and created a meaningful world for others and himself. Paradoxically, the more he told me and the more he became my patient, the more he became my boss – paying me and supervising my work. I understood that at home he was quite literally decomposing; he did not and/or could not make the effort to pull himself together. With me he had to do so both physically and psychologically/mentally: he had to compose a story for me; compose *his* story; compose himself. He was not dead yet or anymore. And I did work hard for him.

After a while I wondered out loud what had happened to the man he used to be: who came to this country with nothing and built a rich life; who faced challenges head-on, and who always looked for and found solutions. This felt risky. Consciously, I anticipated him responding in a defensive way: being disappointed in me for not understanding the depth of his losses, his suffering, and helplessness. I expected him to lash out at me and say that he would obviously have found solutions if there were any to be found, and the whole point was that there was nothing to do anymore when everything had been lost. (No wonder his doctors felt lost and helpless, too.) I braced myself for his anger. Although I did not expect him to say so explicitly, I surmised that what he was feeling was that if he could no longer be the man he once was – competent and in control – he did not want to be a man at all. My suggestion that he try would be threatening to him, insofar as trying would just make him sink more deeply into his losses, and bring on a sense of failure and shame. I thought that maybe unconsciously he wanted to preserve his current situation in which he was actually looked after and in which he did not have to try – similar to a child.

But I asked my question anyway, despite these anxieties about his reaction. To my surprise, none of what I anticipated actually happened. Mr. Z did not defend his symptoms, he did not seem to be threatened, and he did not blame or attack me; instead he looked at me – bemused by my youthful ignorance and showing a little pride at being flattered. In retrospect, this makes some sense at least in the context of my dream. The dark cloak, representing his depression, could be lifted (shifted) because it was only covering what was underneath: a disintegrating body that housed a live spirit.

Over the next few weeks our conversations became unusually practical. To my surprise, Mr. Z's son had been trying to convince his parents to move to California for months (if not years), but this possibility had been categorically rejected by his parents. To my inquiry, Mr. Z explained that for that to happen, he would have to sell the house in New York, which he was not willing to do under the current market rate. This was his last possession and he was not willing to lose money on it, especially because he needed money going forward, and he certainly would not stand for his son paying his way. He added that he had never lived in an apartment before, and he was not about to start at the age of 79. And while his son wanted to be considerate, he did not understand the full burden of actually having two old people around to take care of when he also had a child to raise. He spoke strongly, articulately, with conviction and a lot of judgment – so I thought this is exactly where I should take him on and challenge him.

I began to see Mr. Z's initial depression as a result of an internal conflict: he had very much wanted to move to California on the one hand, but he did not want to acknowledge the necessity of moving on the other. Given that he had always been a man who took care of others, it was hard for him to face up to the fact – especially to his son – that now he was the one in need of help and care. From this angle, his main goal was to avoid the humiliation and shame of being seen in peril as he physically deteriorated. Hiding out in his house allowed him to remain prideful and to hold on to the last vestiges of his old, successful life and the illusion of living independently. While he could not remain independent of his wife, he sure could from his son.

Perhaps there is another layer. I suspect that Mr. Z would have been even more ashamed of his *desire* to be taken care of by his son (if he had been aware of it) than of his obvious deterioration and need for that care. The losses that he had recently endured actually made him freer – they opened the door to the possibility of something new. The loss of his friends, his work, his card collection all made him *lighter*, less tied to New York City by his circumstances. Moving to a warm place to be with his family and *not* having to work extremely hard anymore actually became possible, within reach. However, wanting to take it easy, rely on others, not to be the one who worries and provides for everybody else are all in direct opposition to how he had always lived his life and how he had thought of himself for decades. Allusions to his childhood gave me the sense that his counter-dependence was rooted in early traumatic events that he had conquered by assuming responsibility beyond his share; he took full charge of situations and made things work despite the odds. Releasing control would have been terrifying, yet inevitable if he were to move to his son's apartment.

In this context, my dream gained another meaning, a less concrete one. I think of the decomposing skeleton that was first hidden under the cloak as a metaphor of transformation. It was "easy" to react to Mr. Z's losses (losing flesh) as a horrifying, negative event, but it was also something that needed to be fully completed and be done with. Losing everything meant that he indeed possessed only the skeleton of the life that used to be his – only the bare bones. At the same time, the skeleton still provides a solid, supportive structure; he retained enough of himself and his family and possessions that he could move on and start something new. This brought into focus for me an aspect of the transference that was never made explicit. I think it helped Mr. Z that he came to see a relatively young, female therapist. My interest in him, and more specifically the man he used to be, may have facilitated the analytic process. It may have been revitalizing that he could form a new, intimate relationship with a woman. This may have been an important piece in contemplating moving to California to be with his son, and notably his son's new wife, with whom he would then be living in close quarters. As I dealt with my initial difficult countertransference, the daughter-in-law would need to do so as well, but now that did seem possible.

In summary, the transformation which Mr. Z was going through both in real life and in terms of his identity and self-concept had been extremely difficult (the death of an era), but it was not the ultimate end. In my dream, the decomposing person was sitting in my office after all, looking at me with aliveness and expectation – so ultimately has been enduring, perhaps even looking forward to going through changes as a result of therapy. Perhaps what he needed was to see and accept the possibility of living as a skeleton, a trimmed version of himself: that, although he could no longer be the full man he used to be, he would neither die nor become a child.

Our tone with each other had remained friendly and relatively free ever since my "risky question." I felt more comfortable broaching with him the ideas outlined above, and while he never directly picked them up and did visible, clear psychological work around them in session, I knew privately that he held on to them, because Mr. Z's depression started to loosen. He kept complaining, grumbling, and being agitated, but he also watched me working hard for him. He regained some control, and I kept some to myself: I required him to actually show up and to speak for himself; he couldn't relinquish all responsibilities to his wife or to me for his own well-being. He had to listen to and think about the connections I made for him, even if he didn't make them, and our expectations therefore became mutual for the treatment. The cloak shifted, because I searched for his eyes and because he raised his head; his decomposing face was seen, but his gaze was also met. He was then ready to be received by his son and daughter-in-law, I suppose, because he told me in a few weeks' time that he had put the house up for sale, although he felt pessimistic about the prospect of selling it at the right price. They were going to move.

After a few more sessions the first snow fell, and Mr. Z "put the treatment on hold till the spring," when it was going to be easier for him to make it into Manhattan again. He informed me over the phone, and it was significant that he called instead of his wife. I knew I would not hear from them again, either in the spring or later. Sometimes I wonder what happened since then, and what decisions they made; whether he is still around. As I am writing about him now, I feel the same bitter-sweet closeness that characterized our final sessions, and I know that I have to release him to whatever his fate holds, because he has already moved on from me.

As I wrote about the details of these two cases, I became increasingly aware of how subjective my point of view was in reconstructing the narrative of each treatment. Sally and Mr. Z most likely would have described, understood, and punctuated our work together very differently. As much as their experiences are always of importance to me, I cannot directly speak to them. I can speak, however, to the intimacy, the personal nature, and the depth of our work together, and using my own dreams as starting points enabled me to do this. Both of these people led me to difficult places in my own psyche while they were going through their own struggles, and I feel grateful to them that our conversations and emotional involvement convinced me – and not just them – that change is possible.

Commentary on Hunyady's case

The "see" between us – closeness and connection in psychoanalytic psychotherapy

Cory K. Chen

As I reflected on Orsoly Hunyady's chapter, an image of two people swimming in the sea appeared in my mind. As therapists, we may make a conscious decision to remain on land and look out on the sea that affects our patients – shouting instructions to them from the shore. Alternatively, as illustrated in Hunyady's chapter, one can dive into the water and navigate the waves with our patients. There are dangers and rewards in each approach. To remain on land may allow a therapist a broader view of what's happening, and sometimes what's coming; however, it may also leave a therapist removed and distant from the reality of the patient's experience. In contrast, diving in may bring the therapist visceral knowledge of the patient's experience, and affirm to the patient that the therapist is willing to be "in it with them." But this knowledge may be gained at the cost of a broader perspective on the changing conditions at sea. Diving in also places the therapist in danger of drowning in the same vortex of intense emotion that threatens to swallow up the patient. In addition, the patient's reactions may sometimes be unpredictable – clinging desperately, flailing, or, like Sally, choking the therapist out of transferential feelings of ambivalence at being saved. Diving into the sea with a patient is a riskier course of action but sometimes it may be the only way of saving another. It requires a strong swimmer, entailing both sensitivity to the patient's response to the conditions in the water as well as attentiveness to the therapist's own experience of the water. I know Orsoly well and I believe she would say that she does not know any other way to do this work than to dive in and swim as closely alongside her patients as possible. I also know that Orsoly is a very strong swimmer and the chapter provides a unique and valuable glimpse into what is involved in this kind of work.

Perturbations in the water

Swimming outside of the controlled environment of a pool requires sensitivity to the unpredictable forces existing outside the patient that impact them. For Sally, this included the discrimination she experienced throughout her life and her erratic and unreliable family. For Mr. Z, it consisted of the various losses he experienced and his confrontation with his own mortality. These events illustrate the pushes and pulls of the sea on our patients' lives. These aspects of their histories, societal and cultural forces, contemporary life events, and the inevitable developmental and existential issues which patients face represent the water and weather impacting our patients and also influence us if we choose to swim close to them. Sensitivity to the movement of the water can provide therapists with clues to how our patients are reacting to these conditions beyond what patients may articulate. By feeling the perturbations in the water, a therapist may have a sense of what the patient may be doing beneath the surface. Dreaming of our patients can represent an ultimate "diving in," as these deepened moments of intimacy and connections place patients in our most private and uncontrolled psychic spaces.

Orsoly's dream of Sally opens the chapter and illustrates this powerful process of using the therapist's sensitivity to the space between to navigate connection with the patient. What Sally *says* about her experience (i.e., what is seen on the surface), while relevant, belies the complexity of what is unseen. It is from Orsoly's dream that she comes into contact with these unthought knowns.

> Through the dream I finally became aware of how much I was affected by Sally, how intensely I felt about her anger, how impossible these feelings made it for me to express my countertransferential reactions, and also how intensely connected I felt with her, sharing in her struggles precisely through fighting to keep her at arm's length. I finally stopped pushing back against her push; I no longer needed to intellectualize and stay away from "us" and the touch that existed between us from the beginning – and through these changes we transitioned into the second part of the dream. I realized later, too, that in the dream Sally's anger – which I always experienced as a form of adolescent rage – became unconsciously associated with my younger daughter's tantrums which were frequent at the time and that often ended with us sitting on the dark hardwood floor of our apartment, with me hugging her while she cried. In that sense I brought Sally into my home, into my world; this was another expression of the shift in intimacy that the dream conveyed for me.

Similarly, for Mr. Z, Orsoly's dream provided clues to both his experience and what may have been going on between them in a way that I believe was only possible because Orsoly was "in it" with him.

> [T]he pair of glaring eyes; these were in complete contrast to how Mr. Z spoke in session and the deteriorating, dying face in the dream. However, the glare was oddly reminiscent of the first time Mr. Z and I made eye contact in session. The eyes (Is) were far from being extinguished, empty, or disengaged. I had no good sense of what feeling they were conveying, but they looked directly at me with some expectation.

Particularly with Sally and Mr. Z, both of whom lacked the capacity to articulate certain aspects of themselves, being in the water for herself became a necessary part of the process for bridging the psychic space between therapist and patient.

Knowing oneself

In order to swim with patients, particularly in stormier, more treacherous waters, therapists must attend to more than the patient's experience – they must attend to their own. It is only in understanding the interaction of self and other that we have a chance of making real contact with our patients. Orsoly illustrates this beautifully in the following passage:

> It is worth considering for a moment not only who I represented for Sally, but who Sally represented for me in the dream, given that it was the product of my mind with its own transference to her. Sally probably stood in for my own anger, which I was holding at arm's length because of my own disappointments and losses. It is possible that I have never let myself feel the levels of injustice, outrage, and bitterness that were oozing from Sally, and this made it more difficult for me to connect with and embrace her. She also evoked others in my life who were aggressive and dismissive toward me, and who I have been fighting off for some time. Perhaps the dream also spoke to my own sense of loss which I have felt since leaving my own country. Our power struggle was definitely a way for both of us to avoid the much more deep and solemn tears that followed from feeling unwanted and unseen – and not knowing why. In fact, the second part of my dream may be seen as an elaboration on the first part: perhaps being choked was really about choking *up*. Perhaps we were both holding on tight and struggling hard (internally as well as with each other) to keep the tears away by closing our throats; these tears probably desperately wanted to well up but could have done so only in an embracing, open environment.

I believe that these reflections on what the patient means *to us*, given *our* histories and *our* present lives, are critical to seeing them, particularly if one subscribes to the view that who one "is" may only be understood in the context of one's relationships. Thus, for a therapist to come into contact with a patient, that therapist must also know what the patient represents to him or her. In part from knowing her patient in this way, Orsoly was able to feel differently in the room with her, "less suffocated, controlled, helpless, or angry" and for Sally, her sadness, "became much more pronounced and 'present'." Thus, in finding a way to see each other, Orsoly was also able to find a way to relax and stop unconsciously fighting off the pull of the process. Swimming is often about remaining relaxed and allowing the process to unfold, not ceding control completely but also not desperately fighting for it either. By recognizing the meaning of Sally to her, Orsoly was better able to open herself up to the meaning of the waves between them and to a closer connection with Sally.

> With the loosening of my arm, two things happened: I made myself more vulnerable to her grip on my throat, and also caused an imbalance in her. She had been depending on my counter-resistance to maintain balance. She depended on me for keeping her away, feeling offended or angry, challenging and critical. It was expected that I would not take her in when she was in need; I would not risk closeness with her and would not express my own needs and desires. As I stopped defending myself (unwittingly and unbeknownst to me – not consciously), I created a new situation in which Sally had to regain her balance in a new way. How exactly this was conveyed I am not sure – given that I did not directly share my dream – but something in my demeanor must have shifted.

Reflections on modulating the inevitable distance between therapist and patient

Finding the proper distance is a dynamic process. Although I write about "diving in," a spectrum exists between remaining on land and dragging our patients to shore. Orsoly's work illustrates the ways in which one can both "dive in" but also regulate distance. With Sally, closeness often meant fighting and aggression, as it was her only way of remaining connected to her mother. Coming close and being "struck" by the patient was a way of getting to know her. By taking the risk of being in her grip, Orsoly came to know Sally's experience and thus what she needed. For Sally, a certain degree of distance allowed for growing trust. By Orsoly treading water nearby, Sally could come to feel they were in it together; without the pull to fight that comes with being "too close" and which distracts her from other aspects of her experience, Sally was able to look around and experience where she was more fully.

As I read about Mr. Z, I experienced both an appreciation of the good therapeutic work done while also wondering about the limits of our capacity to "see" and "know" our patients' experiences. Although both therapist and patient are swimming in the water, the water around each person is slightly different, particularly the further apart they are. And although the nature of the water may grow more similar the closer the two come to one another, regardless of how little distance exists between them, two swimmers remain separate in their experience. The waves change as they come into contact with each of their bodies and movements. And their bodies themselves are different and thus translate the movement of the waves into separate and unique felt experiences. Based on the case description, Mr. Z's time with Orsoly resulted in positive changes in mood, outlook, engagement with himself and other people in his life, as well as clear behavioral changes that moved his life toward meaningful activities – these are significant therapeutic successes on multiple levels. I also see the ways in which the work expanded who he could be with others through her efforts to get to know him by focusing on the particulars of his life and not becoming lost in his lack of specificity. And yet something about Orsoly's dream continued to nag at me as I read and reread it:

> I was sitting in my office, and across from me sat a person, wrapped in a dark cloak, head bent down. I was leaning forward to see his face, and as I got closer, he lifted his face; the hood of the cloak shifted backwards, and suddenly the face of Death was revealed. It was a decomposing, skeletal face with glaring eyes looking straight at me. I gasped, pulled back, completely terrified – and was instantly jolted out of sleep.

As with any dream, multiple and layered meanings exist. Orsoly engages a number of them productively:

> [V]isual symbolization of feelings I had experienced earlier in the day: that Mr. Z is dying; he had given up, let go because he did not see any reason to live.
>
> In the dream I had leaned closer to him, and I wanted to see his face. [...] Mr. Z's face in the dream looked nothing like his real face: it was completely depersonalized and generic – and although I did not know much about him yet as a person, I began to wonder whether this was a reflection of some process that had been developing in him as well as between him and his wife. Because the face in the dream lacked flesh, it lacked idiosyncrasy as well. The features that make a face concrete and familiar were absent; it had become non-specific and unrecognizable. The *only* thing that I could see was deterioration itself. This, I thought, probably speaks to his current experience of life, in that his life became almost unrecognizable, dominated by loss and lack.
>
> I think of the decomposing skeleton that was first hidden under the cloak as a metaphor of transformation. It was "easy" to react to Mr. Z's losses (losing flesh) as a horrifying, negative event, but it was also something that needed to be fully completed and be done with. Losing everything meant that he indeed possessed only the skeleton of the life that used to be his – only the bare bones. At the same time, the skeleton still provides a solid, supportive structure; he retained enough of himself and his family and possessions that he could move on and start something new.

Each of these interpretations was an avenue for engaging the patient in the experience of his life that opened him up to new possibilities for being with her and with himself. That said, after the dream, Orsoly writes,

> I was not ready to deal with all of my own feelings around death and loss – as I would have to, if I were to continue working with him. I would have had to come up with something in the face of Death. For a while the terror and withdrawal dominated my response to him and my thoughts about working with him.

Orsoly's reaction made me wonder to what extent *it is possible* to be in contact with certain aspects of our patients' experiences. As close as we may consciously be willing to swim to them, the conditions of the water may make it impossible to reach them, the patients themselves may pull away from us as we get closer, or we may find ourselves involuntarily "cramping up" as we approach the patient. Finally, and perhaps most importantly, we remain self-contained in our own bodies and minds, ultimately mysteries to one another. For all the good work that was done, Mr. Z seemed further away than many of the patients that I have heard Orsoly describe over the years. Perhaps this is even illustrated in Orsoly's use of the more formal (and distant) "Mr. Z" in contrast to the more familiar "Sally" (albeit a generational difference between Mr. Z and Orsoly may have contributed to a more formal/respectful pseudonym). However, I wondered whether Mr. Z, on some level, was communicating that ultimately there are limits to what Orsoly could understand about him.

> Mr. Z did not defend his symptoms, he did not seem to be threatened, and he did not blame or attack me; instead he looked at me – bemused by my youthful ignorance and showing a little pride at being flattered. In retrospect, this makes some sense at least in the context of my dream. The dark cloak, representing his depression, could be lifted (shifted) because it was only covering what was underneath: a disintegrating body that housed a live spirit.

Spirits are more difficult to come into contact with than bodies. Bodies can bump up against one another. They can be known and touched. In contrast, spirits are ethereal. They can neither be fully grasped nor seen clearly. Perhaps, with Mr. Z, that fact was highlighted in a way that with other patients we can more easily deny. In the face of death, aging, and deterioration, how much are we imagining through the patient our own fears of what may await us? I wonder if aging and confronting morality makes us face our own isolation and ultimately unknowable experience of the other. Orsoly ends her chapter with a similar conclusion: that "As much as their experiences are always of importance to me, I cannot directly speak to them." For Mr. Z, and perhaps for all patients, perhaps being fully seen was less important than being with someone who was willing to swim in the same water.

Chapter 9

A lost, depressed woman

Love, Narcissus, and Echo revisited

Carol Valentin

At the age of 11, I was one of seven children living in a five-roomed apartment in the South Bronx inhabited by my mother, my grandmother, and sometimes aunts and cousins. This was our fourth move since I was born in Spanish Harlem in 1954. My mother had moved us from borough to borough each time her intuition told her that the neighborhood was too menacing to stay. We had just left East New York, Brooklyn where, as in most inner-city neighborhoods, the tension of racism was rampant. The self-hatred fueled by racism caused people of color to turn on each other. Family-to-family annihilation was reminiscent of scenes in *The Godfather*. I did not understand the meaning of this, nor did I have a sense of how I would find it, but I was deeply aware of how I sometimes wished I would disappear. My light-skinned, green-eyed, Shirley Temple curled self made me adorable to Whites and Latinos trying to assimilate to the mainstream position. From this sadly "privileged" place, I watched my brothers and sisters suffer. It made no sense to me that adults called my sister ugly. She was told she was mean and would never amount to anything, while I was treated like a china doll, a cherished object by the adults around us.

My mother, a brown-skinned African American woman, spent most of her days and nights working as a domestic in the first years of my life. Sometimes we would go downtown past the barriers of East Harlem and she was often thought to be my nanny, not my mother. When she would clarify who she was I did not feel pride in her voice, but a diffidence which spoke of a feeling I now know as shame. I understood that the man she was married to was not my father and the silence that surrounded who my father was made it clear to me that my mother wished I had never happened. At the age of 11, I felt as if I was in a fog. I had stopped excelling in school even though I could read by the time I was 3. I felt lost [...] recurring nightmares of searching for my mother in a ghost town troubled many of my nights, until one day a conversation with one of my older brothers about God and psychology opened my world to Sigmund Freud. I thought my brother brilliant as we talked about the unconscious and, instead of doing homework which bored me, I helped myself to his library. I read Freud and Jung, and became enthralled with the idea of the unconscious. I felt suddenly alive as psychoanalysis took root in me. There was a way to understand the horrors of my external environment. I pondered "Civilization and its Discontents" and began to feel that I had a purpose. I could use this understanding to stop the hate. I knew little about my own self-hatred then but I was very aware of the hostility I felt from those whom I loved, the pain of seeing my sister wounded, and the pain of seeing her sadness turn to hate toward me much of the time. It was as if the clouds had finally dispersed and I could see a light.

Psychoanalysis became my first path to meaning. I would become a psychoanalyst. [...] Years later when I met my patient, a 37-year-old white female and only my second white adult patient, I was thrown back to a time and a place in myself where feelings of meaninglessness existed.

April

She looked frail but had a beauty that seemed alluring in the same way that pictures of Marilyn Monroe always felt to me. April did not look 37 years old. Her intake form stated that she had come for therapy due to severe depressive symptoms. As we talked in those first meetings there were times when I had a sense of her power despite the severely depressed state that she exhibited. She had little money and we agreed to meet twice weekly. April had been fired as co-director of a performing arts grant that was supposed to last for six months and she could hardly get out of bed. When she did, she would find herself in front of the computer researching the least painful way to commit suicide. Her father, a religion professor at a west coast university, would call her every day but could not sense how close she was coming to wanting to die. I had so many questions. Why did she come to New York? How did she find her way to the William Alanson White Institute? Did she have any friends here? Was she as alone as she seemed sitting in the chair opposite mine, in a very small, dimly lit room filled with books that were remnants of "The Whites'" past? Who and where was her mother? I remember myself wanting to know in a way that made me only partially aware of my countertransference in those twice-weekly meetings. April not only had one mother but two, neither of whom knew about her suicidal thoughts. She came to New York after a confrontation with the members of her dance troupe. Although she was the founder and art director of this very successful organization, she felt something shift inside of her when a community meeting turned into an "intervention." Suddenly she was surrounded by enemies – not friends – as her peers told her that they wanted to disband the troupe. They would keep performing under an acting director if she, April, would take a leave of absence, go into therapy, and figure out why she was such "a bitch." She acknowledged that in the last year her "bitchiness" had come to overshadow her talent, the talent that had made them all a success, the talent that had created this family of friends and peers that she thought closer than any of the members of either of her families. April felt enraged and betrayed but curiously denied feeling a sense of abandonment. Instead she spoke of vengeance, of how she planned to show them that they were wrong for ousting her. She would show them all by signing up to a project in the heart of New York City; she would show them that she did not need them but that they needed her and they would beg to have her back. When the art director in New York fired her after only two months, she, a premier dancer, was "thrown off," but this time she could not find her balance or her bearings. All she had was a profound sense of failure, a feeling that seemed alien to her very being. As she tried to think of reasons to stay alive she could not think of anyone who really loved her, except perhaps her father. She searched her soul for feelings associated with their relationship. They did not seem strong enough to counter the thought that there would be more relief in dying. The tape kept running in her head that she was a bitch, she was entitled, she was self-righteous, that while she had many accomplishments she had no one who really seemed to know her from the inside-out. Her father who had called her every day since she arrived in New York became concerned after asking her about her future plans and hearing that she had none. April always had a plan. He called a long-time friend in New York who suggested she go to the White Institute. Her father agreed to pay for "as much psychotherapy as she needed" but also told her that if she could embrace Jesus and Christianity she might find the real purpose of her life and would not need psychotherapy.

April's father taught religion at college level. He ultimately came to embrace the phenomenology of Christian Science. He met Miriam, her biological mother, after graduating from college. He was a scholar and spent little time socializing during college but somehow when he met Miriam he felt "free." At the outcome of a road trip they decided to get married. When asked by April what he saw in her mother she remembers her father saying that he was fascinated by her. Miriam had a rebellious spirit, she was pretty and not just carefree, she sought adventure, and she seemed unafraid of danger. He admired her for leaving her wealthy Jewish family who cut her off because she did not agree with their values. Very soon after marrying her, the bubble broke. The illusion of who he thought they could be together dissipated, but not before she had conceived. Her voice trails off during one session. "It's as if he never even knew her, as if she never really existed."

April was a heavy chain-smoker. I would pass her on my way to the William Alanson White Institute and sometimes on the way out as she took her first or last drag on a cigarette by the entrance of the 72nd street subway. Often in sessions I would picture a young child not only bruised but broken. There was so much that she did not know about who she was, so much she said that she couldn't remember. I ached for her. I wanted to piece her back together in a way that my analytic words seemed to fall short of. One day as I walked toward the subway thinking of the session we had just had, I encountered her at the entrance. I found myself touching her arm in an instance of tenderness that I could not quell. It was as if we saw each other in a way we had not experienced before. Moments later I was taken aback by my analytic misstep and wondered how I would ever tell my supervisor about this mistake. I remember feeling saved by our next session as I began by saying, "I am sorry. It must have felt as if that touch came out of nowhere. You looked lost and seemed so alone. I felt like I wanted you to know that I understood the pain you were in." April was silent for a long time but finally said, "I was not startled. It only made me aware that I had no memories of ever being physically comforted as a child." Although she had cried before in her sessions, this time seemed different to me. As I talked with my supervisor about this I was cautioned about acting on my maternal instinct. I was not to rob her of the opportunity to feel what it is like to be unprotected. I realized that the lonely, lost feeling that I connected to in her that day came from the memories of days when I too felt lost. Memories of my own mom leaving me lost and adrift were easy to access. My mind wandered back to scenarios of feeling abandoned. There I was just 17 years old being driven to college by my mom and the only person she knew who had a car. I had one suitcase and $15 and wasn't prepared for being left on the steps of Stone-Davis, my dormitory at Wellesley College. As I listened to the laughter of other girls and their parents moving in I sat immobilized. I finally had my own room, something I had wished for all my life, but it was empty and sparse, and I was alone. My mother never visited in the four years of my college career, not even when I had to be rushed into an operating room due to internal bleeding all night from a ruptured ovarian cyst.

It was about four months into the twice-weekly therapy that April's depression began to lift and the discussion regarding three times-a-week analysis began. April had landed a job as an executive assistant in a top-rated firm. She could support herself and her own therapy without her father's help. She had no doubts that while she had never worked in corporate she could use all of her skills to be the most competent executive assistant in the firm. It was her experience that everything she ever touched "turned to gold." She got all As in college and then a graduate degree in the performing arts from a highly regarded school. The brightly lit narrow room with a couch that we used to start analytic sessions seemed to allow for other parts of April to appear. I assumed the couch would make her feel more vulnerable, as it did me when I first lay on my analyst's couch but instead an anger in the form of vengeance toward the world and her parents took center stage. Prior to the couch when April spoke of the history of her father's marriage to Miriam, her biological mother, she appeared detached. As she lay there trying to remember herself as a young child with this mother, she had two distinct images in her mind. One was the memory of pure dread.

> I remember feeling very little, and feeling like I was going to fall off of the edge of the earth and that I knew she wouldn't save me. The only time that I felt safe was when she was baking in the kitchen; only then would I allow myself the freedom to play. I would pretend that I was the mommy, holding and clutching my little baby. I had to even imagine the baby because I had no dolls or toys to play with. We lived in a trailer park where children did not have toys. I dreamed that one day I would have children and a family of my own.

She drifted off. I asked, "What has happened to this dream?" She fired back, "Can't you see that it is dead in the water? No rings on my finger and no man that seems to think I am good enough to have children with." I said, "But surely there are other options, adoption or even being a single mother by choice." She said,

> Absolutely not. Adopting a child means you don't know what you are getting, and a single mother by choice is out of the question. I can only imagine the fragmentation, what it would involve. And how would I explain to the child that she had no father? If it cannot be a perfect set-up, then it cannot be.

April had no other memories of this mother between the ages of 4 and 12, with the exception of one. At age 4 April was sitting outside the courtroom on a bench, seeing her mother wave happily as the doors closed. She then saw herself walking toward a plane. This plane would carry her to her father. I asked if she remembered what it was like to have to separate from her mother. She said she remembered feeling nothing and was having a hard time picturing whether her mother was even there to say goodbye.

Miriam (the biological mother)

Talking about her biological mother during the beginning phase of analysis filled the room with a voice that sometimes did not seem to be coming from April. Holidays, birthdays – there was no sign that she had this mother or the siblings that this mother birthed four and eight years after April was returned to her father. Her father and her stepmother, whom she came to call her real mother, never spoke of her biological mother. It was as though everyone wanted to erase this part of her past. She was 12 years old when she was told that she would start having summer visitations with Miriam, her biological mother, for reasons she was still not clear about. As she approached her teen years she had vivid memories of summers with this mother. It was like being in a play where the mother is playing house and nothing is really real. Everyone in Miriam's life was treated like a pawn. She saw this most clearly in her mother's relationships with men. Some were even worse than pawns: she recounts finding out at the age of 23 that her younger sister had been sexually abused by one of her mother's pawns. He also liked to play house and, as her sister Linda told it, her mom Miriam would dress her up, have her put on heels and lipstick and walk around when Linda was 5 years old, as if in a theater, in front of the man Miriam chose to be with. One of the men would actually hold Linda on his lap in the living room while his penis grew hard. As April spoke of this atrocity she remembered that her younger brother on her biological mom's side told her that their mom wanted to know the size of his penis. Demystifying the pathology associated with Miriam seemed most helpful to April. She would often ask, "How will I ever be able to have a relationship with this woman? She is a pathological liar [...] there is something dark lurking within her." April had stopped talking to Miriam at least two years prior to beginning her treatment. "Miriam," as she called this mother, "has tried to convince me and the world that I abandoned her and so I have." I assured her that this was a place where we could figure it out together, and that I believed she would find a way to make a choice.

Life with Margaret (second mother)

By the time April was in her teens her second mother Margaret and her father had divorced. They had a son, John, not long after April came to live with them at the age of 4. But by the time she was 10 they were separated and filing for divorce. There was never any conversation about why things would change – they just would. Later, April learned that the conflicts started when Margaret used her savings to help her father hire a lawyer in the custody battle over April. It seemed that Margaret had never been able to forgive herself for it, April's father, or April. After this second divorce her father lived close enough so that Margaret could pick April up for visits and also continue a relationship with her younger brother. Margaret took April to the ballet, introduced her to cultural events, and taught her etiquette. She expected nothing but perfection from both of them. While April talked about Margaret as her real mom, I felt no warmth or affection in any of the descriptions of their interactions. April described her as anxiously neurotic and was clear that when she was with Margaret her job was to reflect the excellent "training that she had given her." She couldn't spill her soup at lunch, rip her tights in ballet, ever misbehave, or show aggression. Actually, it was as if none of the feelings that originated inside of April were important. She very soon learned to ignore most of them. She and her brother John were to be a reflection of their fine upbringing that their mother Margaret had given them. April did remember one instance where an aggressive outburst came out of nowhere. She was weighing in at ballet and was told that she was three pounds overweight. She remembered blacking out but was told that she had punched her ballet teacher in the face. I understood how this could happen, as I remembered my own aggression showing up out of nowhere after years of being aggressed against by my sister – the force of it causing me to slap her so hard that she fell to the ground. This, too, seemed to come from nowhere and was so stunningly powerful that my sister stopped whipping me whenever we were alone.

Six months into the analysis April showed few signs of depressive symptoms. Her focus was no longer on her two mothers but on her view of herself as having been dealt a bad hand.

> I never seem to get what I want. By now I should have been married. I had planned the perfect life and now all I am is some girl in New York trying to figure out what to do. I have no real identity anymore. I could have been

> anything I wanted, but I am here feeling angry and adrift. I cannot even find a man who seems attracted to me and I am getting older and fatter by the minute.

The first six months of the analysis felt intense but I was in my element. Having been a child psychologist for 20 years, empathic attunement was the name of my game. Finding ways into her internal world, giving her a way to understand that her depression and sense of emptiness was connected to trauma and her mother's pathological projections seemed natural. But my supervisor, of course, had much more in mind. I was to begin to challenge the idea that she was still the victim. I would interpret her defense of externalizing blame. The complaints about her mothers were valid and my empathic attunement helpful, but her holding on to the idea that the world had dealt her a bad hand would never lead to finding the meaning that she hoped to find or the healing that I hoped to give. I had to help her see that she was participating in her own disappointing outcomes, that the world was not only unfair to her but that the world was unfair, period. It was up to her to take responsibility for change and I was there to help her own her responsibility. As I tried to wonder with her what was behind her need to see herself in these ways, she came back at me with a rage that I am sure her colleagues felt when they tried to confront her concerning her entitled attitude. The more I addressed her obsessional defenses or tried to point out that her relationships in the here-and-now had everything to do with her and the ways in which she had to defend herself in her past, the more combative she became. There were sometimes glimpses that she was aware of something going on in the room between us, but they were few and far between. One example of this was the time when she arrived agitated and commenced to complain about her living situation. She told of her anger and disappointment with her roommates. She is the one who has to keep everything going, she has to keep the apartment clean, to keep the cable bill covered, to keep the landlord on top of fixing the holes in the ceiling. "Can't anyone do the right thing? I am always picking up the pieces of somebody else's mess." I wondered with her about how it was that she could talk about feeling failed by everyone but never talk directly about her feelings toward me. Was I included in those who have failed her? "It feels like you want me to feel your anger but not attribute it to anything that is happening between us. Sometimes it feels like I am your audience and that you are playing out your feelings as if you have a script." April responded, "Well, I am used to being on a stage. What is so difficult for you to understand about that?" I had no counter. There is silence as the session ends.

April started the next session. She did not lie down but faced me and said,

> Last session I felt like I got the wind knocked out of me. I remember everything you said about my anger and how it felt scripted. It felt like the truth. I was angry but in a way that I wasn't even conscious of [...] I realize now that I don't have a way to be angry with someone without wanting to squish

> them – I am an expert at knowing how to humiliate someone in a way that allows me to keep my dignity intact. People may not like me but they will respect and they do fear me – I make myself right and the other person into an asshole.

"You were quiet for a long time before leaving last week. Did you worry that I would retaliate? Could that be why you have chosen to sit up today and not lie down?" I asked. She replied, "I don't know how I was feeling about you in the moment, I just know that I felt exposed to the bone." We were quiet. She looked away and then said,

> But why would I trust you not to retaliate? My real mom was a dangerous person who crushed the fantasy of life and living. My second mom Margaret used me to protect her from her own toxic anxiety, and my father attacked my character whenever he saw my pain.

Toward the end of the first year of analysis and for a considerable time after, I spent much of the time dodging bullets. April felt that after more than a year in therapy I should have been able to assist her in finding and sustaining a relationship with her ideal man. She wanted me to give her instructions. The more I pointed out that the answers resided in her as much as in me, the more frustrated she became. I can recall very few sessions other than those in the early part of her treatment where it felt as though we were emotionally engaged and in the room together. This was very different from anything I had experienced as a psychotherapist – a disconnect that was hard for me to comprehend.

In my attempt to explore her history of relationships with men in depth I was surprised to find that this was a part of her identity to which she seemed quite in touch. She told me with pride that with regard to men she did not feel vulnerable at all. As she talked about her late adolescent and young adult life, my perception of her and herself in the world switched from victim to aggressor. Romantic relationships were clearly experienced through the lens of power. She described herself as a high school student, being a cheerleader who ran with college boys. She knew she was beautiful then and she felt the vitality in her sexual being. "I knew that boys would do anything for a girl who was titillating even if she were not typically pretty. I loved the game of having them pursue me so that ultimately I could tell them to go 'f---- themselves'."

At that time her sexual prowess worked well for her. By the age of 25 she found herself in the middle of a wealthy crowd, pursued by a handsome, rich, older man. She had never really talked about shame in her sessions but as she described this relationship, I was suspicious as to why there was none. She was in touch with a grave assault that she described as changing her life. Contracting genital herpes from this man took away the "best part of myself. When he told me that he had given it to me intentionally, I felt a core part of myself shatter." April blamed herself for not being astute enough to see that he was a sociopath.

But she proudly spoke of the ways she yet found to avenge herself, which "brought a part of his empire crashing down." I asked, "Is this why you feel you cannot attract a man? Does having herpes make you feel you are unworthy?" She replied, "No, not really. Eighty percent of the population has genital herpes. It is really no big deal. It is the world that makes it something shameful – ignorant, stupid people who know nothing about what it really is." In spite of her pronouncement, it felt like a dissociated part of herself that she still hated.

By now, my analytic supervision had come to an end and I was on my own feeling as though I had made very little difference in her life and not really sure where either of us was headed. Her feeling of vulnerability seemed to return when she began to talk about the one man in her life who she felt she truly loved: a loss which she still felt devastated by.

Two years after she contracted herpes she fell in love with Bruce, a man who also had herpes. He was perfect, romantic, smart. They had many breakfast-in-bed mornings and many sexually exhilarating nights. She was sure they would marry. In her words, "we were made for each other with one or two exceptions." He was disorganized, he loved to set her tests, and he did not want her to drink wine. Her compulsive nature allowed her to fix the first problem. She organized his closets, his kitchen, his study, and so on, but there was one problem she could not fix. Not drinking wine took some effort but she felt he was worth it. She knew this meant that there was a part of her that would be harder to reach, as when she drank she was clearly much less inhibited. "He liked giving me tests, challenging my intellect in order to be sure that we were a perfect match. But one day he asked me about the meaning of life. I told him I didn't have an answer." She wasn't sure about her purpose in life. She had not really thought about life that way. She knew she had planned a college career since the age of 5. She knew she would be successful, marry, have beautiful children. She had not really thought about the meaning or purpose of life in that way. April was just happy to be with him. Soon after he asked her this question he ended the relationship. He told her that he couldn't reach her, that she did not know how to be vulnerable. She was confused and devastated. Months later he met, impregnated, and married another woman. The pain of this loss was still felt by her but was entwined with a memory of an even deeper pain.

> When he left me, and my dad found me sobbing in my room, he screamed at me to stop and when I didn't, he became furious. I begged him to understand that I was hurting, that my life seemed to come to a halt and that my heart was broken, but instead the argument grew tumultuous and his anger became out of control. It ended with my putting my hand through a glass door.

She remembered the blood streaming down her hand but couldn't remember how she got to the hospital. I told her I realized the terror in all of this and she responded by saying that it wasn't terror she felt, but torture. No matter what was happening to her, whenever she became emotional her father demanded that she stop. "All he worried about was that I might end up dead like his mother. His memories and pain of her suicide were more alive to him than I ever was." April's rage at her father's being self-absorbed was a part of every session that involved their past and present interaction. He would say, "You have the wrong approach to life, you need to learn what it is like to be compassionate to others. This would be easy if you would only open yourself up to learning about Jesus." This was always the rub: the one thing she kept from her biological mother's heritage was that she maintained that she wanted to be Jewish. Her devotion to her mother's culture fascinated me and I found myself remembering a moment in my life when a wish to explore my father's Jewish heritage suddenly emerged. This new curiosity arose after I had my first child. As I worked on planning his christening and choosing godparents, I was pleased to feel that my very close friend, a warm and loving maternal figure who happened to be Jewish, would make the perfect godmother. When she turned the offer down, telling me that our cultural differences would not allow for it, my heart was broken. I struggled with what she meant and shortly thereafter found my interest in seeing that part of my heritage disappear. It was as though someone had slammed a door on a part of myself that wanted expression and was about to surface. Was April's fierce pride in her Jewish mother's identity the result of a reaction formation? Or was it her only way to defy her father's wish to obliterate parts of herself? It gave me pause and I wondered about my own fierce loyalty to my African American identity. Would it have changed if my friend had not sent the message that I was not allowed the privilege of "entering in?" It had been three years since April had taken leave of her performing arts family but she seemed not to think of them often, or they of her. She continued the connection by editing their brochures and contacting art directors in New York who wanted them to perform. The one relationship she longed for was with her younger sister – the only person besides her lover Bruce whom she felt she truly loved.

In her third year of treatment April complained that she was getting older, fatter, and less desirable by the minute and that therapy had not helped her find the real meaning of her life, nor had it helped her find a sense of purpose. She still felt that she had no way of connecting with a man, that neither of her mothers had given her a roadmap on how to be a woman that a man could love. "How can I be a woman that men want? Sweet, demure and non-threatening." I had the feeling that she was mocking me. I said, "It's as if you think I have the answer and I am withholding it from you." She answered back, "No, it's like every other woman has the secret and no one has ever shared it with me." As she told me of her attempts to date I pointed out that she seems to be attracted to men whose psychic energy was really not available to give her the love she needed. They already had a girlfriend, or children with whom they had visitations, or took themselves and their jobs too seriously. It felt to me that the outcome was predictable and that while she might see herself as trying to date, her choices allowed her to keep her vulnerability out of the equation. She said,

"It feels like you are blaming me. You are saying it is my fault like everyone else. You are supposed to be helping me, not blaming me." I replied,

> I would like to help you. It's as if the part of you that has been hurt and bruised is unwilling to take risks with men who might really be able to connect to you. You are so sure that you will be rejected by these men that you unwittingly set the stage by going after men who aren't interested in getting to know who you are at all.

She was silent but I felt she was withholding. I asked, "Can you tell me how or what you are feeling right now, what it feels like in the silence?" There was no answer.

The following Monday the session was stormy. She started by telling me how she could do nothing over the past weekend. She lay in bed and watched television while her sister and friends went out. She didn't understand why she was becoming depressed again. She was sad; she felt empty. I wondered aloud whether her sadness had to do with feeling that I had let her down. She said that all she knew was that in the beginning she felt transformed by coming to therapy but it was as though the transformation did not stick. She had felt understood and cared for in a way that she had never felt before, but now she felt differently. "So you feel that I have not been able to change you, or that I have changed somehow?" She said, "I feel like I change everyone and that eventually people withdraw from me." She started to talk about her work life and the decision she made to work for the more powerful senior partner and how she hated every aspect of her job. She was really his personal assistant and not in the position that she thought she would be in. But there were times when she felt that he respected her. "He seems to need me in some weird way." I asked her if she thought she was avoiding talking about what she felt was going on between us. She retorted that there was nothing going on between us and asked why I always thought it was about me. I felt that I had made the cardinal mistake as an analyst. Not only was I beginning to feel like the bad mother but now I personified the bad father as well. I felt stuck as if I must move this negativity out of the way, but I continued down the wrong road. "Do you think you chose this man because you wanted him to give you the praise and acknowledgment that your father never did?" April shot back, "And what if I did, don't I have a right to get my needs met somewhere?" The more she complained that her life was empty, the more I dreaded the sessions. She would ask me about books on the bestseller list that I had not read or articles in *The Times* that I had not seen. Had I seen the debates last night? No, I had not. Increasingly I felt the sting of being different, less competent as a person and a professional than she was, less articulate, less well read, inferior, of no use to her. These feelings took me back to my own history and I felt as though I was in the room with my sister but did not realize how angry I was becoming. It did not occur to me that any of these feelings should be brought into the room with April.

We continued to both stay in the cocoons of our dissociated states. As she talked about her envy of her brother's wife for having just had a child, a woman who happened to be black, I began to feel as though there was a cold war going on between us and that the analysis was in grave trouble. As I spoke about this in consultation, I became in touch with how my feelings of inadequacy and her ways of projecting her inadequacy onto me seemed to take away my power to infuse affective life within the interaction and the room. April felt helpless and incapable of bearing the emptiness she felt. I was sharply aware that I could not save her, just as I could not save my siblings from their despair. The guilt was still in the room with me. I remembered the weekly beatings I received from my sister or someone in school who envied me. I realized once again how the depression in my past was tied to my self-hate and my inability to fight back, to the anger at my sister and others in my culture who took their hate out on me. It felt as though this was happening to me now and that I was becoming more impotent each moment we spent together. And I was the one who was supposed to help her make meaning out of what we both were experiencing now.

Four years into the therapy I found myself fantasizing that she would leave, take me up on an offer to seek consultation with a more experienced analyst. Once I found myself asking her if that was how she felt. She replied,

> I doubt anyone can do much better, but it doesn't surprise me that you too would want to leave me. I knew you would come to the conclusion that I was insufferable and abandon me. If I can't trust my own mother, who can I trust?

I became defensive but actually felt my first analytic supervisor in the room, her confidence, and something she once said to me came to mind, and I said this to April: "You could learn to trust yourself, have respect for the decisions you make, to take risks, despite the outcomes and fear of rejection." She replied,

> I don't know what decisions you are talking about. I have been coming here, working my ass off, trying not to be alone in the world and I still feel like I have the mark of Cain. The universe dealt me a bad hand and it cannot fix me, so whatever made you think you could?

The hurt must have finally registered on my face as the session ended. I could tell that she was seeing behind my mask. I felt vulnerable and sad, and perhaps even ashamed. The following Monday I told her that we knew her depression is one of the ways in which she deals with her anger and that it is so much easier to turn the anger on herself than it is on someone she genuinely cares about, especially when she thinks she may have hurt someone. I told her that I suspect she is choosing to hurt herself as opposed to trying to destroy me, but that this time her anger is warranted, especially if she was feeling that I was no longer present, or, worse, that I wished she would just go away. As she lay on the couch she had a memory of her natural mother and how she once told her that if her younger sister had been defective she would have left her out on the ice to die. She wept and so did I.

A month later there was a shift in business as usual. April informed me that she knew the thing that she wanted most in life, the only thing she ever felt truly coming from herself. She wanted to be a mom. As much as she hated her job and the experience of being treated as a narcissistic object by her boss, she was learning how to establish boundaries so that she can still perform competently in spite of his assaults. Besides, she realized that it offered her one thing that being an artistic director had not: health insurance – health insurance that covered artificial insemination. She was now 41 years old and if she were ever going to have a child she would need to start now. There was a man in her life before the herpes. He was older and they still had a connection. In fact, over the past few weeks she had been thinking of him a lot. She felt that he had loved her, but his drinking and his explosive behavior had pushed them apart. They were still friends and as her birthday approached, she was remembering one of her birthdays that they had spent together. He had made a cake for her and they sat on the bed looking at pictures of children all over the world. It made her both sad and happy but he held her and she felt what she liked most about him: his ability to be tender. He was in a relationship now but she wanted to ask him whether he would be interested in being a donor.

He lived on the west coast. She had already called him and they agreed to meet when he came to town in two weeks' time. Meanwhile she did what she did best and researched clinics, found the best doctors, and dove into this project full steam ahead. One of the things that had come up in her search was information regarding an acupuncturist who helped prepare women for the procedures by helping them remove any toxins from their bodies. She would have to meet with her twice weekly. She also looked into alternative medicine and found that one way to prepare her body was to begin a steady regime of acupuncture to have a healthy normal pregnancy. The meeting with the former lover did not go as expected. Whereas he wanted very much to be a part of this experience, his partner, a religious woman, could not seem to wrap her mind around it. April wasn't devastated. Instead her grandiosity kicked in. She would use a sperm bank and this would give her a sense of control that always made her feel on top of the world. She was especially interested in the IQ of the donor, his education, his height, and weight. She wanted to give her best shot at having the smartest, most congenial, high-achieving baby that anyone could have. At this point we had been seeing each other twice weekly and there was more than one time when she had to miss a session to make one of the many scheduled appointments either with the clinic, her doctor, or the acupuncturist. I began to feel as though I was being replaced when she described how wonderful she felt after each session with the acupuncturist. It was as though she had found the ideal mother – someone whose actual touch I could not possibly compete with. The thrill of it all did not last for long. She was able to conceive, but the pregnancy, like transformation in analysis, did not stick. Fifteen months and three miscarriages later, thoughts of suicide were creeping back into her internal life and the consultation room with me.

April said, "I was at the clinic and they changed my doctor without giving me notice. I felt trashed. I went to the park and just sobbed. If I can't have this baby I might as well disappear." I said, "I know that this level of despair takes you to a very dark place." She replied,

> Yes, I am finding myself thinking of suicide. I have no plans to actually commit it, but I think about how it would play out – who would cry, what would change. Nothing ever changes for me. I have taken risks like you said I should, but the outcomes are never like they are for everyone else. I find myself waking up in a meaningless, empty void. I am making more money than I ever dreamed of. I have it better than most people in life but I continue to suffer.

I replied, "I do understand your despair but at this point we need to understand why you are invested in holding onto your anger and giving up on yourself and other options that are still available to you." April then said, "I don't even know what that means – I only know that life feels worthless and it is starting to look like I will have the same outcome of never getting what I want." I replied, "You want to have a child and there are ways for you to have a child if you cannot birth a child." April said, "I want to be a mother, not a caretaker, and when I die I will have a legacy, something to be remembered for."

Here we were again [...] my trying to make her see the possibilities – my feeling stuck and beginning once again to feel as though I have failed her. I had had at least two consultations in addition to my analytic supervision and I could not believe that I was here with her in a hopeless state [...] I searched myself for what was missing, thought about my training and the work that had inspired me. If I could get in touch with how I found my way out of feeling lost, perhaps I could instill hope in her as well. Or, if I could get in touch with her anger without it tripping my own fear of annihilation [...] I sifted through the memories of articles, theories, supervisors, seminars. I found myself going back to the beginning years of my analytic training, as well as to the more recent ones. There were two pieces of work that I feel saved this analysis. The first was written by Phil Bromberg called "The mirror and the mask." Bromberg quoted Bach (1979):

> Bach describes what it feels like from behind the analyst's couch, talking into the wind or writing on the sand only to have one's words effaced moments later by the waves. The patient either welcomes or resents the analyst's words and frequently does not even register the actual content. A session which seems to have led to a certain understanding or experience of some kind may, 24 hours later, be totally forgotten.
>
> (Bromberg, 1983, p. 74)

Bromberg (1983, p. 75) goes on to say:

> The individual tends not to feel himself at the center of his own life. He is prevented from full involvement in living because he is developmentally stuck between "the mirror and the mask" – a rejected appraisal of himself, or a disguised search for one, through which the self finds or seeks affirmation of its own significance. Living becomes a process of controlling the environment and other people from behind a mask. When successful it is exhilarating; when unsuccessful there is boredom, anxiety, resentment, and emptiness. But the critical fact is that an ongoing sense of full involvement in life is missing, often without awareness. The intrinsic experience of accomplishment is transformed into one of manipulation, exploitation, and a vague feeling of fooling people. A state of well-being becomes the goal of living rather than its characteristic quality, and the moment-to-moment sense of being has little relevance other than as a preparation for the next moment. Existence becomes either a search or a waiting period for that moment not yet here when real life and true love will begin. The present is always imperfect in and of itself.

I felt as though she was Narcissus and I Echo, and that our fates were surely entwined. April began to say that she wanted to stop therapy, at least for a while. It was too hard to come twice a week. She could not tolerate failure everywhere in her life and coming here twice weekly when nothing was changing made no sense to her. I tried to interpret her resistance as a way to distance herself as she felt more and more vulnerable and disappointed in her life. I told her I felt that I was in a custody battle, that her acupuncturist, someone who could touch and hold her physically, felt more real to her now. I told her that I was indeed going to fight for her in a way different from her biological mother because I had a love for her that was different from her biological mother's. She listened very carefully and before she decided that she would actually take a two-month leave of absence we had one pivotal session. April was no longer on the couch. She came in and sat up. She said that the last session had meant a lot to her, that she heard me and was touched. She wanted me to know that she was afraid in here, afraid to be vulnerable with me: "I feel like I am going to have a meltdown, one so bad that I will end up screaming, sobbing, and lying on your floor. I can't let myself get to that place." I asked, "What do you think I will do if that happens?" "I truly have no idea," replied April. I said,

> I will pick you up and wrap my arms around you and neither of us will break. I am strong enough to survive your anger, your feelings of loss of control but if you feel you must leave, I will be here when you return. We must keep in touch weekly. I need to know what is happening to you.

In the course of the two-month break she was again able to get pregnant but once again lost the baby. She came back. April planned to try to get pregnant one more time. She had also decided that she was going back to the west coast. Her sister had given birth two years ago and April wanted to be close to the child. She said she came back to therapy mostly to work on intense feelings of self-loathing and self-hate, feelings that she was in touch with during her two-month hiatus but she wanted to come only once a week. I felt distressed at this request. I wondered with her if this feeling might be hiding other feelings, the hatred that she might be feeling toward me for somehow having failed her. She began to listen and then to agree that if she allowed herself to think these thoughts they would indeed make her even more miserable. I countered with the idea that if we could again be in the room together while she was thinking these thoughts and she could tell me about them, we might have a different experience together. April agreed to come back twice weekly until her planned move back home in six months. She wasn't giving up. During the two-month break she was able to allow herself the thought that her sister could be the surrogate for one of her fertilized eggs. As she talked in sessions about her hateful feelings toward her mother and toward me, I was able to feel them and not dissociate them. She became more and more open to experiencing the genuine feelings of caring that I had for her. She was sick during one session and I talked her through what she needed to do. My epiphany about how to be present for April came when I remembered another fine piece of work written by Lawrence Epstein (1999) called "The analyst's 'bad-analyst feelings'." He writes,

> Spotnitz understands the main basis of psychopathology [...] to be the problem of imploded murderous aggression. [...] The primary task therefore is to work not with the resistances to the liberation of object libido but very gradually with the resistances to experiencing and putting into words destructive aggression which is imploded and directed against the mind and the self.
>
> (p. 317)

Epstein continues:

> From this perspective, it can be seen that the negative countertransference experience generated by patients presenting primitive mental states becomes our main instrument of therapeutic leverage. If we can own this experience and inhibit our urges for riddance, retaliation, and counter-projection, if we can address this experience for its informational value, and if we can succeed in determining what the patient needs us to do with our negative feelings, we shall, in effect be performing over what Sullivan called the long haul of therapy, 'a maturation ally corrective, facilitating task which no previous care-giver in the patient's lifetime has either had the knowledge or the will of the capability to perform. [...] All of the internal work that the analyst does with his countertransference – inhibiting retaliatory impulses, holding the patient's evacuated mental contents in consciousness long

> enough to submit them to processes of reverie which cleanse them of their toxicity – is akin to the internal work that the good-enough mother does in both surviving and maintaining her connection to her baby during those episodes in which she "becomes the target for excited experience backed by crude instinct tension."
>
> (p. 43)

As I read this passage over and over again I realized that the break from April allowed me to process the hate in my countertransference; it was the same hate I must have had for my sister, the same sense of being devalued that I felt with my mother which was being dissociated in ways that I had yet to realize. I could now return to the work with a new intention, one of feeling my feelings and encouraging her to feel hers toward me in the present. This transformation of myself by myself enabled new things to happen between April and me. There we were, both in the room, she somehow trusting that she could allow herself to openly hate me and the process of treatment, I also allowing myself to be openly criticized. I could feel her hostility and my own anger at being the object of her attacks. I believe this aspect of her treatment not only changed me as an analyst but changed a part of who I was in my personal life. I began to grieve the relationship that I would never have with my sister as I realized that I would always represent the unprocessed split of hated aspects of herself. I began to see that the process which freed April began with her being able to direct her hatred outward toward me, her symbolic maternal figure, and not have me shrink, withdraw, or become the mask of an analyst that I thought I needed to be. I believe that her body and her mind began working to perform a miracle. Still, I must admit to an act on my part that stood in contradiction to an aspect of my belief in analytic method and technique. I believe that I am free to talk about this now as I end my journey at the White Institute.

When April returned and talked about her last and final attempt to conceive via IVF, I was conscious of a piece of information I had held for at least eight months, thinking it inappropriate to bring into the treatment. A friend had told me that she knew an alternative medicine acupuncturist and professional who had been amazingly successful in helping women in their mid-forties conceive and have their first child. I kept telling myself that I was not her mother in reality and that it would be inappropriate to pass on this recommendation to her. The week before she went to have her fifth and final IVF session I felt that to not give her this information would be experienced by me as a true empathic failure. In spite of my fear that my fellow analysts would see this as a true acting out of my maternal transference, I took a leap of faith. April followed up on my suggestion to see him. He was hours away in New Jersey but she made the appointment, rented a car, and she got there. His method was very scientific. He looked at her bloodwork and explained that there was an imbalance that was not allowing her to hold her fetus. She had a chance of holding this baby if she followed a new nutritional regime and took supplements that should change the balance of her biochemistry. While she did not have the money to take his supplement regime she took his references, took his notes, and planned a do-it-yourself protocol that she would follow. And then we both prayed. When she made it past the danger point and was able to hold the fetus to full term, we felt joy, but I feel we also felt love. She started planning her trip back to the west coast where she would have her baby in the fall.

Before she left I asked her what she thought had changed in her over the course of treatment. She responded by asking me what I thought had changed in her. Were we still Narcissus and Echo waiting by the pool? Without fear and trepidation, I told her that I thought she had become genuinely open to experiencing her vulnerability, her sadness, and her anger in a way that opened the path and allowed her to let others love her. She agreed that there was a dimension of herself that had changed – that she had finally let down the wall and allowed me to love her. Her friends had said that she had softened and she felt a new part of herself open up. After six years of work I felt we were saying goodbye when we had only just begun the real work of analysis. We continued the work via phone over the first three years of her beautiful little girl's life. There were struggles as she rode the waves of single motherhood and times when she needed to understand her own narcissism in order to provide a positive mirror for her child. Time constraints and financial concerns eventually brought our work to a close. I hoped and believed that the "good-enough mother therapist in me" had replaced the harsh, punitive mother that she had once internalized and that the joy she felt as a mother would sustain them both.

References

Bach, S. (1979). On the narcissistic state of consciousness. *International Journal of Psychoanalysis*, *58*, 209–233.

Bromberg, P. M. (1983). The mirror and the mask – On narcissism and psychoanalytic growth. *Contemporary Psychoanalysis*, *19*, 359–387.

Epstein, L. (1987). The problem of the bad analyst feeling. *Modern Psychoanalysis*, *12*, 35–45.

Epstein, L. (1999). The analyst's "bad-analyst feelings." *Contemporary Psychoanalysis*, *35*, 311–325.

Commentary on Valentin's case

A therapeutic dyad in search of a third

David Braucher

This case presentation describes a clinician's evolution from being stuck in one of the potential pitfalls of the developmental/deficit model of psychoanalysis to resolving the enactment through the deft use of some key concepts of the interpersonal model. At the outset, we are struck by the analyst's earnest desire to re-parent the patient, April, by making up for her lack of good-enough mothering. We are also impressed with the analyst's dedication to helping April find meaning in her life. This approach appears to be very effective for the first six months of treatment; it lays the foundation for a strong therapeutic alliance. However, it appears to have run its course once April is stabilized and in a new job. As the analyst writes, "I can recall very few sessions other than those in the early part of her treatment where it felt as though we were emotionally engaged and in the room together."

One might wonder what corroded the ties between April and this analyst dedicated to remaining empathically connected to her patient. What was interfering with this dyad's ability to remain engaged? Is it possible that there are limits to the powers of empathy and therapeutic ambition? Edgar Levenson (private communication, June 9, 2015) would say yes to both. Empathy is always based in *our imagination*. We *imagine* what the other is experiencing from their words, tone of voice, and other physical manifestations of emotional expression. We internalize these and *create* an experience within ourselves, which we only *imagine* mirrors the other's internal experience. As for therapeutic ambition, we can go back as far as Freud (1912/1958) to find cautions against any desire to cure our patients.

Apart from these admonitions, we all approach our work in a manner that suits our personality. Hirsch (2003) states that our preferred therapeutic theory is a reflection of our countertransference. Thanks to the analyst's self-awareness and generous self-disclosure, we know that she suffered significant deprivations and abuse in her own childhood. Consequently, she identifies with April and imagines that April longs for the same empathic maternal presence which she, the analyst, had wanted as a child. Klein (1975) tells us that it is reparative for *us* to experience ourselves as giving to another what we did not get in our own childhood. However, Lacan (1977) reminds us that every identification is necessarily a misidentification; the experience of identification is based in an image that cannot account for the other's depth and complexity.

Once April was no longer in her initial regressed depression, she seemed to reject the analyst's self-prescribed role as good mother. April's anger at this point may have been, in part, an iatrogenic reaction to the analyst's continuing to assert her desire to mother her. We know that April felt coerced to conform to her stepmother's desires that April reflect her stepmother's self-perception as a good mother with well-behaved children. Could April's anger be a result of sensing that she was being encouraged to be vulnerable in a way that would gratify the analyst's desire to feel like a good analyst/mother?

The analyst's theoretical approach informs her that April needs help to access her vulnerability in order to release her anger. From this perspective, the analyst interprets April's combative attitude as a form of resistance. After all, it does impede the analyst's ability to experience herself countertransferentially as a good mother. One wonders whether April experiences this dynamic as a loss of self as she is seduced to collapse into an empathic merger within the therapeutic dyad. April states, "I have no identity anymore." Perhaps the combative tone is an attempt to establish a sense of separateness, a self that would allow her to develop an identity and the meaning for which she longs.

The supervisor must have sensed something along these lines as she cautions the analyst to beware of giving in to her maternal instincts. The supervisor encourages the analyst to confront April regarding her immature perspective on fairness. The supervisor is proposing a perhaps more paternal stance vis-à-vis April – to represent the reality that life is unfair. In response to this intervention, April becomes combative, and the analyst experiences "a disconnect." It is unclear if the "dissing" of their connection experienced by the analyst is occurring interpersonally between her and April, or *intrapersonally* between the analyst's experience and her desire to feel like the good mother/analyst. Anger can be disrupting but also enlivening, and a very powerful form of relating and connection. Moreover, we later learn that April was actually connecting with the analyst in a profound albeit disturbing manner. April was triggering the analyst to relive the painful abuse of the analyst's own childhood – abuse that she suffered without the presence of a protective paternal presence.

The analyst rightly questions whether the anger April was expressing regarding others was in fact a displacement of April's feelings toward the analyst. However, by putting this question in the form of whether April feels that the analyst has "failed her," the analyst seems to be inadvertently expressing her own feelings. She feels that she has failed to make April a less angry child because she is not a good-enough mother/analyst. The analyst may have come across as asking for reassurance rather than conveying a willingness and even a desire to have April express her anger directly toward her. This experience would have allowed April to learn the limits of her omnipotent rage and render the analyst available to her for *use* as a real object (Winnicott, 1971). Instead, overwhelmed, the analyst feels that she must "mask" her hurt, robbing the interpersonal field of a potentially enlivening dynamic.

Constrained in her role as good mother, the analyst doesn't provide April with a reflected appraisal of what it is like for her to be in the room with April's anger. It is no wonder the analyst feels like Echo[1] – she has rendered herself without a voice. One wonders what it would have been like for April to experience the analyst as a spontaneous real other, someone to bump up against and experience the limits of her omnipotent anger. Demonstrating that she was willing and capable of tolerating April's aggression would have put the analyst in a position of strength, a potentially protective paternal presence.

Classically, the father is the third to the mother–infant dyad. He allows the child to experience the limits of her claim to the mother's affections by pulling the mother's attention away from the child. He also provides an alternative attachment figure facilitating separation and individuation. According to Lacan (1977), he represents the symbolic order, a necessity for the creation of symbolization and meaning in life. By interfering with the infant–mother dyad, he instigates the creation of transitional space by helping to create the paradoxical experience of simultaneous separateness and togetherness. This is necessary for a triadic form of relating where meaning becomes possible, as space opens up between symbol, symbolized, and an observing self (Ogden, 1992).

In an attempt to help April experience a sense of meaning in her life, the analyst draws attention to the transitional play April remembered from childhood – she used to play at being a mother. Later, April seems to make an escape into health by taking up the analyst's earlier suggestion that April can find purpose and meaning by becoming a parent by choice. While pursuing pregnancy, April decides to separate from the analyst by taking a leave of absence from treatment.

The analyst uses the separation to reflect on her need to change to meet the needs of her patient, a necessity for any successful analytic treatment according to Levenson (1982). For help, she turns to a theoretical third in the form of articles by Bromberg (1983) and Epstein (1999). When April returns, the analyst is able to relinquish her good-mother stance and brings her own voice into the room. She engages with April's anger allowing for an enlivening interpersonal experience.

After April gives birth, the child becomes the third in the room allowing the analytic space to truly open up. The analyst encourages her to reflect on her narcissistic attitudes toward the infant. While they both imagined that a child would provide the meaning in April's life, it occurs to me that the child provided the possibility for the creation of meaning by opening up the transitional space and making triadic relating possible. Now, April and the analyst were afforded the paradoxical experience of separateness and togetherness simultaneously.

Disclaimer: It is possible that this is how I see the case because, as a boy, I struggled in growing up with a single mother who devalued men and who wanted to be everything to her children.

Note

1 The analyst adopts Bromberg's (1983) use of the Echo and Narcissus myth to illustrate the experience of feeling voiceless with a narcissistic patient. Looking at the larger context, Echo is rendered relatively voiceless as a result of not speaking the truth to Hera regarding her husband's philandering.

References

Bromberg, P. (1983). The mirror and the mask – On narcissism and psychoanalytic growth. *Contemporary Psychoanalysis*, *19*, 359–387.

Epstein, L. (1999). The analyst's "bad-analyst feelings." *Contemporary Psychoanalysis*, *35*(2), 311–325.

Freud, S. (1958). Recommendations to physicians practicing psycho-analysis. In *The Standard Edition of the Complete Works of Sigmund Freud*, Vol. XII (pp. 109–120). London: The Hogarth Press. (Original work published 1912).

Hirsch, I. (2003). Psychoanalytic theory as a form of countertransference. *Journal of the American Psychoanalytic Association*, *51S*, 181–201.

Klein, M. (1975). *Envy and Gratitude and Other Works 1946–1963*. London: The Hogarth Press.

Lacan, J. (1977). *Écrits: A Selection.* New York: Norton.

Levenson, E. A. (1982). Follow the fox – An inquiry into the vicissitudes of psychoanalytic supervision. *Contemporary Psychoanalysis*, *18*, 1–15.

Ogden, T. (1992). *The Matrix of the Mind.* London: Maresfield Library.

Winnicott, D. W. (1971). *Playing and Reality.* New York: Basic Books.

Chapter 10

Rejection by a boyfriend

From idealizing transference to "real" partner

Jenny Kahn Kaufmann

In treatment, patients can develop an idealizing tie to the analyst that serves adaptive, developmental, and defensive functions. It is challenging for the analyst to understand these functions and to know how to respond in an attuned and appropriate way at different points in the treatment. Below, I am going to present a case where I was presented with this challenge. This patient may be seen as pursuing some mild version of the "reparative quest in her relationship to me and in what she wanted from the treatment."

Marie-Helene came into treatment following the break-up of a relationship. She was surprised she felt so badly about this, as she hadn't realized how attached she was to her boyfriend. Although Marie-Helene had achieved a high level of professional success as a radiologist, she had encountered difficulties in her work relationships that reflected the problems of growing up with a mother who was distant, accomplished, and devaluing toward her. Initially, Marie-Helene was admiring toward me, and loved coming to sessions to talk with me. She experienced me as worthy of her esteem and admiration. She appreciated the intimacy of our connection. She felt that I was looking out for her, and that I was supportive of her without being competitive or leaving her feeling badly about herself. She thought that I was able to relate to others because I was a helping professional. I was able to help Marie-Helene quite a lot in her relationships at work with colleagues and superiors, so that she was able to work out relationships where she could hold onto herself and take other people into account. Marie-Helene was overjoyed, as she felt she had better, more mutual relationships here than she had ever had before in her life.

In the context of her increased interpersonal success, Marie-Helene seemed to believe that I knew what to do in every interpersonal context. She started coming to me for advice about how to handle her relationships at work, and how to handle relationships with narcissistic friends who weren't able to take her needs into account. In the transference there was a subtle shift from admiring me to viewing me as an idealized object, someone who had magical powers. While I understood there was more to it, I had the sense that I was helping her by compensating for her mother's lack of involvement and interpersonal obtuseness.

While Marie-Helene did feel more stable in her workplace, she continued to have difficulty in her romantic life. Even though men were attracted to her, they found her to be aloof and/or too controlling. Or, if they did like her, Marie-Helene found fault with them – they didn't have the right credentials, they weren't good-looking enough or, if they were, the chemistry wasn't right. When we explored why she was finding fault with the men or the personal situations, she slowly revealed that she worried that if she didn't find fault with them they would ultimately find fault with her because of her deficiency and flaws. She indicated that she wanted to be more like me, apparently secure and confident interpersonally.

Because of her insecurity, Marie-Helene dated sporadically and went through long periods of time where she holed up and stayed totally focused on work. I made efforts to question and explore the basis for her insecurity. She was able to relate it to painful experiences of being criticized by her mother and rejected by several boyfriends. She began to wonder whether her mother's criticisms were warranted, or whether the boyfriends had been acting out their own issues rather than really evaluating her. Still, she remained feeling insecure and wondered aloud why I couldn't teach her to be more like me.

After this session I was feeling uneasy about her idealization of me. While her yearning to have me teach her to be more like me reflected the lack of closeness and guidance with her mother, her desire to become just like me sounded as though it reflected a wholescale rejection of herself. It was as if she couldn't trust her own capacities and judgment. How could I help her develop this trust? Perhaps I had to help her address and work through the traumatic situations she had experienced with her mother and various boyfriends. She seemed to be utilizing her idealization of me to stave off re-experiencing and better integrating these very painful moments, and I believed she had to integrate these moments in order to become truly centered in herself. In addition, she seemed so out of touch with her own assertiveness and, with it, her own desires and even her aggression. I thought I should be inquiring about these aspects of her at the right time. Again, she was probably using her idealization of me to avoid experiencing and manifesting these aspects of herself.

Having reflected in this manner, I resolved to shift my approach from questioning to finding tactful ways of inquiring about the defensive functions of the idealization. In the next session I brought Marie-Helene back to how we had concluded our previous meeting. I remarked that she had ended the session by saying that she had wanted me to teach her how to be me, but she seemed to be making that request because she was having difficulty dealing with her painful feelings about traumatic experiences in the past. While I appreciated how her request reflected her desires to be close to me and to feel guided by me, I was concerned that if I simply complied with her request I might very well be leading her away from herself and her own experience. I thought it might be more helpful to her and really help her get grounded in herself if I supported her in better understanding these painful experiences. Marie-Helene looked surprised after I articulated this and objected that going back into these experiences would just make her feel bad and probably worse about herself. I agreed that she might experience old pain but thought that ultimately she would feel better for it and even be able to call into question some of the long-standing negative views she held about herself.

She shrugged and wondered where to begin, but soon she began to talk about various moments in her childhood when she had taken the initiative to do what she wanted that was outside what her mother had explicitly prescribed. Her mother had both yelled at her and grounded her. She remembered several times wanting to go out with friends after dinner to parties, to dances without washing the dishes first, and her mother would routinely berate her for her self-indulgent laziness and forbid her to go. Marie-Helene remembered once trying to sneak out of the house to see her boyfriend after curfew and being caught as she walked down the driveway by her fuming, wide-eyed mother who then decreed that she was grounded for the next month. While recounting these memories, Marie-Helene seemed to be feeling more pain. Afterwards she explained how sad and angry she felt about how her mother had tyrannized her. I totally understood, exclaiming that her mother had really tried to crush her independent spirit. In response, Marie-Helene sobbed more deeply, exclaiming that she had almost succeeded.

Over the next weeks of sessions, Marie-Helene described several more painful relationships with previous boyfriends and how they had rejected her. She outlined a pattern in which she had tried very hard to do what she thought would be pleasing to them, but each time they ultimately decided to stop the relationship, explaining that they just didn't have enough of a sense of her to be able to continue. Each time she had felt devastated, believing that she had done everything possible, not knowing what else she could have done to make these relationships work. I reflected that it sounded as though the issue wasn't what she needed to do for them, but how she needed to assert herself more with them. But that had been very hard for her to do because her mother had given her such a sense that her initiative and assertion was bad. Hearing this, Marie-Helene broke down and wailed: "Given all this, what hope do I have?" I said, "Look, I know how you feel but just because your mother had such trouble with your initiative and assertion doesn't mean that other people will."

Subsequently, as you might gather, Marie-Helene began to assert herself more with me. She began questioning comments and questions that I would raise in sessions. Raising reasonable objections and stating her preferences about what she wanted to talk about, at times she indicated some anxiety about how I was reacting to her assertions. We processed her anxiety in terms of how she was assuming that I would react in ways that her mother had done. She also began coming late to several sessions, citing important commitments outside of the treatment relationship that she also had to respect. I saw these moments of lateness as tests of whether I could be accepting of her involvement elsewhere or whether I would react like the outraged mother in the driveway.

Sometimes I inquired about them, sometimes I didn't, and finally I wondered to her if she was being late to let me know that she had involvements outside of the treatment that were also important to her and she was trying to see if I would accept that. In response, she quipped, "It's about time, which I'm saying as much to myself as I am to you." As the culmination of her testing around time, Marie-Helene called me up one evening to say that she was being kept at work by an emergency and she would have to do the session over the phone. Otherwise she'd have to cancel it altogether. At this point I was losing my patience with her shifting the frame and I told her that I really wanted to meet in person for the session. When Marie-Helene came in, she was more enraged than she had ever been with me. She yelled,

> How could you expect me to come into a session when I had to deal with an emergency at work? Hadn't I been dutiful enough in coming to almost all your sessions, even though I was sometimes late at times? Can't I ever catch a break? What is your problem? Why are you so rigid?

When she said that, I saw red. "What? I have been so understanding about all of your latenesses. I ask you to merely come to a session and this sets off your rage?" But Marie-Helene wasn't backing down:

> Sure it does, and this is only the beginning. I'm the Attending now on my unit and I have to supervise the residents who are going to be on call over the next three months, and that means I may have to miss or change a number of sessions. How are you going to react to that if you can't even make an adjustment about this emergency?

Suddenly I was taken aback and I took a step back, realizing how embroiled I was with her. We were back in that driveway and I was warming up fast to be as bad as her mother. The good thing was that she wasn't backing down and expecting to be grounded for the next three months. She was standing up for herself. So I did my best to calm myself down and I said simply, "Okay, you're right. I have to appreciate your situation. But you have to understand also how you've been pushing me." For the remainder of this session and over the next couple of sessions we processed what had happened during this enactment. Subsequently, we did negotiate modifications in our schedule that included several agreed-upon cancellations. Soon after, Marie-Helene began taking a more active role in dating. Here she chose men who she was interested in getting to know better, and she took the risk of asserting her opinions and desires on these dates. At times she did go overboard in wanting the dates to go her way, seeming a little like her mother had been in relation to her. Still, she was able to reflect on these dates with me and gain insight into how empowered she felt when she took the assertion of power beyond mutuality. Her relationship with me and her relationship with men are definitely works in progress. But she has made great progress in terms of having her life become grounded in herself and her own sense of agency.

In conclusion, I have presented the case of Marie-Helene illustrating how she and I developed an idealizing transference and then addressing the defensive functions of this transference state so that she could become more centered in her own experience and more able to take the initiative and be assertive in her important relationships. Her evolution of an idealizing transference in relationship to me may be seen as an example of the reparative quest. In admiring me and trying to be like me, she was attempting to undo the painful disappointments she had experienced with her distant and critical mother and the devastating rejections she had experienced with various boyfriends. Addressing the defensive functions of this idealization in a tactful way at the appropriate time did help open up the treatment.

Commentary on Kaufmann's case

Transforming the reparative quest in the transference

Peter Kaufmann

Traumatized patients like Marie-Helene may begin treatment by developing an idealized tie to the therapist that reflects a reparative quest (Kaufmann, 2012). We term this pursuit a reparative quest because the patient is attempting to experience a relationship with the therapist that will undo significant traumas from the past and secure the future against the threat of re-traumatization. This pursuit may be seen as having developmental and defensive dimensions, with the patient seeking to make up for meaningful experiences that were missing in childhood and protect against the re-experiencing of painful affect associated with childhood trauma. In its self-protective aspect, it reflects and reinforces the patient's disavowal of significant formative trauma.

When patients like Marie-Helene engage in a reparative quest in the transference, they respond to the therapist's empathy by constructing the analyst as a reparative figure that will compensate them for childhood deprivations and thus undo the painful effects of formative trauma. With therapists like Jenny who respond supportively to the patient's reparative striving, patients can feel as though they are having compensatory experiences that are making up for developmental deprivation. Yet, at the same time that the patient's compensatory striving toward the therapist has a developmental aspect, it also uncannily repeats the patient's traumatic past in ways about which the patient and therapist are less aware. This disavowed repetition is linked to all the painful affect associated with formative trauma. Thus, in responding to the reparative quest in the transference, the therapist faces the challenge of how to accept and affirm its developmental aspect while also addressing its defensive function in terms of protecting against the re-experiencing of formative trauma and the painful affect linked to these events. As occurs with Marie-Helene and Jenny, I have found that therapists become aware of the repetition in the reparative quest and its connection with defense against trauma at points when the patient goes "too far" in terms of pushing for their version of compensatory experience. Then, the therapist awakens to the repetition of formative trauma in which she is participating and begins to reflectively question its functions. As Jenny does, the therapist then has the opportunity to appreciate how the patient is using this repetition to both represent formative trauma and prevent a full affective awareness of it.

Through applying this insight, the therapist can craft interventions that address the self-protective functions of the patient's reparative strivings toward the therapist and gradually facilitate the patient's reckoning with formative trauma and better integration of these experiences. Usually this integration process involves a combination of mourning the traumatic past and taking the risk of seeking corrective experience inside and outside of transference. Overall, the therapist facilitates the therapeutic transformation of the reparative quest by combining reparative provision with the full processing of developmental trauma. The therapist potentiates this result by responding empathically to the developmental and defensive dimensions of the patient's idealizing fantasies as each emerges more in the foreground of the therapeutic relationship.

At the beginning of treatment, Marie-Helene and Jenny co-construct a reparative tie in which the developmental and adaptive functions are more in the foreground. Marie-Helene hungers to share her experience with Jenny, apparently seeking a sense of Jenny's interest and involvement. In reaction, Jenny is empathically responsive to Marie-Helene's experience, reflecting it back to her in a way that conveys her grasp and acceptance of Marie-Helene's perspective and her genuine concern for her welfare. As a consequence of this quality in their connectedness, Marie-Helene comes to admire Jenny as a helping professional who can guide her in solving her problems, particularly involving her interpersonal relations. Marie-Helene also indicates that she sees Jenny as being such a guide because she experiences Jenny as being concerned and involved without being self-interestedly critical or competitive like her mother. Thus, she hopes Jenny can guide her effectively in a way that her mother failed to do, providing a much-desired opportunity for her to be supportively affirmed by someone in whom she believes.

In the context of this felt support, Marie-Helene seeks Jenny's guidance in approaching her work conflicts and uses Jenny's coaching in mutuality to both hold onto her own perspective more while also considering the viewpoints of others. She is thus better able to negotiate her work relationships. This therapeutic benefit also provides Marie-Helene with a reparative experience in the transference, as it represents Jenny's being a helpful coach in contrast to her mother who was either uninvolved or critical.

Overjoyed by her success in her work relationships and by her compensatory experience with Jenny, Marie-Helene shifts from admiring Jenny to idealizing her. She sees Jenny as knowing what to do in every interpersonal situation so that she brings all the issues she experiences with her friends and potential boyfriends as well as her work colleagues to treatment and endows Jenny's interventions with the aura of magical power. Marie-Helene indicates that she wants to become more like Jenny as a way of overcoming the extent of her insecurity. Most aware of the beneficial reparative effect of Marie-Helene's transference, Jenny uses Marie-Helene's dependent openness to further her analytic understanding of her insecurity.

Then, Marie-Helene "goes too far" by wondering why Jenny cannot teach Marie-Helene to be just like her, clearly articulating her desire for Jenny to teach her to be just like Jenny. In response, Jenny awakens to the repetitive element in Marie-Helene's idealizing transference state and its defensive implications. Jenny senses how much Marie-Helene's request also reflects a devaluation and even a wholescale negation of her independent will. While she doesn't articulate her formulation, I think Jenny now sees that Marie-Helene's fantasy of becoming just like Jenny does not merely represent a developmental desire to become like an admired figure. It also reflects an implicit accommodation (Brandchaft, 1993, 2007) to her mother who criticized and attacked Marie-Helene's assertions of independence and conveyed that Marie-Helene should stay with mother and be "just like her" instead. Following these realizations, Jenny has an empathic reverie in which she appreciates how she used idealizing fantasies toward her father to accommodate to him and protect them both from facing how hurt and betrayed she had felt by him. Then, grounded in her reverie, Jenny is able to conjecture about the defensive functions of Marie-Helene's idealizing fantasies, positing how they protect her from fully facing her annihilating experiences with her mother and mobilizing her self-differentiating self-assertion.

In the following session, Jenny uses this rich, empathically based formulating to question Marie-Helene's idealizing fantasy of becoming just like Jenny, suggesting poetically that it could lead Marie-Helene away from herself and her experience and serve to protect Marie-Helene from integrating her traumas with her mother from which she derives her insecurity. Although initially resistant to what she sees as the depressing implications of Jenny's suggestion, Marie-Helene follows it. She explores her traumatic history involving her mother's annihilating reactions to Marie-Helene's assertions of adolescent will. Here, she not only recovers the memories but experiences fully her feelings about it. Marie-Helene also recognizes how these experiences have led her to inhibit her authentic self-expression with her boyfriends.

This part of the treatment may be seen as a period of mourning which can occur when the defensive functions of the reparative quest are addressed in the treatment. Frequently, this period of mourning gives patients more fluid access to the diverse range of their affective life, including their emotional vulnerability and their assertive expansiveness. Marie-Helene's mourning culminates in a moment of despair as she sees the link between her difficulty asserting herself with her boyfriends and the crippling impact of her mother's attacks on her will. She feels hopeless; can she ever change? Here, Jenny makes another significant suggestion, indicating that interactions can be different with people other than her mother, including her boyfriends and her therapist. This suggestion implicitly encourages Marie-Helene to take more risks in asserting her independent initiative in her other relationships. As we will see, Marie-Helene takes this leap and uses it constructively. While Jenny doesn't elaborate on her rationale for making this mobilizing suggestion at this point I wonder whether she did, and that it was effective because she had an intuitive sense that Marie-Helene's mourning had sufficiently readied her to take more risks with her expansiveness.

In choosing treatment topics, in expressing her different opinions, and in changing the treatment times, Marie-Helene becomes the willful child and adolescent that she couldn't be enough of with her mother. In the process, she tests out whether or not Jenny can affirm her independent initiative or whether Jenny, much like her mother, will take offense.

Overall, Jenny sees what is happening and maintains the right balance between being the self-maintaining and frame-preserving authority, and identifying with Marie-Helene's limit-testing self-assertion. Again, she uses reverie to enhance her identification with Marie-Helene's foregrounded self-state when she feels strained by the degree of Marie-Helene's testing. She succeeds in giving Marie-Helene a freer rein and surviving, enabling Marie-Helene to rework her grim convictions about the negative consequences of her independent initiative.

When matters come to a head between them about Marie-Helene's resentful coming to the session, Marie-Helene and Jenny do go toe to toe in a moment that could have re-traumatized Marie-Helene, putting her back in the driveway with her enraged mother. Yet through her ability to de-center and self-reflect, even in the heat of this overheated moment, Jenny is able to facilitate a different outcome of the enactment. This powerful experience represents the ultimate test of Marie-Helene's negative expectancies about others' responses to her self-assertion, especially women in authority, and thus serves to really reassure her that others can respond differently than her mother to her authentic self-expression. Subsequently, Marie-Helene is able to carry over this greater self-assertion to her relationships with men in how she chooses and relates to them.

In sum, Jenny facilitates the therapeutic transformation of Marie-Helene's reparative quest in the transference by responding empathically to the developmental–adaptive and the repetitive–defensive dimensions of Marie-Helene's idealizing fantasies as each emerges more in the foreground of the therapeutic relationship. Marie-Helene's experience of Jenny as an esteemed guide not only provided reparative experience, it also set the stage for addressing the defensive functions of Marie-Helene's idealization, which in turn led to Marie-Helene's fruitful mourning process and her gaining more access to her authentic self-assertion.

References

Brandchaft, B. (1993). To free the spirit from its cell. In A. I. Goldberg (Ed.), *A Decade of Progress: Progress in Self Psychology*, Vol. 10 (pp. 209–230). Hillsdale, NJ: Analytic Press.

Brandchaft, B. (2007). Systems of pathological accommodation and change in analysis. *Psychoanalytic Psychology*, *24*, 667–687.

Kaufmann, P. (2012). On transforming the reparative quest. *International Journal of Psychoanalytic Self Psychology*, *7*, 414–435.

Chapter 11

Tolerating his vulnerability

First at age 10, then at 50

Evelyn Berger Hartman

Two weeks before his book *Portnoy's Complaint* hit the stands, Ron told me, Philip Roth alerted his parents. "Look. My book is coming out in a few weeks and I'm already hearing from my agent that it's going to make a fast splash. It's about a family that sounds like ours and it's got some very raunchy material in it. I want you to know this now because it's getting a lot of press and your friends are going to talk." On the drive back to Newark, Roth's mother started to hyperventilate and his father shouted at her, "Calm down. So what if people talk?" Roth's mother yelled back, "People talk? Who cares about *that*? Did you *hear* him? Our son has delusions of grandeur?"

I had come to eagerly anticipate Ron's entertaining stories and Ron took a lot of pleasure in telling them. We are of the same age, and have lived through the same cultural times. When he tells me the Philip Roth story it is clear to us that we are both big fans. It would take me a while before I understood the greater relevance that the Roth story had to Ron, *his* sense of unfulfilled grandeur, and the role that stories played in our relationship. In this chapter I describe the process of the re-finding of Ron's deeply buried vulnerability during the early phase of treatment.

Ron entered treatment at the age of 50 tremendously disappointed with himself. A research physician, married, and the father of two sons, he continued to be depressed after not getting the promotion in his department five years earlier, despite his previous treatment with a highly regarded analyst. His position in his life did not match the aspirations he held for himself; nor did it match the opinion he held of others, whether professionally or personally. Ron now felt insignificant. He had a history of being difficult with colleagues. Intent on producing excellent work, he hunkered down, isolated himself, and when he was offered suggestions for changes he became angry. "I don't have the social skills to work well with others."

As we examined Ron's early history and the good upbringing that he described, we focused on his parents' disinterest in helping him in difficult situations. His parents, he said, avoided distress, small or large. They ignored his struggles in Little League. They ignored his father's deteriorating muscular disease. Ron felt they were well-meaning parents but they believed he should deal with his problems himself and were not very sympathetic to his complaints. Encouraged by his parents to believe that his talents could lead to exceptional success, Ron became depressed and his parents confused when his professional career did not lead to where he imagined.

As Ron described his life's predicament to me, it became clear that despite his ability to describe family members, friends, literary characters, and colleagues with thoughtfulness and complexity, he described his own suffering in simplistic, self-derogatory ways. He told me that he talked too much about himself and didn't show others that he was interested in them. He thought this was because of his insecurities, but, in response to further inquiry about his insecurities, Ron wasn't curious.

Initially, to my attempts at pointing out the discrepancy between his ability to adopt an understanding and reflective stance toward the struggle of others but not toward his own, he responded angrily, again misconstruing what I said and accusing me of believing that he was in fact stupid. And stupid, in particular, for believing that he could achieve success.

Ron concluded that he had been wrong all along, that he *wasn't* as smart as the others, nor as socially adept. In fact, he said, he didn't have the skills to do really great things or to have a really great life as both he and his parents had assumed. I felt stuck by these interactions with Ron. He seemed to have a block that, as rational and insightful as he was, I could not penetrate. I also felt at these moments that this was a mutually shared block, that perhaps there was something that was sticking me to Ron, to this stubborn place in him from which he refused to wander. Perhaps we both wanted to stay exactly where we were.

During our early period of working together, a great deal of time was spent helping Ron with the pain he felt about his son's severe eating disorder. He brought sophisticated psychoanalytic articles to session describing the problem, reflecting on the dynamics within his family. During this time he often felt isolated from other family members who supported his son in what Ron felt were self-destructive acts. They thought Ron was just being difficult. I empathized with Ron's suffering, so it came as a surprise when one day, in response to something I said, he retorted angrily, "So you think, like everyone else, that the problem is just that I won't accept the situation!" I told Ron I was confused about what had just happened. That after all of the time we had talked about his son, after all of the insights we had shared about the disorder, he would think I disagreed with his position and thought that he was the problem. He reviewed what he said and what I said, misaligning phrases. I tried to explain again what I had originally said. "Hm, hm," he said, and was about to go on. I told him that I wanted us to understand what had just happened. That somehow he misunderstood what I said in such a way as to make him instantly feel rejected and isolated by me. *In one sentence.* I wondered whether perhaps something similar happened with other people. Again he said, "Hm, hm." He considered what I said but also dismissed it immediately, rejecting the help he had received. He returned to his narrative. I sat back and listened.

Ron related interesting stories about travels with friends, book group discussions, evenings out with his brother, talks about each other's children's problems. Inevitably, he reflected on how they were all more successful than he was and therefore brought more to the relationships than he did. His friends stayed around with him only for history's sake. His wife's excellent social skills helped *her* navigate the politics of her profession and *his* poor social skills impeded his own success. He felt that his depression brought her down, that she could have a much better life with someone who was more successful and he wondered whether she contemplated leaving him.

When he told me about their fights, he felt empathic toward her but also hurt that she didn't feel apologetic. "I guess I was the kind of kid who needed a lot of hugs." "What kind of kid is that, Ron?" I asked. "Is that some kind of unusual kid who needs hugs?" He said, "A kid who is weak or very sensitive, who doesn't have the resilience to get over the slight. They need the hugs." I pointed out how much empathy he felt for his wife, her issues, her history, her family of origin. He said, "She just doesn't feel empathy. She has no interest in empathy." "Like your parents?" I asked. "Like times when you struggled, they turned away, they weren't empathic, they were not interested in being empathic when you were struggling?" I saw that Ron was staring at me for a moment longer, as if wanting me to say more, to stay in this state in which he felt my empathy. But our time is up. "Oohhkay." He says and got up. I wondered, nervously, what, if anything, he would do with this. Would he reflect on this, would he return to this in the next session?

Why did Ron, so emotionally attuned toward others, struggle to reflect with empathy toward himself? How could I help him to be empathic toward himself? Where did eloquent, sensitive, psychologically minded Ron go at these moments? When would I get to hear that voice toward himself? When would he reflect, with passion and feeling, toward Ron? Frustrated, I found myself wishing that he would soon tell me another one of his eloquent stories. I could sit back and listen.

I asked Ron what memories he had of times he had struggled, or didn't succeed at something. Ron had only a few examples. When he was about 10 years old, already having made himself known as a precocious, dependable boy, he was asked to take care of the neighbor's dog while they were away for a week. He wanted a dog and so he welcomed the opportunity. His mother made it clear that she would have nothing to do with it. Ron understood the deal and agreed. Unexpectedly, he became frightened of the dog, didn't understand why a dog needed to be walked, and the neighbors returned home to a mess. Ron remembered this experience as being a failure. I wondered why his parents didn't step in rather than let him fail. "Well, my mother made it clear that she was having nothing to do with the dog. I think she was afraid of it." "But wasn't there anything that they could think of doing so as not to leave you alone to fail? After all, these people were your neighbors." With his full attention, I wondered with him what it would have been like if his parents had helped him. If they would have recognized his vulnerability, that he was only 10 years old. They may have convinced him not to take the dog on, explaining that he was too young. Or, they could have taught him about setting an alarm clock to remind him about walking the dog, made some other arrangements to avoid the mess. Having heard Ron describe his parenting of his children, how involved he was with their music lessons, how much careful thought he put into teaching them how to drive, how he considered his children's self-esteem when helping them take on tasks for which they lacked the skills, I imagined with him what he might have done if one of his children had been given a similar task. Would he let them just fail? "Ron, when you can't ask for help it becomes really hard to achieve your potential." There was silence. What is he thinking? "You're saying that I think I have more potential than I actually do," Ron says. As much as Ron seemed engaged in my examples, nothing seemed to penetrate. As if all of the sensitivity that Ron conveyed when describing his relationship with his wife, his children, his understanding of literary characters, indeed a keen emotional intelligence, stood outside his consciousness when we spoke about his vulnerable self, at times as if he refused to let it into his consciousness. And, despite my efforts and even my sense that he appreciated my empathy, he refused to allow me to be successful at this. We were stuck again.

At times his aggression was more pronounced. He reported back a misconstrued version of what I had said, said there was nothing new about what I had said and that he's been talking about the same thing with me for all of this time and for five years before me with the other guy. At times this self-defeating stance seemed insistent and deliberate, as if he was actually refusing to accept my empathy. His anger and aggression, misdirected, felt impenetrable. I understood that this too protected him from approaching his vulnerability as he directed ten-year-old angry feelings toward his unempathic parents at me.

I wondered what was going on between us with these stories. At times, Ron's stories, sometimes tangents but nonetheless relevant to whatever issue he wanted to discuss, filled in gaps in my knowledge – history, economics; maybe *his* seventies core curriculum was better than my loosey-goosey one. He has read the early classics. He is more up on the news than I am. I soaked up these stories like a sponge. What were we doing with them? What purpose did they serve? Why was I so pulled in by them? Why did I look forward to them, hope that he would start the session with one? Why did I let them sway me from confronting his defensiveness even more? Was I being rendered incompetent as an analyst as his mentors had been, as his colleagues were? Was I letting him fail as a patient? Was this a version of what his boss referred to as Ron not being "a team player?" Would he leave this treatment, as he had left his previous one, as he felt about past jobs, would he leave this treatment disappointed, feeling once again that he just didn't have the skills, the skills to be a patient? And why? Why was I letting myself be rendered incompetent? Why couldn't I come out of this and figure out a way to get to his vulnerability? Staring like a wide-eyed little girl? Like the little 10-year-old girl I once was, listening naively and wide-eyed as my two much older brothers brought their exciting findings from the outside world into my immigrant home, their stories far more exciting than mine, than any I could *imagine*? Political arguments among my grown-up family all too exciting, too abstract for my 10-year-old self to grasp? Was I really in that adoring little sister place *again*, now with Ron? That vulnerable place of *mine*? Captivated but dismissed, all at once, by them, by Ron? Was I really stuck there once again? Ron and I, two 10-year-old versions of our 50-year-old selves, he destined to do really great things and me in awe. Engaged in a latency aged seduction, he seducing me with his stories and me seducing him with my admiration.

Now, *I* will tell *you* a story. A funny thing happened on one of my summer vacations during Ron's treatment, one of those life-changing, treatment-changing things that happens to an analyst. With some lazy time on vacation in Vermont, my daughter and I visited a farmers' market and came away with a puppy. Despite my lifelong ability to push aside my own wish for a puppy, despite my ability to push aside my children's pleading for one, here I was, this 50-something full-time psychoanalyst with three young adult children out of the house, jumping in.

A few months later, with my apartment under construction and nowhere to leave baby Snoopy, I brought him to my session with Louisa, my 10-year-old patient who, for a year, hid under my couch and stubbornly refused to engage. As if she couldn't resist she reveled in Snoopy, taught him tricks, fed him, and we played together with Snoopy in a more interactive way than we had before. I updated her on Snoopy in future sessions and, more than before, Louisa engaged, still barking but playing too.

When we returned to Ron's dog-walking story, I thought of *my* story, I thought of Snoopy, and I thought of what Ron had missed. He could have had a much better story than one just about dismissive parents and a lack of guidance. Ron had got it all wrong. The dog wasn't scaring him, he wanted to play. Left home alone, the dog was probably so excited to see little Ron. In this way Ron misconstrued the dog's approach. He was the object of the dog's joy, not his anger. Ron missed the opportunity to explore his neighborhood with the dog, discover new places, have sweet interactions with other dog lovers. So now when we spoke about the dog-walking fiasco, I thought of my family, of my 10-year-old hiding patient Louisa, glowing and playing with me and with Snoopy.

Now, as we returned to the memory, there was this big, furry, lively being next door waiting for Ron to come and play. Now, when we returned to the dog-walking story, I interjected my story as I listened to his. No longer mesmerized, I interjected myself into his story and enhanced it. Out loud, I began to voice 10-year-old Ron's confusion:

> I don't get it. I thought this was something I really wanted to do. How come the dog scares me? I was so excited about this. But I'm scared of this dog. I told them I'd walk it but I'm scared and I don't know how I'm supposed to do it. And when am I supposed to do it?

I looked up and Ron was mesmerized. I continued, "I wish I could ask my mother. But she told me she wouldn't help so that's that. But what am I supposed to do?" I looked up again. Ron blinked and said, "Even then I didn't have the skills to ask for help." I try again. "How would you know to ask? How does a little boy learn that asking for help when they don't know something is the thing to do in that situation?" I continue to give voice to 10-year-old Ron:

> Well, my mother told me she'd have nothing to do with this. And my father won't, he just won't help. So I can't ask. I guess I'm supposed to know how to do this. I guess I'm not supposed to be scared. I guess the adults who know how to do things know that I'm supposed to be able to know how to walk a dog. I guess I failed. I should have been able to do this. All the adults assume I'd be able to. They know. They know everything. I failed.

Ron is staring at me wide-eyed, as if in a trance, so I continue: "I'm scared of this dog. He jumps on me. What should I do? I just won't go back. He's scary. I don't know what to do!" Ron looks up and asks me, "So you're saying that the adults should have offered to help?" "Yes," I reply. "Imagine what it would be like if they had intervened. What do you think they could have done?" I wait, a few moments of silence pass, and then "So what you're saying is that I didn't have those skills, those social skills to ask for help." I'm getting frustrated that I've lost him again. We are co-writing his story and he is listening to his 10-year-old vulnerable self. Then he abandons him. Ron punishes himself, and me, for feeling empathic. Empathy for his vulnerability and human flaws is insulting and injurious. He becomes insulted, offended, and angry. He barks back at someone trying to help. He barks at himself, berates himself, just when he's on the brink of feeling empathic toward himself. He's barking. [...] *He's just barking.* He wants to play? I'm not stuck now. Again and again, I approach the bark. I give voice to 10-year-old Ron. "Ron, you interpret the situation in the only way a little boy can, which is to blame yourself." Fifty-year-old 10-year-old Ron stares at me, wide-eyed and in a trance, waiting, yearning for more and more.

In time, memories come to Ron of other times when, while struggling with something, his father, curiously but mysteriously, failed to help. He had trouble figuring out piano exercises, and his father didn't help. "That's funny," Ron said with a smile, "because you know he put himself through college as an accompanist." "So what's funny?" I asked. "Why wouldn't he help you with the exercises?" "Hmm," replied Ron. "I think he felt incompetent as a teacher." We wondered about his father's own feelings of vulnerability. I asked, "So he'd let you fail at it instead? Why would he just let you struggle?" Again, I interject his 10-year-old voice wondering and coming up with reasons for why he may have thought his otherwise well-meaning father wouldn't help.

A dream reminded Ron about an elementary schoolteacher who encouraged his talent at painting. Ron's mother converted a small room into a studio for him but never installed the light fixtures properly. "Why didn't she get it fixed so that you could have decent light in that room?" I asked. "Art wasn't her thing," he replied. "Okay, but she gave you the room to paint in. Why wouldn't she get the light in there properly?" "She wasn't prepared to do that," Ron replied. "*Prepared*?" I asked. "What do you mean, prepared?" "It might have been too physically difficult for her to do it by herself and that my father should fix the light. She probably asked him but didn't want to bug him." "Why didn't she get someone to help her?" I asked. "Why did she leave it so that you couldn't paint? [...] *Why won't Mom help me so that I can paint?*"

While I am giving voice to Ron's 10-year-old self he appears engaged, seems interested. I think he's got it; he can see himself as a vulnerable self. When my monologue is finished he asks a question, as if he is on the verge of understanding something in a different way. Perhaps he will understand himself with some of the depth with which he describes Roth's characters, those stories that mesmerize me. I become hopeful. He's going to be eloquent about himself too. More recently, Ron turns on himself less consistently. Entranced or enchanted, Ron uses these play spaces, these stories that we are co-writing, as an opportunity for us to look, however slowly, more closely at the vulnerability he felt during those times when he agreed to take on tasks he could not master. We have examined how hard it was for his parents to step into a vulnerable place of their own in order to help Ron with his, as if they denied that their very smart son could have some areas in which he needed help. With more memories coming up, he has begun to appreciate how mystifying it was for him, how mystifying it *is* for him to understand his father's unwillingness to help him, how painful it is for him to consider his father's vulnerabilities. He has spoken in greater detail about his father's chronic and debilitating muscle illness. As if considering this for the first time, Ron said tearfully, "I wonder what it was like for him to get the diagnosis as a teenager? I wonder what it was like for my mother to decide to marry him knowing that his condition would only get worse?"

With lips quivering, Ron recalled, when he was 11 years old and with his mother by his side, watching his father drive his oldest brother off to college. "I was so sad. My mother said, "Don't be sad, Ron. When you're older you'll be able to go off college too." "That was true, but it didn't help. She must have felt sad too!" Ron remembered feeling deeply lonely when he went off to college, the profound sadness he felt waving goodbye to his son as he went off to sleep away at camp. He wipes away a tear. "Why didn't we all drive my brother together? [...] These separations are hard for a family, all of these different separations, the kids getting closer to leaving for college, and then the reuniting. These separations take so many forms. It's so hard." Then, without missing a beat, "But a parent has to manage their feelings."

Over time, we came to understand that Ron and his department head were engaging in a big-brother little-brother dynamic of their own. Although Ron's evaluations were now very positive, his overall ratings were kept at only average. Ron was clear that his department head didn't want him to succeed, and was frustrated that he had to acknowledge Ron's success. Ron wished that he had a boss who could have warmly praised him, who would want him to advance. I told Ron that I noticed that he hadn't criticized himself as he might have done before, to explain the discrepancy in the evaluation. I wondered to myself whether he would now once again misconstrue and dismiss what I just said. I said a little prayer and waited. Ron looked up and said, "I hear you." I was, at that moment, so moved. Ron felt both my praise and empathy and let it be.

Philip Roth's predictions weren't delusions of grandeur. Luckily for Roth, he was able to turn around his mother's view of him into a joke, to use it in his writing, and, lucky for us, his career has turned out to be grand. Ron's parents did get his precociousness right. Ron was very smart and capable but they didn't accept his weaknesses. Although his parents were mostly a nurturing and loving presence, though they encouraged his strengths with tender gestures, they disappeared strikingly when Ron struggled. In their own delusional state of Ron's grandeur, they wouldn't respond to a needy Ron.

As Ron and I negotiate his transition from the experience of empathy that he has for himself within a dissociated state, to one that he can have in a more fully waking state, we continue to examine the issues that prevent him from doing so. Separations are hard, as Ron says, and they take many forms. Each quiver, each tear, tears Ron away from a pact made long ago with loving, nurturing parents, to deny his vulnerability. His parents could not tolerate it when his needs challenged their own vulnerability and, instead, let him remain unguided and fail. Ron was supposed to do only great things, and bumps along the way confounded and mystified Ron. Perhaps Ron, so profoundly sad when he leaves home, when his brother leaves, when his children leave, is on the verge of leaving home once more as he allows himself, in a full waking state, to feel vulnerable and to confront the underlying pain. As I struggled to uncover Ron's vulnerability, defended against by loyalty to his parents, I discovered some of my own, hidden beneath my delight in his stories, hidden beneath my idealization of my original storytellers, as I persevered in becoming the analyst Ron needed me to be. As we each emerged from that which mesmerized us, from our latency suppressed 10-year-old selves, from that which rendered Ron incompetent as Ron, and me incompetent as Ron's analyst, as we write stories together, as we invite our passions into these stories, as we rewrite *Ron's* stories, we are writing about a Ron who, rather than automatically barking back when he is confronted by vulnerability, can identify when he needs someone, *that it's okay to need someone*, and can wag his tail, walk over, and tilt his head for a pet [...] and then give a lick.

Commentary on Hartman's case

The multiple meanings of parental failure to provide empathic guidance

Brent Willock

Evelyn Hartman provides us with a most interesting account of her struggle to help her patient, Ron, to become more understanding of his long-standing vulnerability and need for empathic assistance and guidance as the foundation for being able to hold a more complex and compassionate view of himself. One could, no doubt, discuss her case study from many points of view. I will focus on one issue that strikes me as particularly interesting and significant, namely the relationship between oedipal and pre- (or other-than) oedipal issues. The former have been highlighted by the classical Freudian model, whereas object-relational, self-psychological, interpersonal, and relational perspectives have emphasized the latter.

Dr. Hartman commences her chapter in an amusing manner. She shares a joke that Ron told her. He describes Philip Roth warning his (Philip's) parents that his book, *Portnoy's Complaint*, would soon be rolling off the printing presses. Roth alerted them to the fact that it portrayed a family very much like theirs and that it also contained some very raunchy material. He anticipated it would be widely read and discussed. His mother was shocked. To Philip's surprise, it turned out that she was unconcerned about the bawdy passages. She was, instead, alarmed that her son, thinking his book would be so successful, had delusions of grandeur.

For those unfamiliar with *Portnoy's Complaint*, it is described in Wikipedia as the humorous monologue of a lusty, mother-addicted young man who confesses details of his sexual life, including interesting masturbatory practices, to his psychoanalyst. On the first page of that novel, Roth defines Portnoy's Complaint in psychiatric-sounding terms as "a disorder in which strongly felt ethical and altruistic impulses are perpetually warring with extreme sexual longings, often of a perverse nature."

With this Rothian beginning to her case study, one might anticipate that Dr. Hartman and her patient would soon be discussing oedipal issues. This expectation does not turn out to be the case. Instead, her chapter focuses on the sequelae of the historic and continuing failure of Ron's parents to be empathically attuned to his vulnerabilities. Nonetheless, if one is open to the idea that the many stories her patient shares, including the previous joke, might constitute a sublimated, oedipally derived romance between patient and analyst, then one could consider that an oedipal theme may subtly suffuse this treatment. Supporting that possibility, on her first page, Dr. Hartman shares: "I had come to eagerly anticipate Ron's entertaining stories and Ron took a lot of pleasure in telling them. We're of the same age." Several pages later, as she continues to explore her countertransferential experience, she refers to Ron "seducing me with his stories and me seducing him with my admiration." While most of the chapter concerns empathic failure pertaining to Ron's vulnerability, some oedipal qualities do seem apparent in the unfolding transference–countertransference matrix and relational ambience.

Ron commenced his treatment with Dr. Hartman when he was 50 years old. After not having been granted a promotion at his workplace five years earlier, he became and continued to be depressed. Both this dysphoria, and the contrast between Ron's reference to delusions of grandeur in his Philip Roth story and his own feelings of insignificance, could reflect the dialectic between oedipal illusions of phallic omnipotence and impotence. Mostly, however, the narrative focuses on self-psychological matters pertaining to failures of empathic attunement during Ron's childhood and later, and to relational matters concerning Dr. Hartman's creative efforts to explore her countertransferential subjectivity and thereby find ways of thinking about and making productive contact with her patient.

When Ron was a child, his parents did not seem interested in helping him in difficult situations. They avoided distress, ignoring his struggles in Little League just as they ignored his father's deteriorating muscular disease. Believing Ron should deal with his problems by himself, they were not very sympathetic to his complaints.

Ron came to believe that he was not as smart as others, nor as socially adept. He thought he lacked the necessary skills for accomplishing great things and having a great life. Imagining that his depression brought his wife down and that she could have a much better life with someone more successful than him, he wondered if she contemplated leaving him. Analogously in the transference, despite the good times he enjoyed sharing stories with his analyst and her steadfast efforts to help him, he was ready at the drop of a hat to feel that she regarded him as stupid and rejected him. These ruminations and reactions may be regarded as those of an oedipal outsider who feels destined to be life's loser. Only others can have truly great lives, including happy marriages.

Despite the seemingly oedipal beginning and some subsequent similar material, most of the case study focuses on Ron's difficulty with his more primary dependency needs. When he mused that he must have been "the kind of kid who needed a lot of hugs," Dr. Hartman asked if that sort of child was not universal. Ron immediately responded to her empathic foray by defining that type of youngster as weak, needy, and lacking resilience to get over slights. Whereas Ron was usually capable of taking an understanding, reflective, nuanced stance toward others' struggles, he could not be similarly compassionate toward his own needs and challenges.

Ron's difficulty with his dependency seems to fit the schizoid (splitting) pattern described by Ronald Fairbairn (1952). Based on his parents' dismissive attitudes, Ron appears to have established what that Scottish psychoanalyst called an internal rejecting object. Identifying with that entity's attitude, Ron seems to have abandoned his needy libidinal ego. Instead of standing by and supporting his dependent self, he formed an unholy alliance with his rejecting object. Together they created a formidable anti-libidinal ego. In the course of her attempts to reach Ron, his analyst felt the sting of that entity many times.

Dr. Hartman worked creatively and hard to help Ron understand that all children need help from their parents. In what might be described as a kind of psychodrama, she voiced the questions and concerns that he was never able to formulate, let alone express. Clearly she was being the opposite of a rejecting object or an anti-libidinal ego. She was being consistently empathic with states of longing, dread, and hope that Ron had long ago dissociated from his conscious awareness. In response to her efforts, he seemed hungry for more, as well as wary and dismissive of her empathic attunement.

Ron had a dream that reminded him of an elementary schoolteacher who encouraged his talent at painting. This memory of a facilitating figure could probably emerge most easily in the context of a therapeutic relationship in which his analyst labored mightily against the grain of Ron's conviction that he did not have much potential for success. The dream-related primary schoolteacher may have represented or at least resonated with his evolving view of his analyst.

Ron's mother once turned a small room in their home into a studio so that he could paint. Perhaps she was responding to that schoolteacher's observations and encouragement. It turned out, however, that his mother never installed proper light fixtures. Her support had been off to an auspicious start, but it was not sustained. In Fairbairnian terms, her apparently ambivalent attitude toward her son's needs may reflect the activities of the exciting object that sets up gratifying situations promising fulfillment, but then typically withdraws and disappoints.

Ron began to realize that it was odd that his father never helped him when he was having difficulty with his childhood piano studies. His father's unwillingness to assist was particularly puzzling because he was an accomplished pianist. In Ron's attempt to comprehend this lack, he considered the possibility that his father may have felt incompetent as a teacher. Later, he acknowledged how mystifying it was, and still is, for him to understand his father's unwillingness to help him with his struggles in life and, also, how painful it is for him to ponder his father's vulnerabilities. He became teary-eyed as he wondered what it might have been like for his father to have received a diagnosis pertaining to muscular degeneration as a teenager, and what it was like for his mother to decide to marry him knowing that his condition would only worsen. Ron's theory of mind – of his mind and of others' – was clearly expanding as he worked with his analyst.

Toward the end of her chapter, Dr. Hartman discusses what she viewed as a big-brother/little-brother dynamic between Ron and his department head. Ron's work evaluations had become very positive. However, his overall ratings remained very average. He was now certain that his department head did not want him to succeed and was frustrated that he had to acknowledge Ron's success. Ron wished that he had a boss who could warmly praise him (as Dr. Hartman at least implicitly did) and who wanted him to advance (as his analyst did). Dr. Hartman told him that she had noticed he did not criticize himself as he used to do in order to explain the troubling discrepancy in his recent work evaluations. She worried to herself that he would quickly dismiss her observation. Instead, Ron responded seriously, "I hear you." To her readers, Dr. Hartman remarked: "I was, at that moment, so moved. Ron felt both my praise and empathy and let it be." Something had shifted significantly, and for the better.

The preceding vignette may reflect Ron's having made sufficient structural changes in his self – embedded at last in a much more supportive internal and external relational milieu, thanks to his analytic work with Dr. Hartman – such that he could begin facing and exploring oedipal conflicts. He could now see himself as not just a loser, and his department head as not merely mysteriously lacking an encouraging disposition. At this point, he can instead generate and contemplate the possibility that this man actually and actively does not want him to succeed. Ron does not say why he thinks his boss would be so determined to thwart his success. He does, however, now at least implicitly situate this frustration in the context of an authority figure maintaining an aggressive, competitive, self-esteem sabotaging stance toward a younger male – a classic oedipal scenario.

Perhaps in the future Ron may extend this understanding that was beginning to emerge in relation to his department head to acquire a more complicated, oedipally informed understanding of why his father never wanted to help him. For example, could his father's refusal to assist Ron when he was having difficulty with his music lessons have been because his father wanted to be forever the maestro of music rather than facilitating his son's advancing and, perhaps someday, overtaking him?

Might Ron's mother making a room for him to paint in, but never installing appropriate lighting, have also reflected her ambivalence toward his oedipal ambitions? Did she desire to encourage him, but not want him to become too successful, too big for his pants? Recall Philip Roth's mother apparently not being troubled by his sexual passions as he came of age in their family, but "hyperventilating" about his vocational "delusions of grandeur." She could support Philip going a certain distance toward realizing his ambitions, but needed to apply the brakes against any fantasies he might have of becoming too victorious, of going all the way. Philip's and Ron's mothers may have felt it necessary to somewhat permit and even encourage their sons' ambitions in the arts and letters (painting, novel writing) and other spheres, and also to squelch their enthusiasm lest things get out of hand.

Dr. Hartman's chapter title, "Tolerating his vulnerability: first at age 10, then at 50," draws our attention to pre-puberty and midlife – two important moments in the arc of life. With respect to Erikson's (1950) important work on the life cycle that encompasses those times, and more, Blatt and Shichman (1983) believed it necessary to insert an additional stage into that scholar's valuable framework. Between his stages of initiative versus inferiority (phallic narcissism) and industry versus inferiority (latency), they placed mutuality versus alienation (oedipal). They believed this opposition is phase dominant from about 4 to 6 years of age. At that time cooperative peer play commences, along with initial resolution of the oedipal crisis.

Ron embodied this sense of alienation as opposed to mutuality that Blatt and Shichman emphasized. For five years before beginning treatment with Dr. Hartman, he had been depressed about not getting a promotion. Intent on producing excellent work he hunkered down, isolating himself from others. When he received suggestions for changes, he became angry: "I don't have the social skills to work well with others." He had a history of being difficult with colleagues. His boss referred to him as not being a "team player." In the dialectic between attachment and separateness (Blatt & Blass, 1990) or identity and relationship (Blatt, 2008) that courses through the life cycle, Ron seemed stuck on the more self-centered side.

Ron's parents seemed to believe that one should ignore problems, or figure them out as best one can on one's own, rather than sharing them and receiving sympathy and help. Leaving him much of the time to his own resources to either sink or swim, Ron floundered. Often he felt he had failed, as in his poignant memory of looking forward to caring for their neighbor's dog, but messing up completely when his desire did not match his ability to engage in that relationship and carry out that responsibility. Later in life, when his own son developed a severe eating disorder, Ron "often felt isolated from other family members," particularly his parents. When it came to life's struggles, Ron's upbringing seemed to foster alienation rather than a sense of mutuality. Silent solo struggle trumped team play. Ego efforts figured more prominently rather than "wego" ones (Klein, 1976).

For a long time, Ron rejected his analyst's empathic attempts and her encouragement of him to be more that way with himself. He seemed committed to remaining in his alienated position. Dr. Hartman reached deeply into herself to find analogous life experiences that she could draw upon in order to not feel excessively thwarted by her patient's initially intimidating resistance. She found a way to choose, instead, to regard his outbursts as an invitation to play. Ron seems to be benefiting greatly from her therapeutic stance. Instead of his continuing to oppose her, they appear to be increasingly on the same team, helping each other out, Ron by his increased openness and his providing relevant memories, dreams, and reflections, and Dr. Hartman by mining her countertransference and offering new perspectives. As a result of his analyst's perseverance and his response to it, their working alliance (wego) continues to strengthen.

In a much-cited article, Hans Loewald (1979) discussed *The Waning of the Oedipus Complex.* I was struck not only by the waning of Ron's Oedipus complex but also by its waxing. Oedipal issues sometimes seemed near the forefront of his narrative but, at other times, they were occluded by earlier dependency conflicts. Both the oedipal and the pre- (or other-than) oedipal are important in analysis. Toward the end of the interesting, productive period of treatment to which we are privy, there were promising indications that Ron had grown to the point where he could begin to more actively confront oedipal conflicts.

Among its many virtues, Dr. Hartman's presentation of her work provides a wonderful opportunity to discuss the important relationship between traditional and subsequent developments in psychoanalytic understanding. My attunement toward and interest in the interplay and evolution of classical Freudian, object-relational, self-psychological, and relational themes in this case accords with my long-standing commitment to comparative–integrative psychoanalysis (Willock, 2011). The combination of theoretical lenses that the comparative–integrative approach encourages us to adopt enables us to perceive the multiple meanings of clinical material in general, and of parental failure to provide empathic guidance in particular. In Ron's case, this parental inability seemed initially mainly due to their difficulties in being empathic with themselves. The psychic deficits of the older generation are visited on the younger one. Later it appeared as though this parental refusal to help their son may not just have been deficit-based but also related to their oedipal conflicts. Unable to identify fully with their offspring's ambitions and strivings, they tended to ignore and even thwart these developmental needs, leaving him in an alienated position. Through Ron's work with Dr. Hartman, he developed a more secure emotional base, characterized by expectations of empathic attunement and encouragement. Increasingly he could think of himself as a worthwhile, promising person who had legitimate needs that could be understood and responded to effectively by himself and by others. He experienced himself as being engaged in a mutually rewarding therapeutic relationship, and he was harvesting the benefits of their labor. This analytic process seemed to have the potential to lead to his being able to work through oedipal conflicts and to become increasingly successful in his work, marriage, and the rest of his life.

References

Blatt, S. J. (2008). *Polarities of Experience: Relatedness and Self-definition in Personality Development, Psychopathology, and the Therapeutic Process*. Washington, DC: American Psychological Association.

Blatt, S. J. & Blass, R. B. (1990). Attachment and separateness: A dialectic model of the products and processes of development throughout the life cycle. *Psychoanalytic Study of the Child, 45*, 107–128.

Blatt, S. J. & Shichman, S. (1983). Two primary configurations of psychopathology. *Psychoanalysis and Contemporary Thought, 6*, 187–254.

Erikson, E. H. (1950). *Childhood and Society*. New York: Norton.

Fairbairn, W. R. D. (1952). *Psychoanalytic Studies of the Personality*. London: Tavistock.

Klein, G. S. (1976). *Psychoanalytic Theory: An Exploration of Essentials.* New York: International Universities Press.

Loewald, H. W. (1979). The waning of the Oedipus complex. *Journal of the American Psychoanalytic Association, 27*, 751–775.

Willock, B. (2011). *Comparative-integrative Psychoanalysis: A Relational Perspective for the Discipline's Second Century.* London and New York: Routledge.

Index